Everyday Poetics

Bloomsbury Studies in Philosophy and Poetry
Series Editors: Rick Anthony Furtak and James D. Reid

Bloomsbury Studies in Philosophy and Poetry explores ancient, modern, and contemporary texts in ways that are sensitive to philosophical themes and problems that can be fruitfully addressed through poetic modes of writing, and focused on questions of style, the relations between form and content, and the conduciveness of literary modes of expression to philosophical inquiry. With a keen interest in the intertwining of poetry and philosophy in all forms, the series will cover the philosophical register of poetry, the poetics of philosophical writing, and the literary strategies of philosophers.

The series provides a home for work on figures across geographical landscapes, with contributions that employ a wide range of methods across academic disciplines, and without regard for divisions within philosophy, between analytic and continental, for example, that have outworn their usefulness. Featuring single-authored works and edited collections, curated by an international editorial board, the series aims to redefine how we read and discuss philosophy and poetry today.

Editorial Board: Daniel Brown, University of Southampton, UK; Kristen Case, University of Maine Farmington, USA; Hannah Vandegrift Eldridge, University of Wisconsin–Madison, USA; Cassandra Falke, University of Tromsø, Norway; Luke Fischer, University of Sydney, Australia; John Gibson, University of Louisville, USA; James Haile III, University of Rhode Island, USA; Kevin Hart, University of Virginia, USA; Eileen John, University of Warwick, UK; Troy Jollimore, California State University, USA; David Kleinberg-Levin, Northwestern University, USA; John Koethe, University of Wisconsin–Milwaukee, USA; John T. Lysaker, Emory University, USA; Karmen MacKendrick, Le Moyne College, USA; Rukmini Bhaya Nair, Indian Institute of Technology, India; Kamiyo Ogawa, Sophia University, Japan; Kaz Oishi, University of Tokyo, Japan; Yi-Ping Ong, Johns Hopkins University, USA; Anna Christina Soy Ribeiro, Texas Tech University, USA; Karen Simecek, University of Warwick, UK; Ruth Rebecca Tietjen, University of Copenhagen, Denmark; Íngrid Vendrell Ferran, Goethe University Frankfurt, Germany

Forthcoming Titles:
Thought and Poetry, by John Koethe
Philosophical Fragments and the Poetry of Thinking, by Luke Fischer
A Philosophy of Lyric Voice, by Karen Simecek
Skepticism and Impersonality in Modern Poetry, by Joshua Adams
A Black Poetics of the Everyday, by James Haile III

Everyday Poetics

Logic, Love, and Ethics

Brett Bourbon

BLOOMSBURY ACADEMIC
LONDON • NEW YORK • OXFORD • NEW DELHI • SYDNEY

BLOOMSBURY ACADEMIC
Bloomsbury Publishing Plc
50 Bedford Square, London, WC1B 3DP, UK
1385 Broadway, New York, NY 10018, USA
29 Earlsfort Terrace, Dublin 2, Ireland

BLOOMSBURY, BLOOMSBURY ACADEMIC and the Diana logo are
trademarks of Bloomsbury Publishing Plc

First published in Great Britain 2022
This paperback edition published 2023

Copyright © Brett Bourbon, 2022

Brett Bourbon has asserted his right under the Copyright, Designs and
Patents Act, 1988, to be identified as Author of this work.

For legal purposes the Acknowledgments on p. xii constitute
an extension of this copyright page.

Series design by Ben Anslow
Cover image: *Still Life with Apples* (1893–1894), Paul Cezanne
(© incamerastock / Alamy Stock Photo)

All rights reserved. No part of this publication may be reproduced or transmitted
in any form or by any means, electronic or mechanical, including photocopying,
recording, or any information storage or retrieval system, without prior
permission in writing from the publishers.

Bloomsbury Publishing Plc does not have any control over, or responsibility for,
any third-party websites referred to or in this book. All internet addresses given
in this book were correct at the time of going to press. The author and publisher
regret any inconvenience caused if addresses have changed or sites have
ceased to exist, but can accept no responsibility for any such changes.

A catalogue record for this book is available from the British Library.

A catalog record for this book is available from the Library of Congress.

ISBN: HB: 978-1-3502-6546-2
PB: 978-1-3502-6550-9
ePDF: 978-1-3502-6547-9
eBook: 978-1-3502-6548-6

Series: Bloomsbury Studies in Philosophy and Poetry

Typeset by Integra Software Services Pvt. Ltd.

To find out more about our authors and books visit www.bloomsbury.com
and sign up for our newsletters.

To my daughters

Paskalina and Georgina

Contents

Preface	viii
Acknowledgments	xii
1 Poems of the Everyday	1
2 Interruptions	13
3 Can We Speak a Poem into Existence?	29
4 Epithalamion	43
5 Is a Poem the Same as Its Words?	55
6 Poems and Bombs	69
7 Crucifixion Can Seem Like Standing in Air	85
8 Does Poetry Exist?	97
9 Where Are Love and Death?	111
A Conclusion in Two Parts	129
Part I: Odds and Ends	129
Part II: Intonations of Form	133
Appendices	141
Notes	166
Bibliography	175
Index	179

Preface

One Monday morning a number of years ago, one of my powerful Stanford colleagues called me up with an urgent request. She needed to talk to me. I walked from my beautiful office on the third floor of Margret Jacks Hall to her even more beautiful office on the second. She held an essay of mine in her hand. She was surprised, impressed, overwhelmed. She had things to say to me. We had been enemies, but now she had become my champion. I was glad. We talked for an hour. As I left, she touched my arm. I wonder about one thing, though, she said: Why do you write so much about theology? I smiled. The third rail. My dangerous oddity. This book is my answer to her question. It is a surprising answer, since I do not write explicitly about God, faith, or religion. I write about poetry, ethics, and logic. The interplay of these three reveals the answer to why theology offers an essential mode by which to understand art and life.

Everyday Poetics, however, did not emerge out of that conversation in Margret Jacks Hall, but out of my own intellectual crisis. A few years before my colleague called me to her office, I had fallen into a radical mistrust of literary studies, philosophy, and art. And yet despite that, poems, often in their very simplicity, continued to claim me with a surprising necessity. Their claim on me was neither psychological nor ideological, but ethical in a sense I did not yet have the means to articulate. So I began to write about the faces of words and the faces of the dead, about gestures and promises, about shocks and interruptions, about various poems that mattered to me, about Alice and her adventures in Wonderland, about pretense and grace. About redemption. *Everyday Poetics* is the result.

In this book, I argue that a poem is not simply a set of words fitted together into a whole. Poems need not be made of words at all. I have come to understand poems as particular kinds of events. In order to explore these poetic events, I could not proceed in a traditional manner, examining poems as episodes in a literary history or as examples of poetic techniques or ideologies. I had to investigate poems that happen by surprise, contingently, as revelations and expressions of our complicated and conflicted lives. I call these everyday poems, one primal example of which is the beguilingly simple phrase: "I love you." There are many everyday poems of love. Finding and revealing these kinds of everyday poems is one of the essential tasks of this book. In itself, this is a way of recovering the deepest sources of poetry, but the importance of these kinds of poems goes far beyond literary studies. They matter because they are fundamental to living a life worth living.

Everyday Poetics consists of a set of interrelated literary and philosophical studies of the nature of poetry and interpretation as a mode of description, which are simultaneously a series of meditations on love, marriage, words, gestures, children, the sacred, and the dead. I am addressing poets, literary scholars, philosophers, and students of religion, and anyone who cares about the ethics of everyday life, about the surprises that punctuate and give our lives form. But the book is not written in order to confirm anyone's preconceived opinions. I am writing for those who suspect that finding genuine poems has some connection with a sense of sacredness, that without a feel for the sacred there can be no poetry that is not propaganda of some kind. By this I do not mean that poems are sacred, nor that the sacred requires religious belief (often what is sacred and what people take to be religious are opposed, negations of each other, as the theologian Karl Barth might say). My point is rather that the kind of meaningfulness revealed by what is sacred is the kind of meaningfulness that makes a poem. (I realize in saying this, I might simply be claiming that if you need love, then you need poems.) In appealing to the sacred, however, I am not offering a prelude for a theoretical treatise on the sacred or on poetry or on anything else. What we need if we are to live with a sense of pervasive and acute meaningfulness are examples, demonstrations, queries, confessions, revelations. I am offering these.

The poems we teach in class are formalizations of the everyday poems we live amidst, albeit blindly and carelessly. I pursue and try to resurrect these everyday poems: the everyday poems we can sometimes find at weddings, in the dead, in our misunderstandings with words, in the faces of those we love, and in the simplicity of the alphabet. My book is a kind of anthropology of form, an anthropology that is centered in our ethical lives with words and with the forms of things. It is a philosophical meditation on the nature of poetry, but also on the meaning of love and the claim of words upon us. It is a mystery, a testament, and a commentary about our own essential involvement with words and with the forms of love and death. My goal is to establish the centrality of everyday poems in our lives.

In six core chapters I investigate the particulars of everyday poetry: the ethos of poetry as it is revealed in the particularities and the arc of a life, from childhood to death. My targets of analysis range from the simple poem of the alphabet to one of the most complex formalizations of everyday poems in T. S. Eliot's *The Waste Land*. My arguments arise out of a tradition in which the philosophical concern for the everyday is paramount. Wittgenstein is centrally important in this tradition, but so are Austin, Quine, and my teacher Stanley Cavell. Interleaved with these six chapters on ethics and poetry are three chapters which cumulatively provide a logical account of the kind of thing a poem is. Poems are odd, peculiar things, as are we. The book demonstrates that ethics and logic intersect as the oddity of poems.

In every way this is a book of recovery: the recovery of poems from the noise of our culture, from our careless attention, from our intellectual confusions. Literature, like life, does not exist in neat and tidy compartments; it is unruly and requires the free, albeit responsible and informed, movement between literary and philosophical analysis. I do not say this in conformity with the now-common notion that theory is a necessary part of literary studies. Rather, I argue that we must integrate our readings, reactions, and discoveries of poems with a very careful, but brutally honest, ethical and conceptual investigation of what poems can sometimes reveal. Poetry in its very human grounding demands responses that do not fall easily within many of the debates, let alone the protocols and borders, of academic discourse. But my goal is not to dispense with the academy. Far from it. I want to reclaim for academic writing arenas that have been ceded to essayists and literary writers, to show how the difficulties of life and poetry require a kind of care and attention that are not easily given or received.

Consequently, this both is and is not an academic book. It makes arguments about language and literature, but it also reaches in everyday ways toward everyday things. It is not, however, two books interwoven, one for academics and one for everyone else. It is one book with multiple aspects and voices which attempt to reveal how we live amidst poems and words in ways that we have forgotten, and how, in that forgetfulness, we have lost a precious ethos. We have misplaced ourselves and our lives.[1]

I attempt to find and delineate the ethos in which everyday poems flourish and matter. Since this book arises out of a vocation and is directed toward our ways of living with each other, it describes an ethics of poetry, a struggle to articulate an ethos of perception and description. Such an ethos is valuable, since we all so easily get displaced into disruption, into cliché, into nonsense, into dismay and distraction. We all get interrupted.

All of the chapters in this book began as lectures. These lectures were given over a number of years at various places, including the University of Chicago, the New School of Social Research, the University of Lisbon, ELTE Budapest, and

Stanford. I have retained as much as possible the spirit of oral conversation, in which I foreground the intimacy of one person speaking to other people. These chapters remain personal attempts to speak in a public way with other people about some of the fundamental challenges in human life.

Acknowledgments

I am grateful to the following for help, support, and good counsel: Robert Von Hallberg, David Mikics, Haun Saussy, Sepp Gumbrecht, Oren Izenberg, Garry Hagberg, Geza and Kata Kallay, Miguel Tamen, my students at Stanford and the University of Dallas, and my teachers David Perkins and Stanley Cavell. I would also like to thank the anonymous reviewers for a number of very helpful suggestions. I would also like to thank my daughter Paskalina for her help in preparing the manuscript.

Early versions of three chapters of this book appeared elsewhere, although they have been both expanded and revised. I thank the publishers of *Philosophy and Literature* and *Modern Philology* for permission to reuse material in Chapters 5 and 8, and Appendix 2.

1

Poems of the Everyday

Poems irritated me as a child. They seemed parodies of counting, chants of rhythm and repetition. I included them, when I was five, in my moratorium against reading fiction. On the other hand, I respected the alphabet, a kind of poem of pure form. It was orderly for no good reason and did not mean anything. So I concluded that poems were meaningless forms that had their uses, but were not serious.

I changed my mind when I discovered a primal poem of our everyday lives, as I think of it now, a poem of determinate form that also meant something. I heard a love poem. I heard it recited in an old black-and-white film, whose name and story I have forgotten. But I remember a character saying this poem to himself, as if to realize the right intonation, in order to repeat it later to a young woman. When he finally confessed the words to this woman, I said to myself—"That's a poem." What the fellow had said was "I love you."[1]

I have not recovered from these two competing intuitions: (1) that poems constitute formally powerful but ultimately trivial configurations of symbols and (2) that they constitute overwhelming accomplishments of human and linguistic care. I do not hope to reconcile these twin intuitions; instead, I attempt to survive them... in a fabulous way. The chapters that follow tell a fable, a literary and philosophical fable, about our dependence on and vulnerability to the simple gesture and to the ordinate and plangent as these are collected and organized in particularized forms called poems. It is a fable about the poetry of ethics and the ethics of our involvement with poems. This fable I mean to be true.[2]

I would make this fable, however, not out of my earlier disdain, but out of my currently recurrent mistrust of poems, matched by an obsessive attachment to words. Every so often I try to renounce poems, to free myself of the disease of their making and their claim on me. I have no single complaint against them, except for a sense that the magic of poetry, beyond its rhetoric and wit, seduces and distorts, distracts and indulges without enough warrant or consequence. Yet I continually discover that I cannot refute or relinquish my need for the attentions of grammar and sense given through poems. I have no faith in the measurements of form my need for poems discovers. But I have no way of giving up my need.

And so it goes. I battle my temptation to renounce poetry with my mistrust of it. My attention to poems guided by my mistrust of them produces a particular mode of interpretation, a mode of description and redescription that never quite settles in a meaning or a frame, a context for understanding. A poem is unsettled and unsettling if taken, as it should be, not as a statement, but as a half-lost, half-directed reaching and withholding.

Consequently, I remain enthralled by my two competing intuitions about poems. Poetry seems a sham, a form of sophistry and fantasy: what Thomas Bernhard, one of the more angry literary mistrusters, calls "a lousy scrap of wind and rot."[3] Absolutely, it can be lousy and windy. *Sed contra*: I love some poems, find them necessary, feel claimed by them despite my doubts. The combination of these intuitions I call mistrust. I hold my vulnerability and need for poems in the solution of my doubts. I give precedence to my mistrust, and my vulnerability motivates its hold. I battle my temptation to renounce poetry with my mistrust of it.

This tension is the engine of my inquiry and my fable—an account of poetry as a beloved presence that I mistrust. This returns me to my initial discovery of poetry as a child. But with a difference. At this point, I re-ask a traditional question about poetry, but I do so in an unusual way. I ask, "What kind of thing is a poem such that 'I love you' could be one, such that the alphabet could give us its mimic form?" Answering this question in the chapters that follow will lead me to some surprising places—to battlefields, weddings, novels, voices, gestures and the faces of people and of words.

My history of poetic refusal and attraction has had an important consequence: I never just accept what looks like a poem as a poem. For me, poems are never given, but always discovered. In that discovery poems are never secure, but always in need of further justification. I think this is how it should be.

Poems are odd things. A poem, like any work of art, is something that sometimes matters. Its mattering is all important. That is one of art's oddities—that *what* it is depends on *why* it is. But its mattering is insecure. Art is easy to dismiss—"Why bother?"; "How tiresome"; "It means nothing to me." With these dismissals, a poem, for example, disappears from view, and thus disappears from existence. What is left are mere words and whatever they might say and mean. But that is not the poem.[4]

This is when the philosopher of art or the art theorist steps forward. The philosopher, for example, might attempt to determine the necessary and sufficient conditions of art (or more specifically of poetry), and in so doing justify what it is and that it is (or as Nelson Goodman suggests—when it is).[5] The theorist might describe art as a performative act or a cultural expression, using those descriptions as a means of offering critiques of the enabling powers of agents or cultures in such acts or expressions.[6] There is a certain prima facie sense to these philosophical and theoretical suggestions.[7] But I want to minimize the need for theories, and emphasize the value of description in order to discover the special peculiarity of poems in our lives and as things. Before I expand on how poems have an important and peculiar role in our lives (even for those who hate poems), I want to first emphasize some of their peculiarities as things.

Poems are peculiar because they are so particular, at least that is the story. If this is true, then when we change the words of a poem or shift their order, we make a new poem. Poems seem to be radically and essentially defined by their words. Ordinary, everyday sentences, on the other hand, are not defined by their words in this way, but by the thoughts they express. We say something one way, then we say it another, trying to get it right or trying to discover what we mean. In our ordinary lives with language, what we say is not (always) equivalent to what we mean. And once we understand what someone else means, we often forget what was said and how it was said; it is the meaning that matters (or the uptake of what we take a sentence to imply). Sentences dissolve in our grasping of them. Poems are not like that. We may never know what a poem means, and yet we can be held by its particular words. With poems, what is said (or written) does not dissolve in what is meant. A poem seems bound tightly to the particularity of its words.

But how tightly bound? Is a poem the same as its words? Or more precisely: Are poems equivalent to the words of which they seem to be made? These questions will be my concern in Chapter 5. My answer, to spoil the surprise, is no, they are not. Remarkable and unexpected things follow from this conclusion, surprising not only for poems, but for ourselves as language users.

I will explore these surprising things in other chapters by asking further questions. Are words objects? Do poems have meaning or are they instead meaningful? Should we trust language? Do poems have something in common? Is there a special poetic sense? How can we give voice to the poetry of poetry? Where is the sense in reading poems? Are poems like analogies?

Each of these questions exposes some oddity in the peculiar particularity of poems. A pattern emerges: the more particular we attempt to make a poem, the more it escapes into analogy and otherness. The paths of escape, however, are various and peculiar, because those paths involve us and our involuted ways with words. There is no reading a poem that is not also a reading of the kind of thing a poem is. The kind of thing a poem is, its peculiar particularity, is consanguine with the kind of thing we are as human persons.

It is this relationship between poems and persons that the traditional range of theories attempts to explain or characterize. Hence, appeals to aesthetic experience, to conditions of possibility for a poem to be a poem, for ideas of truth or poetic truth that are revelations of a commonality between ourselves and the world, and so on. Our ideas about poems that we collect into ideas about what we call *poetry* are invariably question-begging. Poetry, like all forms of art, is a contested thing, which means that what counts as poetry is determined by our ideas of what it is. Poetry isn't anything separate from what we take it to be, which means it is to a very high degree ideologically constituted. (It is ideological because poetry is constituted by our ideas about poetry; these ideas need not be political.) This is a way of saying that any definition of poetry and any criteria of identification for a poem are circular. I can make a poem disappear by refusing to accept or acknowledge it as a poem.

I can imagine some resistance to such a strong claim. Someone might counter: "Poems are just the end result of some action of making, as are all other forms of art." Others might counter in a similar vein, saying that anything can be taken as art: "Art is made by those who see it or interact with it." They might conclude: "Art is made by interpretation." Seeing would then be a kind of making. If seeing is making, however, so is hearing and so is everything we do; this is idealism run amok and generalizes the idea of *making* into obscurity.

But if this makes *seeing* too powerful, we cannot mitigate that power by appealing to some natural set of qualities that make a poem a poem. Many of the questions about poems and art rest on the idea that they are made things. Certainly some art is made by an artist. And all art needs to be recognized (and thus taken up or interpreted as art), but does that mean that art must be made? The only necessary thing here is that we have to recognize art as art for it to be art for us: but such recognition need not be understood as making art.

The premise driving these questions about art, however, is that there is no determinate or determined way to decide what will count as a poem or a work of art. One can always find exceptions to the rule that art is made. One might argue, for example, that art is parasitic on ideas of beauty that are first found in nature, and that art arises out of a particular faculty of perception and that it is also a kind of experience. Again we can call this *making*, but we can also call it *seeing* and *experiencing*, *finding*, and *being found*. I think there is something right about this counter argument (derived from Kant), but the claim that art is parasitic on natural beauty is a just-so story and suffers the same weaknesses of the theories of art as making. My central point remains: if art can be anything or nothing, then there can be no definitive answer to the question asking what it is. There will always be perfectly legitimate different and mutually conflicting answers.

* * *

Let me return to my primal everyday poems—the alphabet and "I love you." I call them primal poems because we learn them not as poems, but as useful tools to help us manage our early everyday lives. And while they have quite ordinary uses, their puissant particularities of form have the force of necessity in a way that is similar to what are more traditionally characterized as poems. The alphabet is a poem because of its contingent, that is, its arbitrary, but once established, seemingly necessary patterned order. This seemingly necessary order describes its form, its particularity. It is what catches us. "I love you" is a poem because it confesses the necessity of another human being in a standardized phrase bearing the sense and implications of that necessity, of the beloved's necessity. As a phrase, "I love you" has the particularity of a word with the meaningfulness of a sentence. The A, B, C's, on the other hand, make a song that once I start to sing, I follow along as if I were falling. That is how its necessity feels to me. I am taken up by its form as much as I take it up in my recitation.

If these are primal poems, then the notion of poetry expands beyond the ordinary model of an intentional object made of words. The alphabet, for example, while linguistic in import, does not consist of words nor does it have any particular semantic sense. It has a particularity, and fits with our linguistic practices. The phrase "I love you," while made of words and having a sense (as much as any statement does, at least), matters because it means so much more and other than simply what it says.

The alphabet and "I love you" are special aspects of our human experience, but they are extensions of a more common, although no less amazing, aspect of human life: language. In the case of these primal poems (and thus of what I call poems) and words (language) something gains a form that seems necessary and inevitable, even if the actual particularities of that form are arbitrary. We do not hear the sounds that make up a word as tones once we know a language; we hear the word. Once we know a language, we have become vulnerable to it. Our vulnerability to language begins as a vulnerability to its form, the first aspect of which is our grasping shapes and sounds as words and phrases, as meaningful in some way, even if we do not know what they mean. The written word has a shape, but a word is not its mere shape. The word is not shaped by the sounds of our pronunciations, and neither is it shaped by its combination of letters. There is nothing to be shaped. The word is revealed and our understanding of it is simply part of our hearing the word amidst other words, and the same with our reading the shapes of letters as words. We see a word as if it were a face that expresses its meanings. The way we hear words or see words as words with possible senses, grasp their countenance, their tonal particularity, constitutes a primal idea of form that matches the primal poems of the alphabet and "I love you."

What I mean by form when I talk of poems, therefore, is not what is normally meant when someone speaks of the form of a poem or the form of a painting. What I mean are the visceral particularities of things, not just words, that emerge as happenings that claim me, hold me. Other particularities of form will claim you. By form I mean those aspects of words, events, and experience, for example, that can only be made visible and understood by means of analogy; not the shape of a shoulder, but its feel; not the meter of a poem, but the pattern of our experience; not the measure of an earthquake, but its significance. All of these figurations involve not only the target, cause, or object of form, but our involvement and interaction with these. This does not make the form subjective, but rather an intersubjective mode of revelation and consequence.

Here is an example. A man who has lived in Israel for many years gets off a train in Szibucz, Galicia. The Great War has ended. The pogroms that followed the war have subsided. The man has returned to his native town. He comments:

> It takes an ordinary man a half hour to walk to the center of town, carrying baggage, it takes a quarter of an hour more. I took an hour and a half: every house, every ruin, every heap of rubbish caught my eye and held me.
>
> (2)

So begins Agnon's great novel *A Guest for the Night*. The narrator as he walks into town gets stalled, his eye held by recognitions, refuse, leavings from his past. "[E]very house, every ruin, every heap of rubbish" reveals itself to him as a poem, not necessarily one of beauty. These are poems of accident and of the eye. These accidents, continuities, and disruptions do not make poems of careful and intentional construction. They are accidental poems that have the feel of necessity; he is captured by what he sees, at least for a moment. These houses, ruins, and heaps are not poems made; they are not constructed art works. Nor are they epiphanic revelations. These are poems, but they are not made of words. They are events of form that happen to that narrator as he walks. These are the kinds of poems I study in this book, the forms of which are not only made by catastrophe and decay, but are with us every day, in ordinary ways, if we can become vulnerable enough to them. To inhabit such a poetic vulnerability constitutes an ethical discovery and accomplishment.

There are two domains of poetic vulnerability exposed in these lines from Agnon: (1) there is the poem of seeing and sight, the poem that is the subject of this bit of narration, and (2) there is the poem of description, the poem of words given to us in the story. We often forget one kind of poem in our focus on the other. Poets of words—the traditional kind of poet—take the poem as just the thing made of words, and usually it is part of some aesthetic set of ideas or it is understood within the tradition of poetry, often formalized in some way. In our everyday experience, however, we see things that we might call poetic or lyrical, imagining these are just qualities of things. Or in the tradition of romantic poetry, we call such special experiences beautiful, sublime, or revelations—epiphanies or spots of time, and in so doing we imagine we are marking these experiences as poems. My sense of everyday poems is not quite so romantic, not bound so much to aesthetic ideas. It is rather commonplace, a question of being claimed, with what import we must discover. It is as much ethical as aesthetic.

"I love you," for example, is commonplace. It first matters as a poem of our everyday lives; it is not of literature. Its form sifts and carries its promise. Love is a natural simplification that complicates my world. And the inverse: love is a complication that simplifies my world, but it is a simplicity in the way a promise can be. John Ashbery uses a common bit of nature to figure love's simplification as promise, and thus gives us an everyday poem of seeing some trees that matches the feel of love, lived within a careful tensing of everyday words strung into slightly disjunct phrases that make his written poem "Some Trees":

> To meet as far this morning
> From the world as agreeing
> With it, you and I
> Are suddenly what the trees try
>
> To tell us we are:
> That their merely being there
> Means something; that soon
> We may touch, love, explain.

The complexities and simplifications of form by which (and as which) poems emerge are both part of our dependency on language and part of our experience with everything. And thus poems are both accomplished and found.

Finding poems of the everyday, however, is itself a poetic task, one that Wallace Stevens, in the tradition of Keats' odes, teaches or, at least, displays as his poetry, describing how poems of the moment can happen in events such as the

> ... potential seemings turbulent
> In the death of a solder, like the utmost will,
> The more than human commonplace of blood,
> The breath that gushes upward and is gone...
> ("Description without Place")

This more than human commonplace of blood emerges in the way a hexagonal pattern emerges from a whirl of gnats, only to shift away. Stevens goes on. The loss of breath breathes, and "speaks for him such seemings as death gives"; the obscurity of this description can be justified only if we sense the sense of such seemings. I will attempt, as I proceed, to discover the seemings "as death gives"; they are part of my fable of both poems and love.

This particular death of a soldier may effect only a small change in the world or it may be itself one whirl of a gnat amongst others, such that in our perception of how things are as they are for us, we see or grasp a greater change than we could have imagined:

> There might be, too, a change immenser than
> A poet's metaphors in which being would
>
> Come true, a point in the fire of music where
> Dazzle yields to a clarity and we observe,
>
> And observing is completing and we are content,
> In a world that shrinks to an immediate whole...

The seemings of life and of death can overstep "[a] poet's metaphors" and a clarity can emerge out of the dazzle. This is the necessary poem that discovers *in what it is what being at all is*; as such Stevens writes a poetic riddle, both in these words and in what the poem describes. What will count as an answer to this riddle? This is a description without place until we find ourselves *as* that place for which this becomes the necessary description.

When she was five, my oldest daughter told me that her eyes sometimes got stuck on things, as if they, without asking her, just wanted to look at the patterns of the moving branches or the colors on the backs of books in the library. Poetry, Shelley suggests, "arrests the vanishing apparitions which haunt the interlunations of life." Some kinds of poetry exist in the arresting and the weighting of the eye. This weighting of the eye, like Stevens' dazzle, claims us, and in so doing situates us with the forms of things that claim us, regardless of whether those forms emerge as shapes and colors or through the patterns of sense and sound of phrases. The measure of a poem, as A. R. Ammons writes,

> ... moves to attract attention ... not to persuade
> you, enlighten you, not necessarily to delight you,
> but to hold you.
>
> *Sphere*, 30

Words must not just be heard, they must happen if they are to hold us.[8] Sentences and phrases, even single words, can at times, like a face or a gesture, catch us and hold us. This is again here love and poems meet in the phrase "I love you," like a face and its expression.

"I love you" can seem a dazzle, but, if it is more than passion, then it will yield, as Stevens describes moments in life, "to a clarity and we observe,/ And observing is completing and we are content" ("Description Without Place"). Or, maybe not. Seemings can shift into discoloration and we with them. "I love you" can become mere discoloration, a bit of emotional currency. These words require care if we are to take them up with justice.

There is a suddenness to the poems of the everyday, but there is also an open-ended need to sift and judge, to find our way with what holds us. If we are to understand "I love you" as a poem, we must understand something of love. We must remember that we cannot choose love, it happens to us, even if we don't realize that it has happened until some time after the fact. "I love you" as a confessional phrase must also have this force of happening, an event of words to match the event of feeling. If this happens, then it is a poem; if not, it is a bit of rhetoric.

How do we hear "I love you" if we hear it as a poem? I can only hint at an answer here, but I will say more later. The phrase can certainly be used as a symbol under which we figure ourselves in relation to the person who says it to us, or to whom we say it. But that is not yet to hear the poem. That is rather to use it as a talisman, maybe giving it a patina of sacredness. For the poem of the words to reveal itself, we have to hear the meaning of the phrase as necessary, as an inevitable melody. We would hear it, then, like a chair speaking, like the trees or clouds gesturing to us: as something given to us by the world as it is, like beauty. That is what love is for us when it becomes a revelation. It becomes a phrase we acknowledge, not one we merely use or understand.

Aspects of the world, like those that capture the eyes of Agnon's narrator, that caught and held my daughter's young eyes, show that the world can speak to us in this way. We do not just see things in the world, but aspects of the world reveal themselves as what they are, as if they spoke their existence to us. And in hearing the words and gestures of things we gain a vocabulary, a means of describing ourselves, of testing ourselves under their description and import. I do not mean this as a mystical, romantic fantasy, but as a hard-headed fact about the way the world is revealed to us as world we inhabit (just as love is revealed to us as a necessity for our living).

In "The Insistence of Things," the poet Charles Tomlinson describes the way we can hear things in this way:

> Towards the end of a warm spring day, the evening air, echoing with bird-calls, prepares the frost. A distant half moon in its halo. No cloud near it, only down low on the western horizon where it lies shapeless, thick and pink-purple, more like a mist. In the east, a few feathery drifters also catching the pink, last flare. The map on the moon is visible. A sound as clearly isolated as the moon (a shut door) breaks off from the farm building…

The sense of this last clause is prepared for us by the obscurity of the phrase "the map on the moon is visible"; a Borges-like description of a thing as its own representation. This might seem a bit of logical nonsense, since in order to represent something, the means of representation must be logically distinct from that which it represents (it need not be physically distinct). The evening air acts in preparation (it "prepares the frost") and clouds become "drifters" because they drift. And then: "A sound as clearly isolated as the moon (a shut door) breaks off from the farm building." The parenthetical explanation—"a shut door," for the sound of a door being shut—is unnecessary, but keeps us fitted with physical events. The sound, itself, becomes something other—separates out from its cause and from what is seen in the way the moon is distant and other in the sky. The personification of the air, the air that "prepares the frost," gets transplanted more aggressively into sound that "breaks off from the farm building" from which it comes.

I will not offer an explanation for these effects, except to say all of the chapters that follow explore aspects of these effects. At this point, I just want you to feel that the world can speak to us in a way that is both reasonable and compelling. But it would not speak if we were not listening.

The phrase "I love you"—like love itself—can gather itself into a force and clarity greater than what either the speaker or listener first understands. In either case, the phrase can resonate, as the sound does with the moon in Tomlinson's prose poem, in a way that gives it a form separable simply as that—as love collected in a sentence. "I love you" can become an event like this sound sounds in the landscape.

I want to stop at this point, but I cannot. "I love you," as an exemplary everyday poem, is not only an oracle or event. "I love you" is a poem because of the complexity it gathers in its simple form, because of how we meet its words as if they carried someone with them—to which we can respond and react with greater force than we might anticipate and understand. Such a phrase is a poem and surrogate for whoever would use it.

People say "I love you" and it means too much, not enough and vaguely. It is not the only way to express love, but to never say it to someone you love requires special circumstances, a particular kind of culture, and in itself manifests a way of life—a reticent, highly mannered order of virtue, for example, as in medieval Japan. Not all phrases when *not* said would show as much about the person who has not said it to the person they should. "Love" is special because love is.

Love poems, however, raise my hackles of mistrust. They are too often targets for fantasy, like platitudes treated as celebrities. You can use them to say, for whatever reasons, what you cannot say yourself. I have always found that kind of reliance on quotation suspicious: as the offering of a kind of unique intimacy in pretense, using someone else's words, expressing love with some common currency of sentiment. But this is maybe unfair. The most significant of feelings can be expressed in the most banal of expressions. I am unsettled about this.

"I love you" can express a significance that may not be understood by the person who says it. The meaningfulness of this poem of the everyday is less like the meaning of a sentence and more like the meaningfulness of an action, whose meanings will be various, bound to intentions, goals, consequences, interpretations, prejudices, saliencies, uptake, and mistakes. If the poem is a complex action, then how to take up the "I love you" is itself a complicated task. How to describe the character and the meaningfulness of the phrase is endlessly difficult. Our intentions in saying "I love you" can be variable and obscure, our goals dubious, the consequences null, our interpretations of what love means confused and contradictory, our prejudices alienating, the saliencies few or too many, our ability to respond weak or selfish, the mistakes in understanding hard to measure. Ethics and art interleave and resonate in "I love you."

Our lives with words (including my own extreme investment and mistrust) describe an ethic—not a morality of simple judgments or of political confession, but an ethic of virtue and vice, of apprehension and attitude, the motives and consequences of which reveal or disguise our character and the challenges poems can offer. What I mean by ethos describes nothing more esoteric than an attitude that emerges or that we confess in our everyday engagements with each other, in love, for example, as that love enmeshes us in negotiations and discoveries of sense and failure, possibility and hope. We might both agree that we love each other, agree in form and formulation, but we might have radically different ideas about love and about each other, ideas which we might not ourselves yet grasp, and so what is meant by our agreement and by our statements must be discovered. The normative sense of the phrase "I love you" fits uneasily with the complex set of associations, beliefs, feelings, and dispositions of we who say it and hear it. This complex set of things defines more significantly what love means than does the simple normative sense of the words and phrase. To understand the statement "I love you" is to situate it within this complexity—and thus we find ourselves intimately supporting or distantly refusing the phrase in ways we may have to discover to our surprise. This is the best model for how we should read any poem.

"I love you," the romantic poem, floats blank, too clichéd to mean much except in the way that hope can mean. I am not attempting to articulate or investigate the love in poems, but rather the poems in love. Life must be the frame for poetry. Understanding the meaning of "I love you" can be expansive or deceptive; deciding which is a delicate challenge, not to be answered by theories or truisms. Our need, however, is not simply to understand what "I love you" means, as if the phrase were a puzzle, and love a mere idea. We have to discover how the phrase claims and describes us; we have to redeem it, justify its sense and possibilities in our life and person. This is one of the oddities of love and of poems. Poems, like love, must be redeemed. In the next chapter, I will explore some of the surprising and deeply shocking ways this can happen.

2

Interruptions

We are all vulnerable in various ways. Life is like that. We live in fits and starts, in monotony—as Paul Valéry calls it—interrupted by shocks and events, losses and gains, disease and death. What Valéry calls the interruption of life we might also describe as a sense of incompletion. Nothing in our lives is completed; we are not even completed by our deaths.

> Then tell me, love,
> How that should comfort us—or anyone
> Dragged half-unnerved out of this worldly place,
> Crying to the end "I have not finished."
> ("Funeral Music," VIII, Geoffrey Hill)

How to respond to my ending and my life's unfinishing? My response is Quixotic. I aspire to write posthumously. But I don't mean what you might think I do; I don't mean to write for the future in hope of fame when I am gone. I mean something quite different. To write posthumously is to write to God, even if God is never mentioned. This is a kind of theological reckoning.

On the face of it, the possibility of writing posthumously can sound like a joke. If I am alive I can't write posthumously, because I am not dead yet; but when I am dead, and if I am known posthumously, then I have already written posthumously (because I can't write when I am dead). So it seems that I can never write posthumously, I can only be read posthumously.

But I think it is necessary to do the impossible in this case, and actually write posthumously now (as if I were writing to no one I could ever know and who could never know me). I do not mean by this that I want to write to the dead, as if I were to send a letter with Odysseus or Aeneas or Dante on one of their trips to the underworld. I actually want to write as if *I* were dead, while I am alive. It doesn't mean that I want to write with stiff arms and glazed eyes. It requires that I give up writing *for* someone, and instead write *to* someone (not as part of a conversation, but more like offering a gift). And those someones I write to are those for whom I am necessarily and permanently absent.

I write posthumously out of my imagined vanishing.

Emily Dickinson, for example, is a posthumous poet—a poet for others only after she is no longer a poet for herself.

Some posthumous poets (and writers) matter, others do not. You can never tell if you will matter posthumously ahead of time. It is an *ex post facto* discovery, and it can be unjust. But there is no court of appeal. For example, the Roman historian Sallust wrote a great, if incomplete, masterpiece on the decline of the Roman Republic. The work has not survived but for a few fragments. How could such a great and central work not have survived? I don't know. It has posthumously vanished. I wish that I could read it, but I cannot.

Sallust was not trying to write posthumously; he was writing for his fellow senators, and by writing for them he wrote toward the future. Emily Dickinson may have been writing posthumously all along. It is not clear.

To write posthumously constitutes a way of life. I think of it as a life of literary espionage. This is why I imagine that Dickinson wrote posthumously on purpose (separate even from the fact that she kept her poems in a box under her bed): she wrote like a spy, willing to remain always a spy.

In my posthumous writing, I write as a secret agent for a republic of words always gone and lost and for a republic never quite made. As a posthumous republican, I write against the *imperium* of fashion and gossip that rules the present, but I do so in secret. Even in confessing this, I do not make public its secretive form. The situation remains as Kierkegaard, in the guise of Constantin Constantius, describes in *Repetition*—a fictional me writing to a fictional you.

Words can matter beyond what they say, and they can do so in a casual and everyday manner. For example, my words can matter beyond what they say for those whom I love and for those who love and care for me. And the same for you. As part of the climate of love, *all* that we say can become the weather for others as well as for ourselves. Consequently, you cannot write posthumously *for* your friends, although you can write *to* them in that way. Posthumous writing is not part of a conversation. It is more like offering a gift.

For strangers the poems of our heartfelt confessions are more likely to be heard as noise or desperation or sentimentality. You can mitigate this by writing through borrowed forms, by disguising your words in common literary currency, by joining our various public conspiracies of convention and conformity. This last is what academic writing too often is. A posthumous writer, at least one who writes as a secret agent, is working against such conspiracies. And so I write toward strangers as if I were already dead, and I leave what I write to find its own way. I don't hide it; I just let it rest in its shroud. This is what it means to write posthumously.

The poems I like best are those written in a posthumous manner confessing or reporting the interruptions and incompletions of life.

* * *

Things happen.

Things happen that unfit us from who we thought we were or from what we were doing. We can discover this after it has happened, as if the world had changed fundamentally but we hadn't noticed the change until a month had passed. Our lives can shudder apart from who we think we are, from our person. I can be driven into disbelief: "Can this be my life?" Or I can in shock ask, "Am I this kind of person?"

We are persons and we have lives. Life is a domain of action and event in which we measure ourselves, protect ourselves, suffer disappointments, and learn that the happenings and doings of our living are not quite all that we are, feel, and need. We are not, however, just our lives. As persons we are the ones who have lives, who are agents, who care and love, who suffer and react. I am something: what I take myself to be, what you take me to be, what someone can love. I live what my life is: what happens, how it goes, limited, fallen, distorted. This is my fate. I may deserve it, or I may not. But who can measure what I deserve, or survive such a measure, the sense and justification of which will be unbalanced, the scales already weighted by that which we are trying to weigh: ourselves, our lives?

And thus we can become disjunct from our lives; feel ourselves lost to the days in which we live, the actions which we perform, the fate we have accomplished or which is completing us. A. R. Ammons tells this story well in his poem "Easter Morning." The poem begins with a thematic preamble organized through a metaphoric description of a person and his life. I will quote this beginning:

> I have a life that did not become,
> that turned aside and stopped,
> astonished:
> I hold it in me like a pregnancy or
> as on my lap a child
> not to grow or grow old but dwell on
> it is to his grave I most

> frequently return and return
> to ask what is wrong...
>
> ("Easter Morning")

"[T]he child in [him] that could not become" dwells with him. We do not often become what we imagine we would. And when we do, it is not what we thought; it cannot mean in actuality what it could mean as hope. The end of that life that could have been his happened by not happening. Its grave is held at the place of his childhood. The possibility of the life not lived collects in his person, as a pregnancy. The loss of that life that did not happen, however, is not so simply his, since it is what happened to him by not happening. It is outside of him, and thus it can sit on his lap. He finds its grave, its baby form, and his own pregnancy with that stillborn life when he returns to the place from which he came.

The idea here is more than the common notion that to grow up is to die in some way. The life that is mine is not all that has happened to me, not all that I have become, but a sense of incompleteness, of what could have been: a pregnancy in me that is never to be born but must be borne. The life that could have been is wound into what I am. My life is not my person, my being who I am with my memories and losses and hopes, and yet the sense of my life and of who I feel I am is nested one in the other. My relationship with my life is intimate and oblique. The delicate contrariness of poetry can sometimes match this intimacy and obliqueness, while at the same time it attempts to figure the nebulous wholeness of life.

Can we avoid our own stunting? Since we cannot avoid our losses, how can we survive them? The answers to such questions will not be simple. In all their forms, they will be descriptions of what we cannot quite know until we have accomplished the understanding that allows for a certain kind of ability to describe ourselves. Poems sometimes can give us the means and the right kind of trouble to prompt just self-descriptions.

Borrowing some lines from Ammons' earlier poem *Sphere*, Helen Vendler characterizes the two parts that make up Ammons' "Easter Morning" as split between grief and joy. Vendler writes that the first part of the poem says, "Grief is all I know of home" and its second part says, "Joy is all I understand" (325–6). She is right. But this seems a weakness of the poem to me. The joy, I am sure, is real, but it does not resolve or even really respond to the grief. It is an escape.

The grief is marked in this way:

> I say in the graveyard, here
> lies the flurry, now it can't come

back with help or helpful asides, now
we all buy the bitter
incompletions, pick up the knots of
horror, silently raving, and go on
crashing into empty ends not
completions, not rondures the fullness
has come into and spent itself…

In this passage, the clauses that describe the poet's grief grate against each other and make a tangle. The flurry of life lies buried. The loss cannot be helped. There is a gentle mocking in the helpful word-play; no help can bring the flurry (people, life, hopes, possibilities, noise, energy) back, not even helpful asides, helpful consolations, comments, monologues, sarcasms. The graciousness of "help" contrasted now with buying—"we all buy the bitter incompletions": from whom? How? With what? And with these questions the sense of "buy" shifts to accept or believe. "We buy, we accept these incompletions." Help has been exchanged for bitterness. The action continues confused—after buying the incompletions we pick up the knots of horror. Knots of horror, like the initial pregnancy of incompletion, convey our being trapped, helpless, convoluted—flurry turned into gnarl; but how are these knots picked up? From where?

The shifting verbal phrases and their obscurity, if not their incoherence, invoke the idea of action that is itself incomplete and stalled. The only clear action of the passage is the saying of the poet—"I say in the graveyard" (a kind of posthumous speech). While emotionally expressive, these lines primarily describe. They offer a voice tracing absence and hurt—"we all buy the bitter/ incompletions, pick up the knots of/ Horror… and go on crashing into empty ends not completions"; we crash into an empty end, into a nothing, into an absence. How does one crash into emptiness and incompletion? There is no sense to this. And thus, we make our sense in grief by finding nonsense.

The second half of the poem answers the particularity of incompleteness and loss with distraction that becomes attention that trumps the initial description. The turn happens as a shift from the barely sayable ("the flash high-burn/ momentary structure of ash") to the clichéd and fatuous ("a picture-book, letter-perfect/ Easter morning"):

The barren air
        Holds the world that was my world
though the incompletions
(& completions) burn out
standing in the flash high-burn

>   momentary structure of ash, still it
>   is a picture-book, letter-perfect
>   Easter morning...

On this Easter morning the poet goes for a walk, and we expect redemption. He finds the patterns of beauty, of order and renewal in the natural world, shifting skyward he sees what he thinks may be two eagles (a transposition of all his dead into birds? Of himself and the lost pregnancy of his youthful life?), who fly themselves into the patterns of cycle and natural ceremony.

He describes the flying of these birds: "the first/ began to circle as if looking for/ something, coasting, resting its wings/... the other bird came back and they both/ circled, looking perhaps for a draft... then flew on falling into distance till/ they broke across the local bush and/ tree... " Ammons attends to their flight and speculates on their actions. In such attention he finds, if not consecration at least consolation. After describing these birds' flights for some twenty lines, he offers a conclusion:

>   ... it was a sight of bountiful
>   majesty and integrity:

It was a sight, both a seeing and what was seen. He calls that a sight "of bountiful majesty," which is the rhetoric of song; but he also calls it "a sight of... integrity," which clunks in its abstract vagueness, a kind of unearned conceptual conclusion. How are the flights of these birds a sight of integrity? How could they be anything other than birds in flight? The integrity is thus just what they are, and not a choice, as it would be for us, especially if this integrity is meant to answer our losses and grief. "Integrity" gestures without much import.

But Ammons refocuses the poem with a naturalistic redescription of the flight of the birds that is also a figure for their own lives as birds, and for ours:

>   ... the having
>   patterns and routes, breaking
>   from them to explore other patterns or
>   better ways to routes, and then the
>   return:

This is a literal description with an analogical and consoling point. The shifting from an old pattern to a new pattern, route to new route, gives the incompletions of life, the stunting and displacements, a hopefulness. As in his earlier use of "integrity," Ammons reaches for a conclusive judgment about these patterns, but this time he earns the abstraction by embedding it in an analogy that redefines it; so he describes the patterns as sacred:

> a dance sacred as the sap in
> the trees, permanent in its descriptions
> as the ripples round the brook's
> ripplestone...

The dance of the eagles, if we are to call it sacred, is as sacred as the movement of sap in the trees. By implication, it is sacred as the movement and insistence of life. But this dance of eagles is as permanent in its descriptions as the ripples of water and the evidence of such movement and pattern in ripplestones, which we might characterize as fossilized movement (or these ripplestones might be the stones that cause these ripples). The dance of birds is like the sap of trees which is like the ripples of water which is like the ripples in stone. The interruptions of changing routes, of sap flowing and forming, of water moving in waves, of stone forming and tracing the geometry of movement provide an ultimate context for Ammons, and become targets for a kind of love, certainly a kind of attention.

Ammons achieves a naturalistic peace with minimal gestures toward conscience and ritual, indicated by the words "integrity" and "sacred." But the integrity in the poem and its sacred force is in the grief of the first part, not in the consolation of joy he reports in the second.

What Ammons offers is an allegory—a figuration of the birds and life that can replace the analogy of a failed and still-born pregnancy of life; a picture of a completion in circles (Emerson echoes here) that is endlessly unfinished but complete. It is a powerful figure, and there is a wisdom in its framing of our human loss in the patterns of universal life and existence.

His strategy is to replace one description with another, to re-allegorize the first description with his naturalized description of birds and the patterns of the world in the second half. This is beautifully done, but it is used as a trump against the loss and despair that motivate the poem. Certainly, this is one way of resolving such feelings of incompleteness and loss, but it resolves these feelings by displacing them out of their human ground and into sky and rock. And thus, Ammons resolves our very human concerns by figuring our human condition within non-human patterns of existence—bird, water, stone. What is lost in such a figuration is not only love and consciousness, but also the very notion of virtue and vice, of conscience and aspiration. Despite its poetic and consoling power, I take this as a moral failing.

In this analogical switch, Ammons has diminished himself, the person who has a life, who acts and does not act, and who feels grief. If joy resolves grief, then what is offered is consolation, a release of emotional despair into emotional appreciation. The disjunction between person and life that begins the poem is answered by its translation into an image of a life with almost no person left, just the natural cycles of life and circles of life.[1] Ammons displaces the diminished person into the patterns of nature, and thus reframes his life within a naturalistic figure of continuity. The disjunction between person and life is resolved by diminishing and subsuming his person within a generalized figuration of life. This is a kind of posthumous writing I want to resist.

The posthumous writing to which I aspire is the *inverse* of that achieved by Ammons. He describes a person displaced into possibilities of life, analogized with non-human life, which is a recognition of our participation in the history of all life and existence *per se*. But not just a recognition, since it does the work of consolation and representation. It is idealized. In my notion of posthumous writing, I want to foreground instead the recognition of life shrinking toward the particularity of a person, acting with as much virtue as a person can muster. My posthumous writing is a choice that remains human-focused, and not, as with Ammons, an idealization of an inhuman fate.

* * *

There is a morality of posthumous writing. Would Sallust have refused to write his *Historiae* if he had known it would be lost? I don't think so. He had the requisite virtue; I think he would write his histories anyway, regardless of their fate. And here is the moral: to attempt to write posthumously is to risk being forgotten posthumously. Hence the need for virtue.

Here is another example of the kind of virtue I mean. I will describe events that took place during the battle of the Chosin Reservoir, during the Korean War, in December of 1950.[2] In this battle the First Marine Division, with an attached army regimental combat team, was encircled by the numerically superior Chinese 9th Army. Many of the US army units disintegrated and were destroyed. The First Marine Division was able to fight its way out, inflicting a disproportionate number of casualties on the Chinese. At one point during the fighting, a Chinese unit overran a convoy of trucks carrying wounded soldiers from the 31st Infantry Regiment. The Chinese went down the line, setting each truck on fire, and shooting any wounded American who tried to escape the burning. When they got to one truck, they couldn't get it to light; there was no fuel left in the vehicle. So they began shooting the wounded in the back of the truck. Each soldier who was next in line to be shot, lifted himself up if he could, staring his executioner in the eye. There was no pleading, no shouting, no crying; just quiet defiance. One soldier after the other did this—shifted upright, staring at the man about to kill him. Then he was shot in the head. We know what happened because one of the soldiers who was shot somehow survived. He was the only survivor from the convoy. He commented years later: "I watched these men... looking their executioners in the eye. And I thought, *I* got to fight with *these* guys."[3]

As each soldier waited for death, as they each refused to show the fear many of them must have felt, as they refused to lose their self-control, as they insisted on remaining soldiers, they each lived posthumously. Why posthumously? Imagine their situation. They would all die, so who would know if they begged for their lives, if they screamed or cried their fear? They would be erased and forgotten. They would receive no accolades, no medals, no record. Only by mere chance do we know what happened. Their bravery was for no one but themselves. It didn't require an audience; it didn't require acknowledgment. Their dying was neither here nor there; how they faced their death was the only thing. It was their last thing. They were not living for any future; they were all already dead to that future, hence all that mattered was how they faced those who were to kill them. Posthumous living is necessarily ironic: to live posthumously is to die in a way that has no concern for the opinion of those who survive you.[4]

The soldiers chose their posthumous attitude, and in so doing manifest an integrity of person that is unlike the integrity of birds flying to which Ammons appeals.[5] Their integrity is not like the beauty of flight, but like the rage of Job. Job's integrity has many parts, and it whistles against the challenges he faces— his wife's command that he curse God and die; his friends who are no friends, unsympathetic and moralistic in their condemnation of him, the strange Elihu, and then God, a whirlwind of puissant assertion and anger.

So, Job speaks in Robert Alter's translation:
—I would speak,
No matter what befalls me.
Why should I bear my flesh in my teeth,
And my life-breath place in my palm?
Look, He slays me, I have no hope.
Yet my ways I'll dispute to His face.

(13.13-16)

Job's courage and anger fit with his sense of righteous clarity, a commitment both to God and to justice. He speaks not about consolation; he has no hope. But he speaks in dispute with God. He embodies posthumous integrity.

Job's friends, of course, insist that he must have sinned; they offer no comfort, only condemnation. Job rejects their pious self-serving recommendations, as well as their vision of God. Job insists on his own integrity before the Lord, and thus refuses to confess to sins he has not committed. And yet, as he asserts his own rectitude, he does not curse the Lord. When God speaks through the whirlwind, Job admits his error in trying to constrain God by human notions of justice and law. He acknowledges God's overwhelming power and the failure of his own legalistic measure, but he does so out of the same integrity that motivated him to resist his friends' explanations of his plight. He has no expectation of redemption or recompense. As Herbert Fingarette describes it in a remarkable essay, when Job's "integrity is at issue, all else, important as it had been, becomes to Job as nothing. Job is unwavering in his refusal to sellout his integrity for the sake of getting back prosperity" (271). Like the soldiers of the 31st Infantry Regiment, Job acts with an integrity that has no justification in reward or mitigation. Death is darkness and nothing. To act with such integrity without belief in future recompense or redemption, without calculation, regardless of consequence, is to act posthumously.

**

To live in incompletion is to live unsettled. I am terribly unsettled. Maybe my unsettledness is just what St. Augustine would call anyone's restless heart until it rests in God, or some might say in the absolute peace of no longer wanting or needing anything, or in the escaping of our dependencies, as Freud believed. All of these explanations of unrest seem to me to be confessions of our being human: our desire for a cure from the unrest betraying our desire to be something other than human.

So I try to jump ahead of my own incompletion and write posthumously. In posthumous writing, one has to write incompletely of incompletion. Hence, my theme is interruption. It came to me as a kind of surprise. As did the realization that there is no completion in our lives or in our deaths; if we are lucky there are interruptions along the way, and they make a life and a story.

To write posthumously would be to take interruption as a principle of life. Why is that? Think of an interruption as a frictionless slippage in your day. All of the sudden you lose control. You can't decide where to go. You just go wherever. Usually, we regain control after an interruption. But imagine that the life that matters is not the monotony of one thing after another, but is rather made by interruptions, slippages; what kind of story would it be if you wrote *out of* those interruptions and *about* those interruptions? You would have to give up your idea that such slippages of the moment were things to escape, irritations to overcome; you would have to build your continuities of sense out of your slipping and sliding.

To write of interruptions as if they were the ligaments of life, and not the mistakes that happen to us, requires a posthumous sensibility. Think again of those soldiers in the truck. Most of them were young, and they were going along doing the things people do—and then they got interrupted: off they go to the army, and then off they go to Korea. And they fight here and there, with their friends, living from day to day, and then they get interrupted by a bullet or something, and so they get wounded. Then they are going along, in a truck on a road near the Chosin Reservoir in freezing Korean winter—not having a lot of fun, but they are going—and things are directed toward a certain goal—getting to Hungnam so they can get on ships and get away from the Chinese 9th Army. But then the Chinese interrupted them, again. That was bad. And then they permanently interrupted them by shooting them in the head. But these soldiers didn't just accept this final interruption. They responded to it with courage and defiance. That is what makes their bad interruption into something posthumously worthy, even if no one living had ever discovered how they had each faced their executioners.

Think, too, of biological history. Every extinct species lives posthumously, not being able to live in any other way. And if that species were to write (as a species, not as individuals) to a future species, to one of their species' descendants, for example, and that future species could read that writing, then that writing would be posthumous writing. Fossils are a kind of inadvertent posthumous writing.

That is an interspecies example. There are many intra-species examples of interruption, as well. For example, Emerson imagined, as did Vico before him, that language was fossilized poetry. Our words are posthumous poems.

The Hittites offer another example of our posthumous dependencies. I don't mean the so-called Hittites mentioned in the Bible. Up until the end of the nineteenth century, we thought the Hittites were a small Canaanite tribe. Those Hittites were misnamed and were not the people we now know as Hittites, the people of the Land of Hatti.[6] The Hittite empire, one of the dominant powers in the Late Bronze Age, had been completely forgotten for millennia. We now know that the Hittites, who began their conquest of central Anatolia sometime in the early Second Millennia BCE, were allies of the much weaker and marginalized

Trojans when Agamemnon landed his Greek forces at the entrance into the Dardanelles.

In 1902, a Norwegian philologist announced that he had discovered a hitherto unknown Indo-European language that we now call Hittite. This is an example of a posthumous language, not only a language recovered after the people who spoke it have died, but a recovery of a language the memory of which had been completely lost.

Later an extensive archive of royal documents was found at the great Hittite capital of Hattusa. One of these documents is called the Annals of Mursili, who was a Great King in the late fourteenth century BC. His stepmother, I am sorry to say, murdered his beloved wife. He writes—

> My punishment is the death of my wife. Has this become any better? Because she [his stepmother] killed her, throughout the days of life my soul goes down to the dark netherworld on her account. For me it has been unbearable. She has bereaved me. Do you gods not recognize whose is the punishment?[7]

This was not the only offense and betrayal his stepmother, the queen, had committed against him. But Mursili, besides being a remarkable king of power and conquest, was a king of mercy.

> I did not execute her, but I deposed her from the office of swanzanni-priestess. And because it was determined by oracle that she should be removed from office, I removed her from office, and gave her a place of residence. Nothing is lacking to her. She is alive. She beholds the sun of heaven with her eyes. And she eats bread as one of life. Mine is only this one punishment: I punished her with this one thing, that I sent her down from the palace: I deposed her from the gods in the office of swanzanni-priestess. Mine is only this one punishment.[8]

As a kind of history of his reign the king's words display a posthumous ethos. But his goals were not posthumous in my sense; they were posthumous only in the sense that he was writing toward future generations of Hittites. The Hittite empire was in apogee, and while he well-knew the precarious fate of human life and power, he could expect that his great reign would be remembered for a long time. But it wasn't. The king died in 1295 BC and the empire continued until not long after Troy fell, for maybe another 100 years, when throughout the Near East peoples, cultures, and cities were destroyed in some kind of massive collapse and military catastrophe. And while the other great cultures of the near east were remembered in later historical times, the Hittites and King Mursili were not. So when these words of the king about his lost wife and his pernicious stepmother were recovered, we can only read them posthumously. Nothing the king said was for us, but his words have now come to us. They are the fossils of lives whose ways of fitting in the world are unknowable but through our modest reconstruction.

I would write like King Mursili, whose style I admire, but I would write such a history as if I knew it was to be forgotten. His words were forgotten, but he wrote them assuming they would not be. We must read his words posthumously, aware that our recovery of them is mere accident. What happened by accident for the Hittites (the discovery of the writings at Hattusa) I assume is unlikely to happen for me. In my posthumous writing, I give precedence to interruptions, to those kinds of interruptions that destroyed the Hittite world. In so doing, I acknowledge the suzerainty of interruption, but at the same time I refuse the power of interruption to undo *what* I am even as it will undo *that* I am. I write reports to those whose world is no longer mine, trying to resist any fantastic hope I might have that my words will be read by anyone, but still writing them so they could be read by someone. This is the goal of my posthumous writing.

I am trying to write a report about my posthumous agency, because it defines how poems can matter to me. By offering this report to you, I am not renouncing my posthumous goals, since I offer it to you as posthumously as I can. Think of my words as confessions of a literary secret agent, who expects that after his trial and execution the words spoken in his trial will be sealed away and lost, erased like Stalin had his companions erased from pictures after he had them executed.

We know what happened on that captured convoy of wounded soldiers. We know it, because one soldier survived. This is how he survived. He was tossed out of the truck with the dead bodies of the men he felt so privileged to fight with. But because he remained alive, his body still generated metabolic heat. So the Chinese beat him with their rifle butts, smashed his head many times, and threw him on a pile of bodies. Still he didn't die. His body resisted its final interruption. The Chinese went away. He rolled off the heaped bodies—and slowly crawled, very slowly crawled away—eventually getting himself across a frozen pond or river always on his hands and knees. Another wounded American found him. As they waited together, they saw two American jeeps driving toward them. Out jumped a Lieutenant Colonel, who got down on the ice next to him, putting his face very close to his, so the badly wounded soldier could hear him. The Lieutenant Colonel spoke very unposthumously. That's important to understand, even if in my reporting of the story I am speaking posthumously for him. The

Lieutenant Colonel said—"tell me, son, tell me where are you hurt, so I don't hurt you anymore."

Interruption and incompleteness constitute a fundamental condition to which our ethical investment in words is a partial (of course always incomplete!) response. And beyond words, all art is a response to counter the incompleteness, to quiet the unrest. But those attempts to make quiet create their own noise of incompletion. Poems and what we say about poems consist of incomplete thoughts and ideas. The incompleteness of poems we attempt to complete with ourselves, with interpretations and with theories.

It is in this incompleteness, however, that literature is like our ordinary understanding, which is also shot through with incomplete thoughts and ideas, implicit theories or images about how things work and how they fit, half-justified if not half-confused.

My life with words is a wrestling with and sometimes a forgetting into incompletion. On the one hand, I attempt to articulate my thoughts and feelings and my life, to cast such articulations into the breaches of incompletion, toward my dependencies. On the other hand, I forget, as we all do and must, so many things, many of which mattered in ways we can never know. I think of posthumous writing as a way of accepting incompleteness and dependence, of our dependence on our own descriptions and on the descriptions of others. It is an attempt to write, act, and stand in the most extreme vulnerability with all the integrity of being that we can muster, without audience, expectation, consolation, redemption; it is to stand before God.

We read and make poems out of our own sense of our own incompleteness. The interruptions of death and love give the form for the interruption of art, the paradigmatic form for me being a poem. A poem has the form of an interruption, the particularity of which depends on what it interrupts and how. Its power of interruption conveys its seeming force of necessity, as if it had to be just what it is, like a melody, like the alphabet, like our confessions of love. But none of these had to be what they are; it just seems like it. A poem is a face that interrupts us. The face of a person whom we love is a poem that interrupts us. This is one way to describe the relationship between poems and the world.

Life ends by being incomplete. The incompletion realized by our deaths is continually mimicked in our living through the incompleteness expressed as hope or promise or despair or hopelessness. The incompleteness we live is just the difference between us now and whatever awaits us. The incompleteness of our lives still ahead or soon to be truncated shows us to be incompletely made. The difference between our being persons and our having lives defines a moral predicament, one that we try to answer with words. If our descriptions of our persons and our lives can accomplish the semblance of completion, or show us what is not yet finished in our days, even if this is only our imaginings, then these descriptions seem to carry what we are. Is this enough to redeem us? I doubt it; but how we effect these descriptions might decide if we are present enough in the world—even to ourselves—to be worth redeeming.

3

Can We Speak a Poem into Existence?

Important questions follow from the previous chapter. How can we sustain a posthumous attitude? Can we instigate our own moral interruption? Before we go on with such questions, we must take a step back. I have insisted that the events of form—certain expressions of love, interruptions that require a posthumous response—are poems; that poems are not necessarily made of words. I want to make a more straightforward argument about how we relate to words and poems in order to demonstrate the legitimacy of this claim. In this chapter, I argue and demonstrate that poems are more and other than words, and in so doing begin to show that we live amidst revelations to which we have too often become blind. I do this by asking, Can we speak a poem into existence? What is the poem that we might hear or find in our voice, in our tones with words?

We must remember that poems have no necessary form. They can be doubted out of existence. "That is no poem," someone says with disdain, "it is mere noise." "Not true," I say, "it is certainly a poem. Can't you hear its music?" This appeal is not likely to work. "Listen," I say, "I will read it to you and prove it's a poem." So I read it and then look up: "Don't you see? It's a poem." "No, no, I don't hear it. Where is the poetry in these words?" I start to explicate its sense, describe its rhetorical effects, offer an aesthetic justification of its particularity. "Sorry, I just don't feel it," you reply. In frustration, I insist, "Just listen," and I begin to recite the poem again. I read the words *into* a particular tone.[1] You hear it. "It is a poem!," you exclaim. The poem is revealed—but where? If the poem is revealed by my tone of voice in reading, then is that where the poem is, in the tones of my reading, in the art of my voice?

A tone of voice can be expressive. Christopher Ricks comments: "Tone has been called the expression on the face of the words."[2] One can analyze the exercise of tone as the face of words in its provocations and intimations, as does

Ricks in his subtle examination of tone in Eliot's poetry. But my task is different. I will explore tone as a way of finding how the meaningfulness of a face models how words, phrases, and poems grip us with power and portency.

Faces? How are we to understand the faces of words? In the physical world, we live on and amidst, against and behind surfaces. We push against them, puncture them, break them, wrap ourselves within them or around them. We also live with words. But they have no surfaces; the shape of a word is not its surface, since the word means within the context of a sentence and that meaning is not bound to the shape of the word. The shape of the word reveals the word that it is, but it does not determine what that word means.

We can repeat a word over and over until it blurs into mere sound, or close to it. The blurring is a double vision, not a blending, because sounds recognized as a word are logically distinct from sounds remaining sounds. We hear the word not as sounds, some odd melody, but as that particular word. The word requires its form (sounds or marks) in order to be grasped, but its form is arbitrary and could be changed. This relationship between word and means of manifestation is critical in understanding tone and our relationship with words (and with the forms of things). It is this relationship out of which poems emerge.

Let me develop the above description of words. A word makes a whole greater than its form. I see its shapes of letters (which are already marks greater than the forms that make them up) *as* what they show, which is the word. And the same with the word given to me in sounds. The word is a whole and the whole is given or manifest by its parts, but it is not constituted by them. A word is not like a car. The parts of the car that allow it to move and function, and therefore constitute the essential aspects of the car as a car, do not dissolve in the form of the car that we drive or see. The parts function relative to a purpose, if all goes well. The marks and sounds that make up a word, however, dissolve into the word when we recognize it both as a word and as the word it is.

Consequently, the word is not its shape. Its shape is just a means of identifying it. The meaning of a word, however this is understood, is expressed by means of the particularity of the word (however it is manifest). A word is bound to its shape and sound, but it is not equivalent to it, hence its shape and sound can alter or even be replaced. The form of a word (again, its shape or sound) is accidental and contingent, and yet some form is necessary for the word to be manifest as what it is. All the means at our disposal for expressing ourselves have a similar logical form: some means of manifestation is required and what is expressed, if it is anything, must have some particular form in order to be recognized. But what is expressed is not equivalent, not reducible, to its means of manifestation.

To see a word in its shape or hear it in its sound is to apprehend its face, even if we do not yet understand what the word might mean in the phrase of which it is a part. A word, of course, has a face by analogy, but this analogy is not mere decoration or exposition. It is an essential analogy, since we have no more immediate way to describe the meaningfulness of words than by some analogical means. The quality of meaningfulness that collects in the form of a word is a revelation; it just happens and we get it. It is both miraculous and trivial. It is miraculous because it collects the complexity of language into a word. It is trivial because, once we understand language (or can read), it is just how we see and hear those things we call words.

But like any analogy, this analogy has limits. We express ourselves through our face, just as we express ourselves using words. The words we use, however, are not as intimately ours as is our face. Words are shared in ways our face is not, although our picturing of our faces and our recognition of similarities amongst faces push faces closer to words than we might first imagine.

We enact a complicated play between our face and the faces of words, especially as the faces are manifest not in shapes but in sounds and tones. We can participate in the form of words by saying them, reciting them, singing them, and in so doing we correlate those sounds with the expressions of our own face. This participation with words is like our participation with forms. It is the intimacy that precipitates those events of form that I am calling everyday poems.

* * *

A tone of voice seems more primitive than language. Dogs seem to have tones of barking. Babies cry in various tones. A tone seems emotionally expressive. And thus it seems a simple observation to note that we can not only alter our tone as we read a poem, but also that we can search for and sometimes find the right tone for a particular word in a particular poem. But that sense of tonal rightness also seems akin to a sense that a word in a poem (or in our everyday talk) is right (or wrong) in a way beyond its sense. This might not simply be a question of connotations, but rather of fitting and effect relative to the other possible tones of other words in the poem. In this case, "tone" means something different than what is expressed by our voice in recitation, but it is analogous. What we call the tone of writing, its *feel*, is parasitic on our sense that we express *feeling* by means of tonal variations and choices.

Words have no inside. They are not mere marks or sounds, however; and we feel that language at least might have an inside, especially when we imagine, as we sometimes do, that we cannot get outside of language (when we think propositionally, for example). Or we can feel like words have insides when, on the other hand, we imagine that we can get outside of words, when we react to paintings or gestures of need or love with a sense that something is shown that cannot be said. Some things *can* be shown that cannot be said; as Wittgenstein commented—the sound of a clarinet cannot not be said.[3] Why would we expect that it could? Similarly, we can describe a cloud, but how could we say a cloud, speak a cloud? Do we imagine that such a saying or speaking would just be a cloud floating? A cloud cannot be said, because to say something requires that the means of our saying be logically distinct from that which we talk about. Plato realized this, and other philosophers have rediscovered it, always with a mix of recognition and surprise.

* * *

Tracing the lineaments of confession in the tones attempted in a poem gives the poem its claim on us. We express feeling by means of intonation. If I read a poem with feeling, then, as Wittgenstein describes: "The sentences have a different *ring*."[4] That ring, that sound and sense, has a rightness that comes from my "careful attention to my intonation." Judgment about the proper way of reading a poem is manifest in both my tone and in how I react to my successes and failures of tone.

Wittgenstein is right to comment, as he does in Part II of *Investigations*, that to imagine a picture might help him to speak a poem with the right intonation; that if he fails to give a poem an adequate shape through sound, that failure can be revealed in his facial expression as he recites the poem:

> "When I read a poem or narrative with feeling, surely something goes on in me which does not go on when I merely skim the lines for information."— What processes am I alluding to?—The sentences have a different *ring*. I pay careful attention to my intonation. Sometimes a word has the wrong intonation, I emphasize it too much or too little. I notice this and shew it in my face. I might later talk about my reading in detail, for example about the mistakes in my tone of voice. Sometimes a picture, as it were an illustration, comes to me. And this seems to help me read with the correct expression.[5]

That a picture might help one read with the correct expression (whatever that might be) already suggests that the poem is not just a configuration of words on the page, not simply the meaning of the phrases of which it is made, but it is rather a meaningfulness that to be articulated must be articulated in a certain way, given further form through my involvement with it. If the poem were simply the meaning of its words, then any recitation would do. *That* it does not mean just what its words do suggests that it is more than such meanings. What is shown through my intonation of the poem is not its mere sound (the sound of its words), but my taking these words into the sounds of my voice, my intonation, into the physiognomy of my understanding.

This last metaphor must be more than decoration. "[T]he physiognomy of my understanding" describes how my understanding is manifest, made apparent as something to judge and understand. My tone in this case is not simply a way of expressing my understanding. Coming to the right intonation in saying the poem can be a discovery of a way of showing the poem as a poem (and that it is a poem). I can realize after saying the poem: "That is the right way to say it!" or even "That is the poem!". It is not my understanding that I am expressing in this tone but the poem that I am articulating into audibility, into visibility. I make it manifest as what it is. Through my own tone (and face), I am giving the poem a face.

The face of a poem does not emerge out of its configuration on the page. Such a look or configuration we might call its clothes or its body. What I am calling the face of the poem is different. The face of a poem projects itself into the world *as* how we recognize it, how we take it up and how it holds us; we give the face of the poem eyes by our ways of reading it, by our expressions and tones. (This is why seeing a picture can orient us toward the right intonation.)

Resisting as he does so the idea that something special goes on inside us when we find our way with a poem, Wittgenstein continues his consideration of tone in reciting a poem: "I can also give a word a tone of voice which brings out the meaning of the rest, almost as if this word were a picture of the whole thing."[6] The tone by which we articulate a word carries with it our understanding of the word—and its place among others. A tone can situate other words before and after in relation to this conveyed sense. The tone is my expression, but it serves to "bring out the meaning of the rest." Wittgenstein's description of this "bringing out" allows that a tone can show the whole poem under the aspect of that tone. But the "aspect of a tone" is an odd description. The tone does not offer a picture of anything, but is only a sound: this sound, however, situates the speaker in relation to these words, so that it is the force of that person speaking the words in the way that he or she does that shows the words of the poem as fitting together. This is not because the words of the poem so spoken somehow become the speaker's. If a tone is to have this organizing and revealing force, these words cannot be ours, cannot be meaningful as part of a conversation. If they were, the tone would express *my* meaning, not the poem's. If the tone is strong enough to absorb the words into a speech act, then the poem is given that single meaning: it would then be illustrative or expressive in the way that any set of words would be in such a communicative act. If the tone does not provide this kind of determinate meaning, then it is a meaningfulness that allows a tone to stand for and frame the entire poem. And a word said with such a tone can show the meaning of the other words as if they all made a face, the surrogate of which is our face in reciting them.[7]

* * *

All art is incomplete, and so we epitomize it into parody to give it a place amongst us by manifesting it despite that incompleteness. There exists no literal face of words or poems, hence their need to borrow our faces in surrogate, just as we give them our voice, our gestures, our belief. In reciting words of a poem that are not mine, I am not speaking in my own voice. I become some kind of mime, or a kind of fictionalized person, speaking the words of the poem that are not mine as if they were, with a tone of investment and absorption. The words of the poem I recite with meaning are not like those I speak in conversation, but they claim me, in some ways more so, since I might be more deliberate, more attentive. I could use a tone, and then afterward renounce it: dismiss it as a failure and wrong. When I recite a poem with understanding, I am experimenting with its words, inhabiting their sense or letting them inhabit my understanding.

A tone symbolizes how thoughts can hold us, possess us, and yet not simply be ours. Criticism would be a way of reading in various tones in order to discover the tone that can take one beyond oneself. One might write, read, or think through poetry in order to discover one's own words. We should conclude then that if our thoughts can be stolen (as they surely can), then our thoughts can steal us. The reason for this is not something that can simply be said.

Every word we speak must be given a tone; there is no toneless word or phrase; a neutral tone is still a tone. The point is more general. Whatever form and sense a word, phrase, or sentences (propositions) has, it must be manifest somehow, open to correction and revision, graspable and deniable (we can at any time say: "that's not what I meant"). Tone is the way we make these manifest aurally. And while we can infuse a neutral tone with great complexity, words and their senses require some manifestation to be what they are, and thus even if there are different tones and modes of manifestation, and even if we have more attitudes toward words than simply our grasping of a phrase's propositional content, that manifestation is part of the word (and thus part of its possible senses). There is no grace in movement if something—our hand, our arm, our torso—does not move. (There is also grace in not moving.)

Tone is accomplished, but in that accomplishment, something is revealed. Any particular tone, in this sense, interprets what could be said in some other tone. The accomplishment of that tone requires appeals to exemplars, to the complexities of judgment and taste that organize ethical judgment. With ethics, we are always faced with an incompleteness in our criteria of judgment relative to the complexity of motive and situation, and are always dependent on the acuity of our apprehension of the situation relative to our various goals and values. This mix of apprehension, judgment, and situation requires that we depend on analogy and example to clarify and simplify our understanding such that we can act. With poems, we are involved with similar types of apprehensions, understandings, and judgments—again bound to complex and incomplete criteria of evaluation and even of identification. (Is this a poem? Is this a good poem?).

To get the tone right I might not have to have a precise idea of the meaning of the poem; a gesture might do. And hence I might find my way with the words by imagining or remembering a situation or experience, by picturing a face or even by watching my own face as I recite. Here meaningfulness guides meaning; it is not that the sense is irrelevant, but that orientation with words is sometimes more important than explicit understanding. This describes a central quality of many poems: meaningfulness often matters more than specific meanings (although these are seldom irrelevant). This is true even when we read in order to interpret a poem into sense. This sense of meaningfulness (as opposed to propositional content or meaning) is cognate with how the human face is meaningful, not simply as human, but when we see (and how we see) the faces of those we love.

A pattern of tones can make a ceremony; a ceremony can reveal a poem. A ceremony is an action trying to become an event. In a ceremony, we act—through repetitions of form or formalizations of some kind, even if only of attention—to produce an event, a happening of form. A ceremony is attempted, and sometimes accomplished. Just as mistrust can devolve into suspicion, dismissal, and disregard, a ceremony can degrade into preciousness, affected gesture and rote form. And if we fear, for whatever reason, that all such ceremonies are caucus races—that is, a running anywhere, stopping whenever, everyone winning and thus no one winning—then with what sense or form can our ceremonies matter?

But they do matter. We can turn caucus races into real races or trump them, survive them in a way that separates us from their pointlessness, transporting us into some other pattern of action and event, reaction, and response. Showing caucus races to be forms of hope is one possibility found in poems, especially everyday poems, if we can find a way to take them up or to find ourselves taken up by them. But how? By reading, by writing, by thinking our way into the right kind of vulnerability. And what is that?

* * *

Cormac McCarthy, in his great novel *The Road*, shows us an everyday poem of ceremony, an event of form, enacted through a tense confluence of hope and fear. In the novel, human existence, after a world-inflicted cataclysmic event, has degraded into horror. A father and son travel the road, searching for food, trying to stay alive, walking forward, half-starved, on the edge of desperation. The father must wash the brains of a man he has killed out of the hair of his child. Afterward, "… he sat holding him while he tousled his hair before the fire to dry it. All of this like some ancient anointing. So be it. Evoke the forms. Where you've nothing else construct ceremonies out of the air and breathe upon them."[8] The life of father and son are made out of little ceremonies of speech and gesture. The father lives through doggedness and love. He finds in momentary simplicities a form of faith to sustain both himself and his son.

A ceremony of this kind holds someone in a community of faith. But the kind of faith needed is special: it cannot be built out of belief, since there is little to believe in for the father. The world is too savage and decayed. The faith he needs and makes must lie in what he can do, what he can find in what he can do in the moment, in what father and son are to each other beyond all ceremony, but shown mostly through ceremonies. Father and son must believe in what the other says, and they usually do; but not always. There is trust; but it is trust in what they are, father and son, and it needs no other name. There is an imperative to protect each other beyond all limit—and that means that they would kill each other rather than let either be used as food for the cannibals that many have become in this world. Facing that need, knowing that there are horrors worse than death, cannot be helped by belief in each other. They must have faith in something more than their wandering, if only to give themselves hope. But what is needed more than anything is courage. Courage is required in the act of making ceremonies: "Where you've nothing else construct ceremonies out of the air and breathe upon them."[9]

Such a ceremony is a form, but less a form of ritual than a way of acting with a degree of self-reflection and commitment that marks a current action as part of some greater pattern of action. That pattern is made by our acting with a sense of self-reflective concern: the father is giving his son a particular kind of attention, which offers in its form a kind of hope provided by continuity and his care. The continuity must be expressed as that hope, a hope directed toward his son, not simply unconscious habit, and it must be taken up as hope, although this only entails fitting himself in some degree into the pattern made through his ceremony.

Again, I repeat: a ceremony, like this ceremony between father and son or like a wedding ceremony, is an action trying to become an event. In a ceremony, we act—we have a certain tone of voice, we repeat phrases and gestures, we can feel like we are participating in a tradition or a sacrament or rite. We attempt ceremonies, and sometimes accomplish them. A ceremony that matters, that situates us within its forms, becomes a happening of form. It is not simply a happening with form, as if the form can be found elsewhere and put on for the ceremony. These kinds of everyday ceremonies reveal the meaningfulness of the forms by which those forms do whatever other work they do. The form is itself accomplished: it happens.

Such a ceremony makes a poem, reveals it, in this case, as a poem not of words, but of gestures. (If you insist that poems must be made of words, then this ceremony offers an analogy for how poems can be more than mere words.) The father tries to fit a faith in life forward, beyond the moments of everyday struggle for survival and against the bleak horror of life in this future world toward some greater hope. He describes, as a way of holding his son within the world of action and threat, a sense of imaginative meaningfulness.

This ceremony of affection arises after the washing away of blood and brains, after a purification of the consequence not only of the violence of the fighting and killing, but of their survival. They were under threat, and they live and struggle through a world of unmitigated aggression and danger. The act of caring through attention is a ceremony if it marks or expresses a difference between the domain of father and son and that of everyone else. The act is ceremonial because it is an assertion, an acknowledgment of the difference between these two domains, and thus is itself a domestication of the violence the father used to defend his son. The ceremony shows what that violence means—a caring motivated by love and an expression of how father and son are separate from the degradation around them.

I recognize the rightness of McCarthy's description and of the act described because of how it fits and arises in the story; we have seen a pattern of interaction, in which father and son demonstrate their mutual love and commitment. We could make this explicit by citing the examples of care, responsibility, generosity, and selflessness: the father shows us what it means to be a father. Our recognition is also bound to our own moral understanding and experience of love and family.

But there is one aspect of what is offered to us in this description that goes beyond this recognition. The ceremony is made through breath, or the invocation of breath, in analogy with breath. At first the act and the breath gather a complexity of sensibility, linked as it is to our living and to long-standing ideas and descriptions of God's creation. The moment of ceremony described is like what the narrator of Agnon's *A Guest for the Night* says about the young nubile Rachel: "every word that comes from Rachel's lips seems to me like a complete conversation... when she let fall a word or two they won a place in your heart, so that you gave up part of what was yours and it became hers."[10] Words are shared like our breath can be shared. We breathe the same air and if we recognize that, then our intimacy becomes a sharing exchange. This poem of the moment is given to us by analogy: "every word... seems to me like a complete conversation..." It seems; a word (every word) seems like a conversation, a whole and complete conversation. Her words are concentrated with implication. And much else—promise, possibility, a wholeness: we have no way of knowing what but by discovering some kind of sense through imagination, memory, sensitivity.

A ceremony is the display of a form, made meaningful, even if without some specific meaning, through our commitment to the lives it sustains or cherishes. Reading such a ceremony is itself a form of cherishing it, of breathing into it. Reading with such breath requires an active attention in which one situates oneself within what is read. One must find oneself amidst such ceremonies, responsible for them, but not fanatic about them, since we must protect particular human beings within the ceremonies of our attention, and not replace the living with ideas or beliefs. These ceremonies are for the living and motivated by love.

Remembering the living and this love of particular persons and not of ceremony *per se* requires a mistrust of the ceremony, guided, however, by an extravagance of attention. The ceremony is not the point, the person is. So the ceremony cannot be allowed to become too strong. But ceremonies, like those between this father and son, help sustain our lives together, just as our ceremonies with words help us sustain ourselves with words and our words with ourselves.

I am trying to suggest that the ceremony of art is a moral act, similar in kind with this ceremony between father and son. Such ceremonies require choices that are explicitly commitments: but their moral content is not determined by this alone. What matters most is to what we are committed and how.

But there is a problem. Ceremonies of love whose targets are people are different in kind from those whose targets are poems. Poems are forms, words, gestures. They are not people. Not only are poems not people, they have a different kind of claim on us than even the conversations of others have.

We can give poems special authority or respect, but this is exactly what I want to resist. Poems are the means of some further love. They should not be the objects or targets of love, except in a secondary sense. To make a case for this claim, I must step back a bit.

I love poems, not in spite of, but through my mistrust of them. In this I treat poems in ways that are similar to how I treat people, but with a significant inversion. It seems to me justified to mistrust, in some general way, people who are not my friends or family. I can of course mistrust friends and family, but that mistrust would be a consequence of knowledge and experience. With strangers, since I lack adequate knowledge of who they are and what they are like, I am naturally wary, a bit cautious, even if still open. Wariness or mistrust of this kind describes a questioning of appearances, a tendency not to take things at face value. This mistrust of others can be taken too far. We should not get lost in pathological distrust, imagining that others speak in secret codes, assuming that they lie most of the time, that they don't know what they mean (although in a certain mood I think all of these things are true). But one lives with one's mistrust, and it does not debar one from helping others, interacting with them, and valuing them. This changes the more one becomes intimate with someone. The closer one is to someone the more destructive mistrust becomes. If you love someone, then regardless of what they have done, regardless of your own judgment, you must trust them and risk your disappointment or worse. To not trust them will simply produce what you fear most. I find that many times poems are like people I do not know, and thus I begin with mistrust, and settle there. But some poems claim me with the force not only of beauty, but of love.

If the analogy with people holds, then I should give up my mistrust. I might, as C. S. Lewis suggests in *An Experiment in Criticism*, refuse to use poems for my own interpretative or emotional reasons, and instead, as if toward God, receive the poem, open myself to its claims and discipline. For Lewis this idea of reception is modeled on prayer and our attitude toward sacred texts. Poems, however, do not have the authority or warrant that a believer would give to sacred texts or to God. Without the warrant of authority why would one trust the dictates of what we read as poetry? Lewis appeals to the model of prayer to distinguish how we should stand toward literary art from our egotistical use of it for entertainment. Lewis gives art a quasi-sacred power. In any case, I refuse to give it that status. But that does not mean that I then think one should use poetry for one's own ends.

Lewis is right, as is Iris Murdoch in "The Sovereignty of Good," in seeing our attitudes toward art as too often symptomatic of our own human egoisms.

Poems do matter and are meaningful beyond what they say, and thus their value and content do not lie in our grasping of them. They grasp us. And this is what I mean by love—my love of a poem. But at this point I have to qualify the analogy between poems and people: this love survives for me through mistrust, not despite it, and my mistrust does not threaten my intimacy with the beloved as it would if she were a person. A mistrust of poems is a mistrust of certain pretensions of meaning, significance, and implication with which we might surround a poem, or even which seem carried by the poem itself, in its tone, sense, and import. Such a mistrust is itself an ethical stance toward the ways we imagine ourselves to ourselves, to the ways we succumb or do not succumb to the attractions of ideas and words.

This mistrust is not to be alleviated or assuaged; I can find no answer or solution to it. Reading poems is only trivially like being a detective. There is no killer to find, no doubt to remove. In poetry what would count as a crime is a riddle and thus always open to further consideration. Instead of catching the criminal, we have to catch the crime, or let it catch us. Poetry should remain always a trap in order to work its prize into what we prize. Our attitude toward a poem determines how we are vulnerable to it.

A poem is not just what it is, but it is an example of something—of a poetics, of something we can care about, of a feeling and a thought, and so on. But if I read in order to justify it relative to my own involvement with it, then I must in some way take it as an example of something about me. But this is to take the poem as an object over and against me, something like a tool or a picture. To read a poem, given our own involvement with language, is more like taking myself as an example of the poem (maybe an exemplification). That would be like taking myself as an example of what a photograph of myself shows. This is the wrong way around. But our relation to words and to ourselves is such that this is what poems offer, and it is the way in which poems are redeemed: I become an example of the poem, and in my reading the poem I discover this or I do not. If I do not, then the poem is a mere poem. And this is not an all or nothing thing: parts of a poem might claim me in this way and other parts might not.

Tone is an infusion of intention or suggestion, of meaningfulness and emphasis. It is expressive and indicative. We can speak it, sing it, gesture it. And through our correlations with language, we can order words in ways that give a tone, albeit more indeterminate, in what we say or write, even if we take up these words silently in reading. The reciprocal relation between how we read something and how we might picture ourselves—the ways in which the face we give to words through tone can correlate with our face or another's—shows how we can be captured by tone, which, like breath, can be shared. We hear the tone of a phrase relative to other possible tones. Tone, therefore, is a mode of analogical suggestion: as if I were saying, "Listen, hear the word (phrase, poem) like this."

We inhabit a world of tones. Our ideas of tone extend beyond sound not only into diction and the art of putting words together, but into how we inhabit spaces and interact with the world. Situations have a tone: streets and houses have tones; the past has a tone; hope is a tone. This is not mere metaphor, but a consequence of how tone correlates things, situates something with the complexity of our person and our lives. A tone is a mode of simplification that collects much that we can only guess at in a normative pattern that we can recognize.

With our voice we can seem to inhabit not only what words reveal, but the words, themselves; we might call this a kind of investment. We say—"Recite the poem like you mean it." But this *meaning it,* while conveying the idea that the words are mine, that they are expressing me, and thus that I am somehow in them, can be imitated, mimicked, put on—and thus, I would inhabit these words not as I might my skin, but like my clothes. That is not the only way of inhabiting words, however. I am claimed by a poem and reveal its poetry when its words are not mere clothing, but when I inhabit them as I do my face.

All art is incomplete. We do something with it in order to give it a place amongst us, by manifesting it despite that incompleteness. Our tone helps complete art by binding it to us, to our voice and to our face in its expressiveness, even if this binding is only temporary and is really our binding ourselves to it—to the poem through our voice and in our face.[11]

4

Epithalamion

I have never liked weddings. Too often, when I have been forced to attend a wedding, whenever I have gotten married, for example, I have found the mix of opera and pot-luck dissolves what Spenser, in his *Epithalamion*, characterizes as the glorious wonder of love made sacred and ordinary in two particular lives. So weddings distress me. This is as much my fault of attention, or rather of distraction, as it is the fault of the fissures of sentiment that brittle marrying couples to their fates.

To put on a marriage of forms requires very little to accomplish. An actual marriage of intimacy and stability, however, requires virtue, luck, and persistence, and mutual and reciprocal descriptions. So as much as the wedding is one thing and the marriage another, how one accomplishes the wedding suggests what one understands a marriage to be. But the wedding is not the forms and rituals, in whatever variation; it is the sacrament by which a commitment to mutual description, at the very least, becomes an event and a power, a necessity through which two lives must be organized. We can only get married through a kind of linguistic and descriptive surrogacy. Such a surrogacy mimics the process of reading and of rational negotiation within a broader social and a more intimate attempt to find ourselves held together with someone. To describe a wedding in this way shows how, if successful, it would be a poem, a poem of the everyday, even though one does not get married every day.

Usually it takes many years to accomplish a true wedding of lives and possibilities, and too often it never happens. At the very least, a wedding should be a way of taking responsibility for what we mean by marrying each other. That is a difficult thing to do before we have lived our marriage. Praise and lament are attitudes we can take toward things we only half understand. If those two extremes seem inadequate, what kind of faith can support our commitments to each other? How do we translate our anxieties and failures into intelligible patterns that can still support our loves?

A wedding is an attempt to share in our responsibilities to each other. How can we do that? My brother once upon a time asked me to speak at his wedding. What could he have wanted—entertainment, stories about his joyful three-year-old exploits or his humorous adolescent missteps? If I spoke after the minister, I would be part of the consecration of the marriage itself, not simply a speaker at a gathering of people. I did not want to tell stories of commemoration, like those performed at receptions in which everyone acts as if they were in a movie. My first wife had a friend who rode to and from her wedding in a horse-drawn carriage, waving like Snow White before she went to live with her dull husband in a mobile home. One is supposed to get lost in these weddings, like at a dance or carnival, papered with sentimental confetti. A wedding speech can always turn into a carriage, the words the waves of the princess in her *a la mode faux* parade.

But who should speak at a wedding? Who does speak? A priest, a minister, a justice of the peace, a person with the authority to establish a contract, all licenses in place. The marriage is an entering into that contract, an elaborate way of signing it, of agreeing to the binding. Do we need marriage as a commemoration of love? By what authority does anyone enter into his or her own marriage? We stand in such a ceremony as free agents, trying to show we are not puppets, trying to display our acceptance of a new form of social obligation. We speak, two people to each other. But after this formal speech what else needs to be accomplished? Mock ritual readings of hallmark sentiments, music symbolizing symbols of love, hearts and doves, glitter and rented opulence, gifted extravagance, or nothing, an honor to our various poverties?

To speak at a wedding is to stand as some kind of ministering priest, even without the sanction of the church. My brother's wedding was Protestant. So I stood there as a representative of something: I was a representative of the democracy of spirit that makes anyone who can be designated responsible for consecrating the wedding agreement with extra-legal spirit. I was there to offer a form to what was done and what was happening that was not a contract. I wanted to point like the ghost of Christmas Future to some mark of the inevitable that we should all avoid. Not the wedding; it was too late for that. A wedding is already a push against fate.

If marriage like love resists the fates, it pushes against the necessities that bind us, attempting to domesticate those necessities into greater kindness, I would hope, although that is probably not usually successful. Kindness is a grace that is hard to sustain. We are too prickly in our desires and anxieties. Kindness is a great virtue.

Pushing against fate is pushing against necessity. Only necessity can resist necessity. Marriage is an attempt to imitate necessity. Why only imitate? How can a promise and the laws that support it make a necessity for us, a necessity out of our choice to get married? Promises fit our actions and feelings and fall out of our actions and feelings, so we can fall out of promises since the promises we can make are often really expressions of our wants and dispositions. Our fate is not quite ours to promise, although it is ours to pursue and resist. Laws, on the other hand, are unseemly attempts to order what is surprising or to make something of what is mostly an accident. What is to be done let no one undo by any means that is not as great as the means of doing it in the first place.

The necessity of marriage is communicated by the necessary 'I do' of the wedding. But this last necessary act does not make anything else necessary. Hope is stronger than promises; but also weaker, since it can follow the birds in winter. Still I can only sustain myself, and yet I cannot sustain myself. Hence our need for imitations of necessity. Also for prayers and sex. And for special powers.

We too often mistake authority for necessity.

Priestly power was once immense. Authority can attach to someone and make them special. The authority of love is meant to do that, can do that to anyone. Priests once matched that authority with their own. If he said you were married, within the proper form, you were married. This power was similar to the power they had with bread and wine. Their power was circumscribed by religious and social constraints, thank God. People believe too much. Mischievous priests might spring on unsuspecting couples walking innocently down the garden path: "you're married!," "you're married!." That is the wrong kind of glee with which to bind people together.

Not everyone believes priests really have this power anymore. Still, marriages remain marriages. They remain bound to the same social and legal constraints to which they have always been bound, more or less. They still entail social and legal obligations. These obligations, however, are certainly diminished.

Since I could not speak as a priest, I was not quite sure what to say at my brother's wedding. My goal in speaking was simply to see if I could talk myself into the right way of saying the right words, and thus of finding an end to my words.

I could not discover or even rediscover the right words unless I try to speak them to someone: a wedding is after all not a fiction. Nor is what I am writing here. But to protect the actuality of speaking, to protect these words I am writing now against fictionalization, I will pretend that I am still speaking before those actual people who got married. To speak in this pretend way is not quite decorous. You, who are reading this, must stand in for the audience at that wedding. And in this too, the fictions of weddings are like the demands of poetry. Poems are challenges for you to take them as your own. You need not; you usually should not, but it matters if you do, and it matters in a way not dissimilar to how one takes up a marriage. How far away we each are from the wedding couple will often be shown by how our partner responds to us and we to them after the wedding, on the way home; a dangerous time of retrospection.

I am standing now in front of these people. My brother and his new wife standing too, but to the side. I have to speak. Do I wish I could have the priestly Eucharist power with words? Poets do; they want the ability to say something that alters the world, to transform something from one state, the unmarried state, for example, into another, the state of connubial bliss.

The priestly Eucharist power has its residual traces in how we ordinary people can use our ordinary language. If, for example, I were to curse in front of the wedding party (pretend that it is you here), undoubtedly the blood pressure, heart rate, and flush response of my parents would increase. Any of us can say something that can make someone blush. Words in this way can alter the world, maybe not alter wine, but they can alter physiology. They can make things happen.

Or I might break down and cry. Some of you might feel sorry for me then. Someone might even cry with me. My wife would think I was silly. Notice, however, that I don't say that my brother would be mad or embarrassed. I suspect that no matter what I might say he would be amused. My words for him, no matter what I say, as long as with kindness, will mark the event. He would not expect that anything I could say would sanctify the occasion. What is required is that the particular commitment between husband and wife be matched with symbolic expressions of recognition of that commitment.

Making my parents mad, my wife embarrassed, and my brother amused would mock the occasion, not further it. If what priests can say now is more conventional than theological, the marriage ceremony still rests on the special power of words. There are two special powers of words that matter in marrying. First, we can say things that matter and that mean to us personally, individually, with words that are shared, borrowed, not only as all words are, but also in patterns and forms that are given to us. And second, one way to speak in the midst of such forms is to perform something, to perform the speech act that J. L. Austin calls performative. Regardless of the logical difficulties in providing an adequate account of such uses of language, it is certainly true that we can perform certain speech acts in which what we say does not just mean something but does something.[1] When I christen a ship I do not just refer to it, I actually name it—even if that means I am the owner of the ship and I write my chosen name on a legal register. When I name my child, I really do name her, at least for the time being. When I promise something, I really do make that promise, even if I do not keep it. When x and y say "I do," by that statement they commit the act of marriage. All of these are less acts, however, than activities, sanctioned in various ways. They are activities by means of which we attempt to produce the event of the promise, of the marriage.

We get married. A wedding is not a stage for marriage itself. It is a mousetrap, but not just to expose the guilt of the guilty. Hamlet's play to catch the king's guilty countenance as he watches a brother murder a brother is a parable of our ambitions and fears, not just of our crimes. Marriage can be an allegory of our lives in a way that we have to discover: the order of life cycled through attachment and withdrawal, commitment and knowledge, the purposes and accomplishments traced between two people and the family they make or lose. Should we believe that if our marriage is true, our wedding a promise we keep, that our lives will then gain a point or a depth? Or is marriage a way we describe our lives in order to see what it would mean for our lives and our loves to have a point or depth beyond satisfying our wants? Marriage can be either. It can be either, because at any time amidst our living we can shift out of our lives and see them from the outside, as if they were pictures or parodies of what we imagined our lives would be. "Is this my life?" is a question that can trap us and come unbidden. The wedding is a play in a play of our lives, or at least a play in the play of the marriage that begins with it. A wedding is a parable of what the marriage might become or be. The play in a play is just all one play; it is our pretending that makes it more. We can give depth to our lives by pretending, but at some point the pretense will give out and we will find that our lives are the mousetrap for the wedding we once had. We will find ourselves guilty or saved. At that point, we will have to find ways of recovering our hopes or of renouncing them.

A wedding is a time of anxiety, or it should be. Anxiety is one state of being alive, being uncertain in our certitudes; do I know if I love her? Yes, I know this. The real fear is that she will not always love me or that I will not always love her. But love is not love that alteration finds: should we vote to see if this is true? If we are lucky and good enough, we will discover that it is true. Cast your mate as one of the continents and then look to discover constancy. There are lots of models for such expeditions, some hopeful and some terrible: Marco Polo to China,

Scott to the pole, Cortez to Mexico, Burton to Lake Victoria, and long-forgotten travelers from one town to another, one village to another, a picnic to the hills, a walk from one room to another.

How did we get here? How did I find you? Love you? "Oh dears, we are all chance and flotsam." That is the wrong tone for a wedding. Maybe this would be better: life is an optical exam. You go back and forth between types and options, "is this better or this?," until it is right. It is, however, a dual optical exam, and you have to match your better and worse with someone else's. We are often cast into our actions like fish cast by the currents of the sea, the conventions of our school turning us left instead of right, into the net. For us our actions string the net of our personality. There is an important conclusion from this. There is little that cannot be bettered by love, and marriage can consecrate love. Still, a marriage is living a life, not loving a person. This is the hardest thing to accept.

It is not a mistake to recite poetry at a wedding. We can use poetry to recognize ourselves, not just to give ourselves away. That is how poetry can become like Hamlet's mousetrap. A wedding is a great poem. Not like a sonnet. But like *ring around the rosie*, your pockets full of posies; or like the first time your child says she loves you and understands fully what it means to say it to you. We play the forms of commitment into a story that we can now tell about ourselves. A poem is nowhere in the poem. It is not simply the words or their meaning; it is something which is more or other than anything we can call it. That is why poetry can amaze and be like love. Thus, if a wedding is like a poem, it is collected in the event, in what happens, not simply in what is said.

I can find the moment, those particular few seconds in which my brother and my sister-in-law got married. 4:32 p.m. on that day in that year. A wedding is an event. But can I find the fulcrum, the means that turned their belief (love is a belief) into an act (being together is an act) into a state (a marriage)? That is the actual wedding, and that is the poem. These are events, but of a special sort. They are something we discover like a proper description of a person or a day. It is a plot made into a poem of the moment.

I am writing now more than what I spoke then, but my goal is the same: can I find the words that will not lie and that will not lose what we call the truth of love and marriage? But it isn't a truth; it is not an assertion about a state of affairs; it is not to be evaluated as consistent or coherent. The truth we call the truth of love is better called the meaning of something. We can describe it, but not really know it. It slips away and can slip back.

But if we can speak too much, we do too little. Calling speech an act does not stave off what should be done that is more than talk—carrying your child to bed after she falls asleep, cleaning the garage, holding hands, caring for parents. But then calling your wife, or your ex-wife, on the phone is an act beyond what you say.

Lying and being lost in our words—Hamlet's fate and contrivance—slip him into moral danger. He can seem to prevaricate, to delay, to weaken into impotence as he waits to act. Or, in his pursuit of revenge, does he fling his intelligence against the simplicity of the decisions and fears that surround him? He loses his world because he finds he is only half in it. Hamlet, dispossessed of his father and thus of his place in the court, remains a prince, but unsettled. He is bound to his father, and in setting himself astride sense, his nonsense casts him as a ghost at court. He is, as Ophelia describes him, undone, not himself, "as if he had been loosed out of hell/ to speak of horrors" (2.1.83-4). His deceptions or insanity or moods match uneasily with his revenge, his betrayals (of Ophelia, of Rosencrantz and Guildenstern), his mocking cruelty of Polonius, such that what his true goals are and who he is for himself and for others—and for us—is undecidable. But he is an enigma that we recognize.

Stendhal says love has to hide: if you cannot contrive, then you cannot love, and thus you have to hide, and if you hide you are never fully anywhere. Hamlet is only half anywhere, but without the love. Hamlet, the cynic, exceeds his world by hiding himself from it, losing himself in half disguises, without hope in actions, losing himself in too great a belief in words, in what he says and unsays, intimates and claims.

He loves the form of words as if they were enough by themselves to populate the world, as if the deceptions of art were as much revelations as disguises, the words of the ghost a more compelling target for compassion than Ophelia's despair and weakness. This is why Hamlet matches the tragedies of Romeo and Juliet. Both Romeo and Juliet die from the consequences of believing that romance believed is all there is to love. How comic. Hamlet lets his belief in words carry their meaning. He lets all words become poetic excuses to believe or reject. His world is infected by mousetraps, word games against others and against himself. Hamlet believes too much in words, and yet he also uses them carelessly as tools, masks, and toys. If words are not binding, then neither is the world: psychosis, hysteria, invention, imagination, projection are always carried with both our words and our senses of how those words or our thoughts show the world and lose it.

Marriage matches the temptations we face when reading a poem or a fiction. We should include love in this matching; both love and marriage in this are the same. The danger of reading a poem, in living in this world, would seem to lie in the way anything can be lost to fantasy, to doubting others and ourselves. The *force of poetry* to claim our attention would seem to lie in the way it encourages our denial of it, a denial of meaning, the acceptance of nonsense into our lives as something people make.

So we can also say: the *force of love and marriage*, like the temptations of poetry to claim our attention, would seem to lie in the way it encourages our denial of it, a denial of meaning, the acceptance of nonsense into our lives as something people make. And since we are people, we are made and unmade by such nonsense, not just our own but also that made by others.

Descriptions of people and events can collect our memories, or they can lose our memories in distortions. A friend of mine admits that she does not remember the feel of the pain of childbirth, instead she remembers her own description of the pain—and through that description she remembers the pain. Our mutual descriptions hold us together or shift us into distortions, losing us to each other. We look into each other's eyes, and the circuit of understanding is completed not just in mutual desire, but in something more; but the moment shifts away, and if we describe it one way we find each other again, if we do not, then we may not. Things proceed differently.

Our descriptions, like our memories, are kinds of witnesses to what happens. At a wedding, we are witnesses of the wedding. A witness guarantees little. Certainly, the witnesses of a wedding need know little if anything about the parties involved. We need other guarantees. Witnesses ensure that a ceremony actually took place, if such reassurance would be legally required. At wedding ceremonies, friends and family parody this role of witnessing.

If witnessing for the law is not the point, maybe our witnessing remains part of the ritual transformation of man and woman into bride and groom. This ritual transformation for the woman was traditionally cast as the death of one life and the birth of another, marked by her being given from the authority of her father to the authority of her husband. Such weddings are gift exchanges; the woman is one gift among many. But can this be true anymore, even psychologically? Should we construe the bride as giving herself to the groom? Would this be like the old practice of selling oneself into slavery out of dire necessity in the ancient world? Our communities are not so dependent on ritual status, nor do women suffer the bonds of male authority in the same way or anything like the same degree as either the classical or the village societies in which such rituals would have a place.

There is another sense of witnessing that carries with it an ethical seriousness that few marriages can match. Witnessing has become a form of remembering, and hence a way of defying forgetfulness.[2] Witnessing seems the last recourse with which to challenge overwhelming loss. We can attach our moral fervor to the idea of being a witness to something. We try to stand as witnesses to what is lost in order to resist the fear that our losses are meaningless and nothing.

Such witnessing is an attempt to replace a God we might fear is already gone or never was. No matter how necessary or honorable such witnessing is, it can only become a parody of what we have lost. Another parody. It may be that when we die, our memories of love will be the final witness to the hate or pitilessness of whatever kills us. A wedding should not be a parody of anything, even in its repetitions, clichés, and rituals. But without a belief in the sanctity of these forms, how can it not become such a parody?

While my brother and his love say and do that act of marriage, what do we do, we who watch the ceremony? One would think that we watch their act of marriage as a way of recognizing their new status and relationship within our community. This was certainly the role of public marriages once, when communities were more stable and stationary. I am not sure we fully understand our role anymore in watching marriages. It can seem a bit like watching a football game. The "I do" is the winning score, which we can all cheer. We can say: "Did you see how she tilted her head before she said—'I do'? What great style." But how does that contribute to the marriage? I am no longer even in the stands watching the game. I've been asked (I was asked) to come onto the field and make a few comments. I feel like I should interview someone. The winning team goes to some holiday destination, another symbolic diamond. But the winning team never stops playing, and the "I do" is never an "I did" within the marriage. It can only be a continual act of agreement. I can say that, but the reality of saying "I do" every day is only something one can discover. It is pointless to give advice about such things.

If priests do not have Eucharist-power, they still have social power. And the married couple can say those special words that make something happen. Still what can I say that can be part of the marriage? I can't say—"welcome to the community of marriages"—without sounding silly. I do not think I can speak for any community. I can recognize, as we all can, that something is happening here today (then, on that day) and what is happening is something that has the weight of an entire life. I seem to be trying to say something like "I recognize and acknowledge this marriage." Which I do.

But I don't think my words can do any more than I could do simply by watching from the audience. Whatever I say must have a special character, if these words are going to do something and not just mean something. They must have, I think, an ethical character and they must be part of a moral act. There are in a certain tradition seven virtues (we have probably all heard the names), although they are more or less out of fashion. They are the four cardinal virtues—fortitude, temperance, prudence, and justice; and the three theological virtues—faith, hope, and charity. Since this is a marriage, the virtue that will help me figure out what to say here, the solution of which will mean that I will stop talking then and stop writing now—has got to be the greatest of all theological virtues, charity, what we translate as the theological virtue of love. The famous wedding passage, which is really about God, at *1 Corinthians 13*, which says love is patient, love is kind, and so on, could also be translated as charity is patient, charity is kind. What we translate as love in the modern Bible is the vulgate Latin word *caritas*, which is itself, used to translate the Greek word *agape*. *Caritas* and *agape* mean love, not romantic love, but the love that is expressed through charity, our cherishing God and our loving our neighbor as ourselves.

What I should express here then is *caritas*. That is not easy. Saying it is not enough. There is no magic in a word just because it is old and foreign. What can I say in English that can express charity? "I love you" will not translate *caritas*, but that phrase might give us a clue. "I love you" is not much of a phrase. Anyone can say it, God knows what it means. It's a bit of a mystery. If you say "I love you," someone is bound to ask why. Why do I love my wife?—because she is kind, smart, loving, and brought me a large dowry? Well, yes and no. The question "why do you love me?" is rightfully dreaded as a trick question, without any really good answer. You can give reasons why you love someone, and those reasons will matter. But love is not love that is justified by reasons; reasons certainly do not supply the content of the statement "I love you."

It is not the content of "I love you" that matters so much as that I say it to some particular person. I have to be able to stand behind it—and how I do that is something I have to discover and do, something she and I have to decide together. In saying "I love you" to her, I provide her with a way to describe me. What I want to say at this wedding, however, is not the romantic "I love you." I want to express charity. An act of charity is an act one cannot quite control. What it means is not fully up to me, like all expressions of love the meaning grows and is re-made through everyday, ordinary acts. When we all say, in whatever way we do, "I recognize and acknowledge this marriage," we are expressing an act of charity, of *caritas*, as much toward ourselves as toward the marrying couple.

Our charity is not in saying this; our charity is in being a part of the wedding. Can we decide or choose to be a part of it? Is our charity a commitment or a disposition or a feeling or an action? Do we have to dance, drink, or kiss the bride? Thank God, none of these are required. We allow ourselves to matter for this couple in a way *beyond* our control, *beyond* our feelings and beliefs in love and marriage, even *beyond* our feelings and beliefs in the people getting married. My speaking must not quite be an event if it too is to fit into this wedding.

What I have to say is what someone can only say of me; I cannot quite say it myself. What they have to say of me is only what I can say of them. A mousetrap is what we set for each other in this case, but it is a mousetrap in which we want to get caught. It is like being caught in our words, or rather the words said to us; words like "I love you." But not any mousetrap will do—and it cannot be set by anyone. We are invited to find a way to risk our being trapped. What that is for me is not what it is for you. The risk lies in accepting that a wedding is a contingent act, in which we let words stand in for us; we risk cynicism when we give words this kind of power. But if we do not, we are in a greater danger of losing the person we love amidst the changes and flow of feelings and moods. A wedding is an act of description in which the couple getting married describe together how they are together. This is true for those getting married, but how can it matter how the audience and the priest and the commentator describe the wedding?

We can say more than we mean and know how. It is in this way that what we say is also an act—its consequences gather in how others respond and remember us through what we say and mean. The pattern in which what we say means is not just expressed in what we decide and claim to mean. The pattern and sense we imagine that we express in our words and acts remain only an idea for us; it is for others to describe us or forget us in their own expressions and actions.

There is no us but us. We have to do this for each other, knowing our descriptions will be incomplete and mistaken. The chorus for this love must find a marriage greater than this, greater than any marriage. We must become a chorus with a belief in love greater than anyone's particular love.

We might find a final form for this wedding in its symbols and repetitions. God and tradition could be useful. But where are the peeping eyes in the flowers, the chattering feathers, and scandalized petit fours to watch us, to comment? Where are the emissaries with the treaties or resolutions that would give us our proper form?

As a chorus we would voice a final frame for our human aspirations. That frame must be what we find in our lives. We are trying to see beyond our hand using only the light we shine through it. We see our glowing enlightened hand; not much else.

Our aspirations frame our aspirations; I want to become a chorus here, to make explicit what is possible by the frame of *caritas*. All I can do is try to make explicit the possibility that this marriage will say more than anyone here means by singing "*caritas*" into our memories. And by saying this I do; "I do." The single quotation marks mark the poem or the cliché. You have to discover which it is, and act accordingly.

5

Is a Poem the Same as Its Words?

In all of the preceding chapters, I have been arguing and attempting to demonstrate that poems should be understood as events of form that may depend on words but need not be constituted by words. An important counter to such an idea would be to insist on a poem's linguistic particularity—that it is made of words and made of particular words. But is it? Is any given poem the same as its words?

A poem, certainly, is not particular in the way a painting is particular. A copy of a poem is still *the* poem, while a copy of a painting is not the painting. But a poem is still particular, since it seems to be constituted by a specific set of words in a specific order such that to alter that order or any of those words is to make a new poem. Marianne Moore begins her poem "An Egyptian Pulled Glass Bottle in the Shape of a Fish" in the following way:

> Here we have thirst
> and patience, from the first
>   and art, as in a wave held up for us to see
>   in its essential perpendicularity[1]

She might have revised this (she often radically revised her poems) and replaced "perpendicularity" with "verticality."

> Here we have thirst
> and patience, from the first
>   and art, as in a wave held up for us to see
>   in its essential verticality

This says the same thing, but it is not the same poem. The particularity of a poem, relative to the words which make it up, constitutes a minimal description of that poem, a description independent of almost all aesthetic ideologies and philosophical commitments. The point is not that poems, like everything, are self-identical, but that for poems made of words, what seems to define them is not what is *meant* but what is *said*, the particularity of the words in their particular order. While this is a minimal description of poems made of words, it fails, as I will argue, as a definition of such poems.

The particularity of a poem motivates various aesthetic ideas. For example, Malcolm Budd begins his account of poetry by recognizing the particularity of a poem relative to its words. He writes, "The value of a poem as poem does not consist in the significance of the thoughts it expresses, for if it did, the poem could be put aside once the thoughts it expresses are grasped."[2] This fact prompts him to suggest that what matters to us is "the imaginative experience [we] undergo in reading the poem, not merely the thoughts expressed by the words of the poem." This is not a necessary conclusion, but it a very common way of understanding the value of reading a poem, which would consist, then, "in an awareness of the words as arranged in the poem."[3]

Many literary critics and a number of poets imagine that the particularity of a poem allows for the expression of new kinds of thoughts (either ineffable or grasped in some putatively non-normative way). Poems are called particular and not general, and thus poems become situated in arguments about knowledge (which is general) and freedom (often understood as particular). I want to turn aside from these aesthetic ideologies and theories, in order to investigate the logic of a poem's particularity. If we take a poem as constituted by its particular words in their particular order, we produce a surprising (often ignored) logical pressure on how those words can function and mean. If we follow out this particularity, we discover that poems are odd logical constructs. The more explicit we make the logical particularity of a poem, the more logically strange it becomes. In fact, if poems are logically constituted by what they say (their particular words) and not by what they mean, they become parodies of language, faux-language.

* * *

I understand what each sentence in *Middlemarch* (or any novel) means, but by virtue of that, do I know what *Middlemarch* as a novel means? Clearly not. Because we can know and understand the specific meaning of each and every sentence of a novel, we do not by virtue of that know and understand the meaning of the novel. The meaning of a novel is not a concatenation of the meanings of its sentences (or phrases), partly because a sentence has a different kind of meaning than does a novel. We can replace "novel" with "story" and make the same argument.

This argument can be made even more general. If I were asked to describe my day in ten sentences, I could. And those ten sentences could be perfectly intelligible. If I were then asked "What does your day mean?," or rather, "What does your account of your day means?," I might legitimately not know. I might not even know what would count as a meaning. This is seemingly the kind of meaning we are after when we talk about the meaning of a novel or a story. We could reduce these ten sentences to one sentence, but still the meaning of that sentence need not be the meaning of my day (or of my account of it) in that one sentence. The sense of "meaning" is different in each case. And thus, the sentence, what it says and means, is not equivalent to the story; it is something different than the story it tells.

One can make the same argument about poems: that knowing the meaning of the phrases that make up a poem does not mean that one understands what the poem means, suggesting again that this second use of "meaning" means something different than the first. But there is a problem in the extension of the argument to poetry. A poem need not be a story. And if a poem does tell a story, that does not mean the poem just is that story, which could, of course, be told non-poetically. Before we can extend the argument from story to poem, we, therefore, have to show that they are similar kinds of things (which seems unlikely), or we would have to show that a poem is *not equivalent* to the phrases and words of which it seems to consist.[4] With this last possibility, I have returned to the question of how a poem is defined by the words that seem to make it up. Maybe a poem just means what its sentences mean, especially if it tells no story, but expresses some emotion or makes a statement of some kind. I can reformulate this challenge into a simple question: is a poem (however defined) equivalent to its sentences? Or to make it clearer and more difficult—if a poem consists of one sentence, more or less intelligible, is that poem equivalent as a thing to that sentence, and does it then mean whatever that sentence might mean?

Before I answer that question, let me examine the easier case of a poem made of multiple sentences (or phrases). If the relationship amongst the sentences and phrases is unclear, ambiguous, and multiple, then those disjunctions and their effect prevent any equivalence between those phrases and the poem of which they are a part. The poetry of John Ashbery offers many examples, one of the more extreme being "A Last World":

Yet having once played with tawny truth
Having once looked at a cold mullet...
He wished to go far away from himself.

> There were no baskets in those jovial pine-tree forests, ...
> In that foam where he wished to be.[5]

Is playing with the tawny truth the same as looking at a cold mullet? Who is the he that wished to go far away from himself? Are we relieved that there are no baskets in those jovial pine-forests? Maybe, whoever the he is, his being far away from himself is being in some kind of foam; that sounds like a joke. The poem, in effect, includes these questions and the problems of sense they reveal. The poem cannot be the sentences because we do not know how these sentences fit together as thoughts, except as possible thoughts (or effects) in a strange thing called a poem. The disjunctive character of these sentences allows us to take the poem as separate from the sentences that make it up.

But poems are not all of one kind. A more challenging case would not be a poem of fragments, but a poem of one sentence, the sentence perfectly intelligible, thus supporting the idea that the meaning of the sentence would be the meaning of the poem. Ben Jonson writes a poem in praise of Benjamin Rudyerd, consisting of a single intelligible, if complex sentence:

> If I would wish, for truth, and not for show,
> The agèd Saturn's age, and rites to know;
> If I would strive to bring back times, and try
> The world's pure gold, and wise simplicity;
> If I would virtue set, as she was young,
> And hear her speak with one, and her first tongue;
> If holiest friendship, naked to the touch,
> I would restore, and keep it every such;
> I need no other arts, but study thee:
> Who prov'st, all these were, and again may be.[6]

Thus, the poem forms a clear argument: *If I would wish for truth, if I would recover the good of the past, if I would try the world's purity and wise simplicity, if I would return to the uncorrupt virtue of our nativity, if holiest friendship were restored without disguise and dissemblance, then you (Rudyerd) would be who I could study now to show what these were and could be.* The repeated phrase—"if I would..."—is part of a rhetorical fiction that situates the speaker within the degradation he would wish to overcome.

Why not say the poem means what the sentence means, and in the same way? If I utter the sentence in conversation, even with its cadence and ambiguities ("try" in line three), the poem will not sound like a poem; I will be accused of being pretentious, making speeches. But I could say it in praise of my admired friend, Benjamin Rudyerd. I could say it as a general comment on our degraded society. I could say it. Or write it in a letter. I could send it to anyone as a comment on how things are and how I wish they would be.

If a poem is simply highly rhetorical language, organized according to particular notions of genre, governing diction and topic and modes of address, as it seems in this case, then poems would not have any special meaning beyond their constituent sentences. They might have effects (like any rhetorical statement), producing feelings, engendering associations, suggesting allusions, and so on. But this just means that some other sentence saying the same thing would mean the same thing, although it might have a different set of rhetorical effects. In which case, the initial poem would not mean what its sentence means. It in fact would not mean at all—only its sentences would mean. There would be no poem. Until we say how a poem is different than a sentence, it is a sentence and not a poem.

If we ask how Jonson's poem-sentence is more than a sentence, we might point to its rhetorical effects and putative allusions, its implications and associations. None of these, however, need to be understood as poetic such that they make it a poem. They can just be clever ways of speaking. Nothing in the sentence makes it a poem; only our taking it as such makes it that. And when we do that, we take it as not simply a complex statement which could have been written in a letter to Rudyerd, but as a complicated and subtle poetic performance that is part of a particular social and moral context, and given its particularities of form, is separable from that context, recoverable for us as an attitude, as a set of thoughts about both morality and poetry. The sentence is not just a sentence when we take it as a poem. Our taking it as a poem has to be justified in some way. This may not seem earth-shattering, but, in effect, it makes a poem not only contingent and undefinable relative to the words of which it is made, it means that there is no integral relationship between poems separate from our construing them relative to each other, bound to our ideas of poetry. And if we take a sentence as the poem, then we take it as meaning more than what it means as a sentence. But that is to step away from sentence-meaning and to take the poem as meaningful in some other way. What is this other than a way of meaning?

Jonson's words are equivalent, as they stand, to a sentence that could be said non-poetically. For example, one could say the same words in a speech, not as a quoted poem, but as prose. In this case, we might still infer that the point was to praise Rudyerd as a way of criticizing more common behavior, the form itself giving grandeur to the wit of criticizing by praising. Or we might embed the sentence in an oration with other goals and motives. In both cases, we would evaluate the words relative to their effect and our putative goals. We might conclude that the words were perfectly chosen. The same poetic effects would be present in the speech, but none of these would turn the sentence so presented into a poem, even if we found the sentence had a special kind of interlocking integrity of effects.

The words of the speech, of course, constitute the oration as what it is. A speech is formalized, after all—and is also defined by the words which constitute it. This last is to say everything is identical to itself, and that again is not interesting in this case. The particularity of the words, in a speech, is justified relative to their effect and to the point of the speech.

This is a general point. The particularity of words (or of forms) has to be justified relative to some criteria. In many cases, the criteria constitute the particular language practice as generally understood, such that there can exist broad agreement about what those criteria are. This is the case with orations and, in many ways, with stories. It is not the case with poems.

One can react to a poem without understanding the criteria by which to judge its words as necessary, but one cannot justify those words without having a set of criteria by which to do that. When this is not the case, when the criteria are contested and thus subject to some prior commitment or investment, then either the aesthetic manifest by the poem (and our commitment to it) or the words in themselves count as the criteria of justification. In the first case, a poem is just what we take as a poem; there is no such thing as poetry separate from our ideas about it. In the second case, when we take the words themselves as constituting the criteria by which the poem is defined as what it is, the poem is self-defining and is understood separate from effects and from any justification we might offer for those words.

Consequently, a poem is equivalent to the words that make it up or it is constituted by an idea of poetry that turns its words and phrases into more than words and phrases. In the first case we have a sentence not a poem, and in the second case we have an idea and not a poem. We seem to have a problem: we can't find the poem.

To ask what Jonson's poem "To Benjamin Rudyerd" is about, and to answer "Rudyerd" or "the moral degradation of society" will not be enough to capture the content of the poem as a poem. If Jonson's praise of Rudyerd is more than a rhetorical exercise, more than a way of making it more vivid and memorable, then the poem-sentence has some significance beyond what it says. Why write a poem of praise? Why not send Rudyerd a letter or comment about him in conversation? And, of course, how you write the praise matters. Figuring out why is to go beyond what the sentences mean—but to do so is also to leave behind the idea that the poem means (at least in the way sentences do).

A poem *qua* poem is not logically distinct from its sentences in the way fictions and stories are. For a poem to mean more and other than a sentence might, it must be other than a sentence, even if it is a poem of one sentence. Poets can create logical complexities of ambiguity, disjunction, distortion, and nonsense. None of these, however, necessarily make a poem, but rather prompt a challenge to make sense of the phrases so deformed in themselves and relative to each other. To take the complexities of form as part of a poem, a poetic whole, is a further idea, and one we bring to the poem. Our attitudes and beliefs (ideas) give a sentence a promise greater than what the sentence offers as a sentence. Unlike fictions and stories, poems are conceptually other than their sentences in contingent ways, and are, therefore, dependent on our attitudes and beliefs.[7]

* * *

In ordinary situations of communication, I can fail to say what I mean (and fail to mean what I say). I can also mean (assert or state) the same thing using different, logically synonymous sentences. In all of these cases, there is no necessary relationship between what is said and what is meant; we can say and mean whatever in multiple ways. The particularity of a poem, on the other hand, seems determined by the particularity of its words. We can revise a poem, alter it significantly, but when we do so, we have just made another poem with a variable relation to a previous version. There is no ontological mystery in this. A poem is a string of words in a particular order, in which that order defines that poem as that poem.

Can this particularity of words of which the poem seems to consist function as the primary criterion for its *existence* and *recognition*? (These are two different things, but they are strongly related in the case of a poem). We might balk at using the particularity of words that make up a poem in this way, since we might describe any sentence in the same way. If we understood a sentence simply as the words that make it up, then of course it would be self-identical. But a sentence is not simply the words that make it up, just as a word is not simply constituted by its orthographic marks or its phonemes. A sentence also involves in some essential way what it expresses, its meaning, reference, significance, and so on. (I can be agnostic about this for my argument.) A poem is somehow different from how we ordinarily use and understand sentences. If we take its particular words in their particular order as constitutive, we do so by refusing to understand another sentence as equivalent (in the relevant ways) to the original poetic sentence. And thus, we would be refusing to take a poetic sentence as equivalent to a proposition that might be stated in some other way.

If this is the case, then the determinate form of the poem underdetermines the putative meaning of the poem. What are the consequences of the asymmetry between the determinacy of form and the consequent underdetermination of meaning? In other words, if we take seriously the possibility that the words of a poem would constitute it in this radical way (so that the meaning of a sentence would be necessarily underdetermined relative to those words), then what does that show a poem to be? To answer this question, we can set aside the complexities of poems, and simply examine the logical consequences of treating a simple sentence as if it were a poem constituted by its words such that there would exist no equivalent sentence in the same language. I will use the sentence "The bookcase is filled with objects."

The sentence "The bookcase is filled with objects" means that there exists a bookcase such that it is filled with objects. We can find many examples of such bookcases, although there might be some questions about what "filled with" means: How many objects on a bookshelf (in a bookcase) will make it count as "filled with objects"? This does not mean that "filled with objects" has an indeterminate meaning, but rather that its vagueness underdetermines the meaning, such that it can become problematic. If there is no way to adjudicate what is meant (because, for example, the person who said this is dead), then we can guess or have some general sense of what "filled with objects" means; but in so doing we further under-determine what the sentence means. (Again, the meaning is not indeterminate, but is generalized among various possible judgments).

We could take (in the relevant circumstances) the new sentence "The bookcase is filled with things" as logically equivalent to our previous sentence: "The bookcase is filled with objects." Both sentences could be used to refer to the same bookcase, and the truth of the sentences could be determined in the same ways (beset by the same ambiguities). If, however, we insist, that in changing "objects" to "things" we have changed the meaning, then we are claiming that the sentence is not about any particular bookcase filled with objects, since we would either be suggesting that there would be *no other way* of referring to such a bookcase except with this sentence (which is silly) or we would be using the sentence in some new and mysterious way (which is maybe the hope).

If the object-sentence and the thing-sentence cannot be used as synonyms in the way we would ordinarily use them, that is, if they cannot express the same proposition, then there are two possibilities. Either there is some special distinction being made about *things* and *objects*, or else these sentences cannot pick out what they ordinarily do anymore. If we mean what we ordinarily do by "objects" and "things," and if these cannot be used as synonyms, then these two sentences have lost the world: they cannot be about anything we could identify without further stipulation.

There is an alternative; if the object-sentence and the thing-sentence are seen as not synonymous and as having no referential overlap, we might understand them as names, in which case each sentence would be attached to some particular bookcase. If we take the sentence as a name, it has a determinate referent, but no meaning. If we do not take the sentence as a name, and we hold to the necessary particularity of the sentence, then it is no longer a sentence about bookcases. It would instead express some special and specific thought that we have yet to determine.

What kind of thought? If we insist that the sentence be treated like a poem, such that the thought about a bookcase filled with things is different than the thought of one filled with objects, then we might imagine that by insisting on this difference, we make the thoughts expressed more particular in each case. Object-thoughts would be distinct from thing-thoughts. The issue for me is not whether these are different thoughts, but whether by making a specific set of words essential to the thought, such that just those words are the thought, we make that thought (or, in this case, the meaning of the sentence) more or less determinate.

We cannot grasp the difference between object-thoughts and thing-thoughts by example, since we lost our examples once we made the sentence determinate in form. (Unless, as I have suggested, we treat it as a name). Even if we used examples to differentiate between these two thoughts, we would require further explanations, and not just a general explanation. We might argue that the word "objects" marks a special category of stuff (decorative stuff, for example), but that the word "things" describes anything—paper, old tickets, coins. Such an explanation would allow for cases of overlap (objects are always things, but not all things need be recognized as objects), and since these are thoughts (and not statements about the world *per se*), the only way to express our thoughts would be by further talk, open to further ambiguities. In effect, even if the thought putatively expressed or produced by the sentence had a particular, repeatable, and thus determinate form for me, I could not know it (nor could you) without explanation. All of this means that the thought would be logically dependent on the explanation. It would be logically dependent because the truth or falsity of the sentence, let alone its meaning, could not be determined separate from these explanations, all of which would be subject to various ambiguities. It should be emphasized that there is no fact of the matter about the truth or falsity of the sentence, and thus no epistemological ambiguity. The issue is logical, or as Wittgenstein would say grammatical. The thought and the sentence would not be and could not be determinate.

Therefore, a sentence, if radically dependent on such explanations (since no example will count as decisive), would necessarily underdetermine our explanations, and thus the thought that sentence would express. Consequently, the sentence could not differentiate between various thoughts I might have, all of which could be prompted by the sentence, nor could it differentiate, in itself, amongst various thoughts it might be taken to be about. My concern is not with how the sentence means. (Nor does my argument require a decision about the logical priority of sentences or mind-states relative to our general linguistic understanding, an important question in the philosophy of language). The initial premise of my thought experiment is that the sentence, in its particularity, has logical priority relative to any thought or content we might ascribe to it. This priority is what makes it like a poem.

The more specific and particular and necessary the words are, the more difficult it is to support the idea that there is a specific meaning of those words that could be correct or incorrect. Instead, the specific sentence has possibilities of meaning. A sentence taken as necessary in its particular form cannot be necessary relative to its meaning, since it has only possible meanings. We might, therefore, construe the sentence as like a word (as if the sentence were a single word), and, therefore, distinguish it from an ordinary sentence we might use. Under such a construal, the sentence would, like a word, have possible meanings, not a determinate meaning. Words gain specific sense within the context of a sentence. A sentence construed as a poem has a sense within the context of my interpretations of it. This is to say my interpretations have meaning, the sentence (so construed) does not; it is merely meaningful. It might be meaningful in the way an action or event can be meaningful. This argument is not an argument for any general indeterminacy of meaning, either Quinean or deconstructive, but for the peculiarities that follow from making the form of a sentence primary instead of what we might mean by means of it.

Although mathematical statements are not equivalent to sentences, the consequences of asserting the radical uniqueness of a sentence can be illustrated using mathematical formulae. The situation is like this. I believe 3+3=6, and I take that statement to be radically unique. Consequently, I deny that it is equivalent to (3)(2)=6 and I deny that it is equivalent to 4+2=6. If so, what can I mean by "6," let alone by "3+3=6"? By so asserting, I have removed 3+3=6 from mathematics; I have denied addition, equality, and the relationships of numbers. I must either imagine some special unspecified quality or meaning for 3+3=6 or what I mean by that statement is nonsense. Similarly, a unique sentence, if it could be uttered or read, would be displaced out of language, becoming a faux-sentence like a mask is a faux-face.

Thus, any ordinary sentence like "This bookcase is filled with objects," if it has no relevant equivalent (synonymous) statement that could mean the same thing relative to its truth-value (or whatever rubric of content one wants to appeal to), then such a sentence would no longer express a thought; it would become a target for interpretative speculation. If an ordinary sentence is understood as articulating a unique thought (according to whatever theory), and if no other sentence, no other logical structure can be the means of articulating that same thought, even if the sentence or thought seems ordinary to us, then we can only understand that thought by grasping not merely what we take it to say, but by excluding any other single equivalent thought (such that no sentence could say the same thing under some reasonable interpretation of "same").

It might seem to express a thought, but since it has to be a unique thought, it would also have to exclude and have different content different than any other seemingly equivalent thought-statement. (This follows from taking the words as decisive). Such a sentence would mean something we could never grasp, and it would cease to function as a sentence within our language. Such a unique thought-sentence might be meaningful in some aesthetic way, relative to some theory or interpretation, but it would no longer be a sentence. It would be a faux-sentence, the sense of which we do not know (and about the justification of which we could only speculate). To read "This bookcase is filled with objects" under these special conditions would be equivalent to understanding the words but not what was meant (or could be meant) by the sentence. The sentence "This bookcase is filled with objects" would become nonsensical, although it would still look similar to an ordinary sentence. To read the unique kind of sentence would require that we find and then reject all other possible synonymous-seeming sentences, which would then reveal the sentence as lacking sense.

* * *

I can now collect my arguments about the attempt to allow the particularity of words to constitute a sentence as a model for how a particular set of words might constitute a poem. My arguments lead to three conclusions, three different ways we can respond or construe such a unique sentence: (1) we can exclude it from the language, (2) we can treat it as a parody of a name, or (3) we can understand it as analogous to a word (or to the kind of thing words are). To exclude the sentence from the language is to say it is nonsense or it is to imagine some occult sense of meaning. If the unique sentence is construed as a name, it then has a referent and not a meaning. Reading such sentences, and such poems, would be like reading the phone book. Such a sentence would be a mere name of whatever we might take it to stipulate. If we take the unique sentence (the entire sentence) as *analogous* to a word (a single word), we would understand it as having possible meanings, not yet specific meanings. Such a sentence would not be meaningless, rather it would be meaningful in ways that have to be determined. Such a sentence might lack any particular semantic sense, but could be meaningful in ways analogous to how actions or events can be meaningful (which is not to say that it need be understood as an action or event). In other words, we have to determine how such a sentence-poem would be meaningful (not what it semantically means) through our reading of it.

A poem, if it is constituted by its words, becomes an analogical structure relative to ordinary language, and not only if we understand it as analogous with a word, as in option three above. If we understand the poem as excluded from language, for example, then it looks like an example of language, but isn't; it is nonsense. To see the poem as a parody of a name, since it would never be clear what it named, is again to see it as analogous to a name. And, of course, if we take a poem as an analogue for a word, it is analogous with one aspect of language. In all of these possible cases, the poem has become a parody or caricature of the sentence of which it is made, and thus of language itself. A poem can look linguistic, but it isn't quite. If it is defined by the particularity of its words, then it has become a parody of a sentence and of language. So what a poem *is* is already an analogy, and this before we make any sense of it, and discover (by analogical means of course) other analogies it might offer.

When we read a poem as if it were constituted by its words, *it is as if* we are mimicking ordinary reading, imagining that the words we read are ordinary words. But if we also insist that those particular words constitute the poem, then the words in the poem only approximate ordinary words. We read them that way because we have no other way to read. But we must then remember: "These are not really words but only like words; I must decide what else to do with them." With this reminder, we can then offer an interpretation of the specialness of the words, again modeled often on what we know of language, but also relative to our ideas of poetry. The oddness of what a poem is (and of where it is) requires that we figure out what to do with it. The poem becomes an ethical challenge, first given in the simple phrase "What should I do with this thing?," but then modulating into "What can this thing have to do with me?" I take this last question to be one of the gifts of poetry.

If we define a poem by its particularity (insisting that it is equivalent to the specific words of which it seems to be made), we find that this definition fails. But it reveals how poems, if understood as radically particular, pressure poetic words into faux words, or words that only look like words (are analogically words). In so doing, our relationship to language shifts (or aspects of it become more visible). If we try to reduce poems to their words, we fail and find poems elsewhere; if we give up that attempt, then we begin with an idea that poems are elsewhere. No matter what poems are, they are elsewhere than their words.

The attempt to define the poem by its particularity displaces it elsewhere. A poem as a name refers to what it names, and thus the poem is elsewhere, since it would only stand in for what it refers to. If we take the name as without a referent, as a mere name, then it collects whatever we associate with it; and again, the poem is elsewhere. If we imagine there is no adequate synonymous proposition for any particular poetic phrase, then we exclude that sentence (that poem) from the normative modes of language. In that exclusion, we would have to reject the poetic phrase as pointless, alter our own involvement with language, or find ourselves held by the phrase as a kind of nonsensical event. The poem would be elsewhere than language and we too might find ourselves elsewhere, in something like Wonderland. If a poem is like a word, then we must fit it into a sentence, what we call an interpretation. So again, the poem needs an elsewhere to be somewhere. What we see in all three of these possibilities is that poems are dispersed, never more so than when we try to make them as particular as we can. They escape us. And yet what motivates the attempt to get the words to be the poem is the fact that those words, that particularity claims us, constrains us. With poems we can find ourselves intimate with words whose sense we may not be able to fathom, and yet we are held by those words, by their form and promise. This is what poems do—they relinquish determinate meaning for the intimacy of being held by the particularity of form.

Poems are in-between: a spoonful of intersubjective soup and with each bite we eat the spoon. Poems are not in one place, and yet they are someplace. This is the riddle of poetry. But the words? Surely, specific words in a particular order make a poem. Nothing in the words makes a poem. If a poem is a set of phrases, it is not simply these phrases or even the meaning of these phrases. A poem, if it is a sentence, is always more than that sentence; otherwise, a poem would not be a poem but a sentence.

If a poem is not an act of communication, which it need not be, and if it is not a mere illustration of a poetic idea, which it should not be, then it is natural to imagine that it is constituted by the words of which it seems to be made. If it is, however, then we find the poem displaced out of language, reduced to a name or transformed into a word. In all three cases, when a poem is understood as constituted by its words (logically and thus essentially), it becomes faux-language, analogous to the words and phrases that seem to constitute it.

A poem is more than its words and phrases because it is also analogous with those words and phrases. It is elsewhere than simply in its sentences or phrases or words. If the words are strange or the words make more nonsense than sense, then we can either normalize those words and phrases into sentences that make sense (and thus they are simply code for some other sentence) or we give up taking those words as giving us the poem in themselves. Their deformation, like a parody, gives us analogies or demands theories of justification or relies on our reactions, and thus the poem shifts elsewhere from the words that prompted it. A poem is potentially something somewhere, potentially itself, just not yet.

As are we.

6

Poems and Bombs

In this chapter, I return to poems of the everyday, poems that are akin to the poem of the wedding I described in Chapter 4. A wedding attempts to produce an event, to transform the accidents of a personal relationship into a social necessity. Weddings and their aftermath are political events, infused with tensions of power. Weddings hope to accomplish a unity. Other political events attempt to create disunity. The detonation of a political bomb is one such event, an event of power. In this chapter, I investigate the everyday political poems that we can find revealed as political bombs, bombs that also reveal the grounds of poetry in what I have been calling events of form.

Power is a form of necessity that is specific to a situation. A bee flying near my face has the power described by my flinching. The bullet that kills me has the power described by my death. If it misses me then it is powerless, at least if I don't flinch. The manifestation of power (my flinching) describes this power; it does not only show it. To say that the bee's power is *described* in my flinching captures that my flinching is the actual power the bee has.

Political acts are those acts by which we attempt to produce or do produce, in whatever way, a necessary response in or by the target of the action. Politics attempts to produce, manipulate, and manage these putatively necessary responses and reactions. Thus, "power" is a name for the attempt to produce the sense of necessity in other human beings. The highest goal in politics is to mask the contingent as necessary. It is also a motive for throwing bombs.

Blown-up-people, by being blown up, get dangled and shoved by force and shock, metamorphosed into unstrung puppets of bits and pieces of themselves. Their form is broken. Bombs bomb form. But some bombs attempt to bomb more.

Terrorist bombs, for example, do not just want to go **boom** and kill people. A terrorist bomb is meant to have political effects. It is exploded for motives and reasons. The motives for a political bomb would be something someone would state, display, comment on. Of course, they could be lying, deluded or wrong. What this tells us is that a terrorist bomb has to be understood as that to be that; and so even if the motives for a bombing are unclear, mixed, or suspect, what matters is how the community targeted by the bomb understands the bomb relative to those motives that they understand as political. Admittedly that is a bit convoluted, especially given that a bomb has initially rather simplifying destructive effects. I feel my own impatience here—an x amount of explosive results in the production of y force, which has the effect of blowing apart the bodies of those who are within z yards of the explosive epicenter. But that is the bomb—not the politics of it.

I want to suggest that the kind of thing a political bomb is shows something about how we are involved with words and shows how that involvement is the ground of poetry. Consequently, we can learn something about our literature, our minds, and our everyday aspirations with poems when we look at the extraordinary aspects of political bombs. And by looking at the attempted explosive force of poetry, we might learn something about the aspirations and ironies of terrorist bombs and what they might mean beyond propaganda and fear.

Political bombs, like education and art, attempt to change minds. One history of literature might be an account of the overlapping ideologies of revolution and aesthetics, a story about how imagination came to embody freedom, how social virtue lost to self-interest, how self-interest became desire, how desires encouraged fantasies, and how fantasy and realism became moral distinctions. Luckily, I attempt a simpler task in this chapter: to describe how the political bombs inside stories are poems gone awry. They can show us how any one of us can ourselves become a bomb or find ourselves exploded.

* * *

A paradigmatic political bomb goes off at the end of Alice's adventures in Wonderland. Alice destroys the fear-inducing, albeit toothless tyranny of the Queen of Hearts during the trial of a feckless knave accused of stealing tarts. It is a mock of a trial and an example of literary criticism run amok, for the trial consists of the allegorical reading of a poem to prove the guilt of the accused. But the trial ends politically. In the face of the absurd questioning, authority, and practices of the court and its presiding monarchs, Alice refuses to recognize any more the claims to personhood and significance that have sustained the society and political order of Wonderland. She says "who cares for you?... You are just a pack of cards"; and in this non-mattering, the card-persons unshuffle back into things. Alice destroys the society of the Queen of Hearts.

Alice has been learning how to make this bomb for some time. She did this by learning to survive challenges to her own personal and species-identity and then by remembering a trick a pigeon had tried on her. Early in her adventures, amazed at how queer everything had become, especially herself, she begins to wonder who she is. She imagines she might have become one of her friends, Ada or Mabel. This is a joke. We find it funny, and she finds it bedeviling because she confuses the criteria for identification of herself, whether she has ringlets or not, for her identity as some particular person. In effect, she allows that third person descriptions of herself might determine who she is. In her bewilderment, she does not appeal to a first-person sense of herself as an I that can ask questions of herself. Instead, she decides that she will ask someone from the upper world who she is, and if she likes the person named, she will come out of the rabbit hole, if not, she won't.

She reacts better when a pigeon doubts her species-being as a little girl. Her neck has grown quite serpentine. Her head finds itself in some trees, near a nest of eggs. A mother pigeon squawks and complains, accusing Alice of wanting her eggs and of being a serpent. Alice protests. Their debate is not a conflict of opinions, but a debate about relevant intersubjective norms. For the pigeon, to eat eggs, and secondarily to have a long neck, is just to be a serpent. Alice believes that there are distinctions that importantly distinguish little girls from serpents. But these don't matter to the pigeon; and Alice must insist that criteria of identification do not determine identity *per se*; just because she can be described as a serpent does not make her one.

The argument between the pigeon and Alice does not mark a conflict between incommensurable concept schemes. The pigeon's normative distinction between serpents and non-serpents can be described relative to Alice's different set of norms. They each can learn how the other understands what they take to be the relevant distinctions. The difference that matters here is found in how they situate themselves relative to these distinctions. And given that the pigeon is a pigeon and Alice a human being, for Alice to accept the pigeon's characterization of her, to accept that someone else's third person description of her would constitute what she is, would in effect destroy her as *Alice the human being*. Understanding the pigeon's norms of judgment is one thing, accepting them as necessarily binding would in effect blow Alice up and make her something else.

Alice and the pigeon situate themselves differently within their respective intersubjective understandings of things. They exist in different ways relative to the different criteria they each use to define serpents and little girls. There is no question of subjective or objective definitions in this case, but rather two overlapping but still distinct ways of understanding the same world relative to what one values and relative to who one is, or what one is relative to the distinctions at issue. It is not, therefore, a plain fact of the matter that Alice is not a serpent, since Alice, herself, could not distinguish egg-eating-long-necked creatures from herself. The pigeon could be taught to make the distinctions Alice would want to make, but such distinctions would not matter since they would have little role in the pigeon's life. In calling Alice a serpent, the pigeon distinguishes herself as a not-serpent and a pigeon. And in her world, these are the three primary categories that organize her life of egg laying and protecting: serpent, non-serpent, and pigeon.

For the pigeon there does not exist any more abstract realm of interaction in which individuals can exist separate from how they fit within the fundamental categories of her own life. The pigeon does not have a self-definition that situates her within civil society, since that socio-economic mode of reflection and action is specifically determined by interests, although those interests allow for particular forms of abstract individualism that the pigeon can also not participate in. The pigeon recognizes no particular reason to allow persons to exist in terms that they use to define themselves, fitted within their interests, and not her own interests.

What the pigeon had done to her, Alice does to the Queen of Hearts and her fellow cards. She does it in a very careful way. She does not say—"I don't care for you silly cards"; she says "who cares for you…," generalizing the *not-caring* beyond her opinion into a set of general norms for a community of which she implicitly claims membership. From a generalized intersubjective frame, she re-establishes the norms that define the kinds of things humans and cards are as persons and things.

Alice is not trying to kill the Queen of Hearts in order to install the Queen of Clubs in her place. Alice's anarchic political bomb destroys the idea of playing card queens as queens *per se*. Alice denies the legitimacy and reality of the cards' social world. She does not do this by waking up, but by attacking the kind of thing the cards are in Wonderland. Within her dream, she re-establishes a set of norms that alter how *she* relates to things. Alice's bomb is the dissolution of one set of norms for another, both internal to her dream.

* * *

Alice's bomb uses norms to counter norms: in other words, her verbal bomb is intersubjective, a force of language and judgment that shows the world in a particular way. But what if everyone pigeons others and themselves like the pigeon attempts to pigeon Alice? Alice's bomb goes boom because she has the power to re-situate herself in the everyday world of persons and things. What if there were no escape clause that allowed one to recognize one's executioners as just cards? If so, you would find yourself in the world of *The Secret Agent*, Conrad's *tour de force* of novelistic irony, published in serial form in 1906 and as a book in 1907.

I fear our modern situations make us more like secret agents than little girls.

The Secret Agent is a tragedy of temperaments finding temporary accord, but no intimacy or understanding, and thus when the form of that accord is threatened, its collapse quickly follows. In the novel, Adolph Verloc is a secret, double agent. Disguised as an anarchist revolutionary, he imagines himself a protector of the English social order his anarchist friends want to destroy. Although he is half English and does not want to overthrow the English government, he works for the Russian empire, for reasons we only half-know.

A new Russian diplomatic regime installs itself in London. The new order does not pursue protection (the putative project of Verloc's indolent political activities), but provocation. Vladimir, the new ambassador, wants a terrorist bombing incident to prompt the English to reverse their shameful toleration of anarchists and revolutionaries in London. Vladimir wants to provoke some civilizing political oppression.

Vladimir has a theory which is the lever by which he wants the weight of the terrorist bomb to move the social order. He does not want the typical bomb that kills and maims: the passé execution of royalty or presidents or the destruction of churches, museums, or towers. Vladimir wants a terrorist provocation that cannot be rationalized away as the work of fanatics of resentment, of derangement, of special interests and needs. He wants a bombing that will be pure politics.

The bomb should express a motive and purpose which cannot be understood as personal; the motive and the cause of the bombing should not be curable by curing the perpetrators. He wants instead to produce for the middle classes a fundamental political dilemma—either the perpetrators should be destroyed, since they cannot be cured, or political society will be destroyed. Given those two choices, he believes England will revise its open-door policy for foreign dissidents.

He needs, therefore, a target that cannot easily fit with any defined interests or psychological fanaticisms. In Kantian terms, he wants a motive (and a target) that expresses something objective and universal and that cannot be reduced to psychology. If it cannot be so reduced, so the argument might go, then the force expressed will be understood as impersonal and, in some sense, universal.

Vladimir provides a parodic inversion of the Kantian aesthetics of the *Third Critique*. For Kant, what universalizes in our aesthetic judgments is the harmony of our cognitive faculties, which do not in this case grasp knowledge, but produce the experience and judgment of beauty. Beauty is the harmony shown by the form of our cognitive faculties disengaged from the world. Vladimir does not want to produce harmony, but fear. He wants something that universalizes as disharmony. This cannot be our capacities as human beings, but something that threatens those capacities. What threatens those capacities? Nonsense does. The ordinary nonsense that we can produce for others is our talk and our actions. But talk is just talk; what Vladimir wants is a fact. A nonsense fact would be a nonsense action.

Our social and political actions and relations are both harmonious and disharmonious. How they are harmonious is particular, determined by specific configurations of agreement and accord. We share our harmony in particular ways—in our social practices, values, commitments, political arrangements, and so on. We call such harmonies families, communities, and in a much more general way, States. Disharmony, on the other hand, we all share in a different way. Whatever harmonies of association we manage and participate in, what threatens them all is the noise of disharmony. So regardless of the particular social harmonies in which we live, we all share the same relation to disharmony. Thus, disharmony universalizes in a way that harmony does not. And this means that nonsense is always threatening us.[1]

What Vladimir is after, what he calls the pure political, is not only a universal force, but a necessary one. Vladimir wants to produce a necessary disharmony. Disharmony is nonsense, the unintelligible that still has the force of intention and a kind of faux sense, just like the harmony of beauty, for Kant, is meant to show the form, the faux sense, of our cognitive faculties.

The inversion of harmony into disharmony with universalizing effects has, of course, certain similarities with Kant's theory of the sublime. I do not think, however, that Kant's theory is coherent enough to work as a model for terrorist nonsense, beyond the universalizing power it shares with beauty. The sublime is a species of nonsense; but Kant's understanding of nonsense is rather different than mine. The sublime is certainly not a necessary category—one can package our sense of awe and dread and amazement in many different ways; nor do I think it can be characterized as a definite state of mind, in the way that Kant requires for his redemption of reason. Thus, I think it would burden my argument unnecessarily to clarify how the species of nonsense imagined by Vladimir relates to the "limitless" prompt for sublimity, especially with its "superadded thought of its totality" (*Critique of Judgment*, FI.I.2: §23). Vladimir's idea, and the logic of nonsense on which it is based, is not organized around the concept of reason as Kant understands it. What is critical for Vladimir is not the idea of totality in formlessness, but an overwhelming sense of challenge to social conditions. He doesn't want the dread of the nonsense of the bomb domesticated in any aesthetic sense (although how to situate the negative pleasure of the sublime with the harmony of the faculties produced by beauty is obscure in Kant). The world of politics lives in the delusions and the managements of harmony and disharmony, and thus its nonsense remains more an inversion of beauty than a case of sublimity.

A bomb is an attempt to focus a necessary disharmony in a pitiless act that others will experience as an event, and thus as unavoidable. If the motive for that act is unintelligible except as an expression of destructive force—then the force is itself just the fact of disharmony. Such an uninterpretable action that is somehow still meaningful is what Vladimir calls a fact. The bomb itself he understands as a mode of speech. He needs the bomb to be expressive of an intention, but that intention cannot be personal. It must be objective, necessary, a fact. He wants a bomb to say a fact: the fact of the political will that detonates it. He needs the bomb, therefore, to be focused, so that its unintelligibility will seem directed.

Thus, he wants an *intentionally unintentional act*—a purposeful purposelessness—but cast not as our minds or as an artifact, but as an act-event challenging the form of society and its political management. Such an act-event must be something that English society cannot subsume relative to the personalities and actions it domesticates within its civil arrangements. Relative to that society, the act-event must be inescapable and unintelligible.

But we all want things we can't have. Still, Vladimir has a plan.

Ideally, he'd like to throw a bomb into pure mathematics, for who could justify that? Of course, he admits that is too difficult. So he suggests attacking astronomy instead. Science, he argues, is the fetish of the moment, what is understood by the middle classes as the foundation of their prosperity. Therefore, science should be attacked. For this to work, the middle classes would have to see the attack on science as a threat to their prosperity and for them to understand their prosperity as constituting their lives and persons. At best, an attack against astronomy as a symbol of science would be a symbolic attack on their prosperity. Of course, this still fits with Vladimir's theory, because the bomb attack shouldn't attack prosperity (although that would be more useful given Vladimir's practical political goals) but be an expression of nonsensical force directed against the foundation of society. This is awfully subtle and implies something important about symbols. Regardless, he wants the attack to be pure form, without any real content, because pure form would be the most terrifying. There is some sense to this. An example of the pure form of a human being might be a corpse. There is an analogy here: the bombing is to society as a corpse is to a human being.

Vladimir demands that Verloc blow up Greenwich Observatory (which *was* attacked in 1894). Verloc decides after much struggle and panic to use as the bomber his simpleton brother-in-law, Stevie, a young man of great loyalty and sympathy. The young man stumbles on his way to the observatory and blows himself up.

This is bad enough, but things get worse. Mr. Verloc believes that he is loved for himself. He is not. His wife, Winnie Verloc, has sacrificed herself to him for the sake of her brother, Stevie, whom she loves with a ferocious maternal protectiveness. For her, their marriage is a contract. It is not, however, a disaster because of this. It is a relationship sustained, as the narrator comments, by a kind of temperamental superficiality of character. He says:

> Their accord was perfect, but it was not precise. It was a tacit accord, congenial to Mrs. Verloc's incuriosity and to Mr. Verloc's habits of mind, which were indolent and secret. They refrained from going to the bottom of facts and motives.
>
> (222)

Against this fragile but perfect accord, Stevie explodes. And Mrs. Verloc discovers that the cause of Stevie's death was her husband. The accidental husband has caused the accidental death of the necessary brother. Winnie Verloc's life had been a life of "single purpose" (219), in which her self-understanding and social roles and relationships have been defined by this purpose and sustained by her incuriosity. Stevie's death removes the organizing principle by which these relationships have sense and justification. Mrs. Verloc is bombed free of her life. She suffers the force of the bomb in the way Vladimir hoped, but not for the reasons he imagined (she was not shocked by the attack on science).

She then oppresses Mr. Verloc, the secret agent, severely by stabbing him with a kitchen knife. Vladimir's political bomb goes off in the Verloc's home. This means that the bomb only universalizes over a few lives. The force of the bomb, however, is of the exact form that Vladimir wanted—an explosion of nonsense that unjoints the basic social relations of people.

* * *

Verloc becomes to Winnie, following the logic of Alice's pigeon, nothing but a serpent, who has struck and killed her brother. Given her ferocious maternalism and the deal she has made with herself in order to live as Mrs. Verloc, she is maddened to desperate fury. This thought, that her husband "took the boy away to kill him," the narrator comments, "in its form, in its substance, in its effect, which was *universal*, altering even the aspect of inanimate things, [was] a thought to sit still and marvel at for ever and ever" (emphasis added, 225). This is the universalizing effect Vladimir was after—but the universal change is only locally consequential and ultimately without content.

All that is left for Winnie is the residual accident of her marriage contract: that accident is the person of her husband, who thinks he is loved for himself. The murdering bomb that Mrs. Verloc becomes is a consequence of her own suffering shock. The narrator comments that

> … this creature [Winnie Verloc], whose moral nature had been subjected to a shock of which, in the physical order, the most violent earthquake of history could only be a faint and languid rendering, was at the mercy of mere trifles, of casual contacts.
>
> (229)

How can this be true? Her shock of losing her brother has greater force than the most violent earthquake of history? Hyperbole! A joke!

But I think this is meant seriously—and rightly so. One is tempted at first, I think, to emphasize the analogy—it is as if an earthquake shattered Winnie's world, an emotional earthquake that seemed to come from beyond her understanding as if a cruel act of God. This analogy is built from other implied analogies; that the physical ground and buildings are like Winnie's moral emotional states; and that the effect of losing one's home suddenly in an earthquake alters one's sense of the world in the same way that losing her brother has for Winnie. The analogy can be justified because both earthquakes and moral shocks produce similar emotional states. But the claim is that the worst earthquake doesn't compare to Winnie's distress. The point of the analogy is to make a distinction—of mock degree. While the analogy appeals to a scale of emotional degree—the further point is to show the futility of such a comparison. The difference between the worst earthquake and her moral state is a difference not of degree, but of kind.

The narrator claims that the most violent earthquake in history (how much of the world would that destroy?) is but "a faint and languid rendering" of her moral shock. Again, I think the extremity of the comparison is correct, but we must be careful. The claim is that the earthquake is a faint rendering of her moral shock. A rendering. In other words, nothing can render her shock. Why not? The shock is not a fact of the world, it is the dissolution of the intelligible forms of Winnie's life and social world. The point of the comparison is not to situate two kinds of facts next to each other in order to express the severity of the one over the other. That comparison again sets up the distinction between them as if it were of degree. But it is not, it is of kind. The use of rendering indicates this—an actual earthquake would be a faint rendering of her moral shock. If an actual earthquake were a rendering, it would be a faint inadequate rendering of her moral shock. A shocking rendering shocks me in my grasping and understanding what is rendered, since it does not shock me because it falls on my head. An earthquake, however, shocks me not because it renders something, but because it crushes things and kills.

The analogy is a riddle: what cannot be rendered (or can only be rendered badly) by the most devastating earthquake possible? Someone's death? No; the vicissitudes of a marriage of convenience? No. The answer: a life made nonsensical. The existence of Stevie had organized completely her life and existence as sister, daughter, and wife; so this murder dissolves all aspects of her life—except the effect on her of that dissolution. Thus, her life becomes nonsense. She does not know what to do, where to go, how to live—not because the world is inhospitable, which it is, but because she no longer has any reason to do anything. She has only one thing left: the accident of Verloc's existence.

Stevie was Winnie's fetish, an idol not to worship but a factotum of purpose and commitment. This fetish was protected by an unspoken and secret contract. Mrs. Verloc refused, with the condign acceptance of Verloc, to ever question or think beyond the appearance of things, beyond the accommodations of their marriage. They never pried into the ground or reality of their relationship. Verloc thought he was loved for himself. But he was not.

And Mrs. Verloc? She had reduced herself to conform with the terms of the unstated contract she had made in order to protect her brother. With her brother dead, she is freed from her previous condition, except for the residuum of that contract. But the residuum is unaware that he is that to her. He argues, in the face of her distress, that she should buck up: what if it had been him who had been killed, and not the unfortunate Stevie? Where would she be then? For Winnie, this is just noise, evil blather, that cannot be borne. With her pigeon logic, her husband is simply a serpent of destruction; but he imagines he has a claim on her, that he has a sense as someone who is loved for himself. For Winnie he exists as solely part of the deal she made for the sake of her maternal career.

So she kills him to free herself from what is nonsensical.

* * *

Alice's mother-pigeon is who and what she is within a primary distinction defined by her political enemies, who are all egg-eating serpents. Thus, the world for the pigeon is reduced to nothing more than serpents and non-serpents. Vladimir wants his bomb to be like this, but in his case, he wants the State to recognize the anarchist's mad fury as an existential threat, so that it will act to remove those that are madly furious. Verloc is killed because he insisted on being loved for himself, and in so doing forced Winnie into a corner in which she would have to accept his claim on her, which was to her nonsense, or remove him, as the accidental residue left over from her previous life. These are all cases of pigeon logic. Something is either only x or y; and I am like x, but not y; so y is nonsense, and so forth.

We can find these pigeons of nonsense not only in the world, but inside ourselves.

One winter day in the sixth grade I had lunch with Jonathan, a friend of mine. I remember his skin looked oddly dry, as if overlaid with lines of white filigree. It seemed disturbingly unnatural. Later that day he was killed riding a motorbike. His bike slipped. He went headfirst into a car pulling out of a driveway. I keep picturing how it would have happened. The angle of it, the force of it, his surprise. But before I could fully grasp the action of the car pulling out, the bike sliding, his head hitting him dead, I saw his dry skin. I could imagine it all happening, but I could never see the aftermath, never see him hurt or dead afterward. Only, I saw his dry skin, with its white lines against the tan that looked fake somehow. I couldn't get the brittle lines of what I saw at lunch out of my mind.

The memory of his dry skin spoke a message it shouldn't have. It said: dry skin means you are going to die. I couldn't shake that foretelling sense. I was being ridiculous and irrational. Every day I began looking at people's skin. If their skin seemed dried into the similar filigree pattern that had marked Jonathan's skin on that day, I feared for them desperately. I wanted to warn them that they were in danger. That they had to be careful. I didn't say anything, but I felt sick with fear for their lives.

At school we planted a tree for Jonathan. It seemed a terribly contingent way of remembering someone. Standing next to that tree, I remembered something I hadn't before. Two years before, I had seen another motorcycle accident. Playing baseball, my teammates and I had heard an awful crunching metallic noise. We ran to see. When we got close, we saw someone lying on the street. There were people about. The rider had flown through the air and speared the curb headfirst. His helmet had split and he flowed into the gutter in both directions. Helmets shouldn't split like Styrofoam. People shouldn't lie so still on the street. My friend Chuck, who was standing next to me, started moving funny and moaning. Then he started screaming and screaming. The boy on the street was his sister's boyfriend. At first I just stared at him; I knew why he was screaming but it still didn't make sense to me. Then I just picked him up and carried him away from that place as far as I could. I thought: *Chuck has gone hysterical.*

When I remembered this standing in front of Jonathan's memorial tree, I figured that what had happened to Chuck was happening to me, just more quietly. I had become hysterical. About Jonathan's skin. I am not sure I felt any better for thinking that. I didn't want to be hysterical. His dry skin meaning death and my hysteria was a bomb exploding. It was like being shaken and strangled.

Jonathan's skin had become an awful poem, which had meanings beyond my ability to deny them. The cracked dryness of his skin made a net, it trapped me, it happened to me, like an assault, an earthquake; it was an event whose sense held me despite whatever I thought and wanted.

The fact of the rain and the thought of him sliding his head into the wheel of the car: this makes one picture in my head. And then the sight of his skin, our sitting at the blue tables, the pale light that was still bright during lunch: this makes another picture. Both pictures overlap, blur like the fast flutter of a bird's wings as it lands; Jonathan's skin and its cracked white lines make hieroglyphics in a death's head language. The ruins of his skin say death, death, death.

That is nonsense. It is hysterical. It isn't my opinion that his skin speaks death, you know. That is the strange thing. It is a fact. I see it, not like I might see a shape in a cloud, but like when I know my parents are upset, even though they haven't said a thing. Except there is no mind behind his skin expressing itself, it is instead the indifference of things, death, itself, revealing itself like a skull sucking our faces into its insides leaving bone on the outside like the exoskeleton of an insect. I can't shake that thought, that Jonathan's skin spoke Death before he died. That if he knew how to read his skin, he would have known that this was his last day alive. This is how the secret things of the world show themselves. It is as if I learned a new secret fact about the world. A fact like Tuesday is a fact. That it is Tuesday is not an objective fact about the universe, nor is it a subjective projection.

It is an intersubjective fact.

No theory or fact about hysteria could change the sense of hysteria I had discovered. The nonsense of his skin speaking death, a nonsense I can still hear, is fitted with the possible ways I can tell the story. I learned a sense of hysteria that is particular but not private. That sense is not my opinion, but a normative distinction that I can share with you. You might want to call it something else— and that would be fine. We would only have to agree about the fundamental description of the events and their effects on me. Those effects are something only I can share, but their sense is not something only I can understand.

It is as if I discovered a new day of the week. So there is Monday through Sunday—but then there is a new day called Deathsday. No one else knows about that day. They can't find it. Jonathan exists only in that day. I can see him and his skin, but that's it. His skin makes the calendar for that day.

My friend had lost his name to his skin. His skin names him now.

* * *

I am still held by the answer to a question I don't want to ask: What was the meaning of his skin? The form of his skin holds not just his death but me. The two accidents of that day—his skin and his death—make a necessary link. And they fit with Chuck's distress. I had discovered a normative sense over these examples of what I called "hysteria." Because this notion of *hysteria* is defined by and is a constituent part of these experiences, the word and his skin describe for me a necessary distinction. This sense of necessity is all important.

Jonathan's dry skin really does *show* me death—not in the way I feared, as a premonition—but as an example of how anyone can turn unintelligible to themselves when things turn unintelligible in the world. Such a dynamic is what I have been calling a bomb—whether it is moral or political will depend on how it fits with other stories, with our senses of things, and with its scope.

Recognizing my reaction to Jonathan's skin as like Chuck's hysterical panic does not explain anything. It provides me with a new target for interpretation. My interpretation may express more hysteria. To make sense of how the meaning of my friend's skin can actually have the meaning of death but still not be an oracle of the gods, I have to recognize that I am pigeoned by my friend's skin in ways that Alice was able to resist when the mother pigeon tried to pigeon her as a snake. I am afflicted by wild pigeons calling me names, unable to do anything but survive my belief that the skin saying it is death is Death.

I have already suggested that the most famous poem many of us have probably learned is the simple sentence "I love you." The words are simple, but how one says them is all important. When your child says that she loves you with understanding and feeling you are amazed. It is something you can hear in her voice and see in her eyes. It is a statement of the most immediate expressive meaning and a statement of the most obscure and indeterminate sense. It requires and prompts interpretation. I call it a poem because our initial response is almost as if to an action, one that is meaningful but the meaning of which we have to discover. And we discover it through our sense of its form and through all that we understand about life and love—and all that we understand of the person who says it.

I am using "hysteria" of myself in this story like I might use the phrase "I love you" in expressing love to someone I love. My story itself shows you what I mean by that. You might resist my use of "hysteria." You could only do that not by offering some authoritative definition, but by retelling my story in a way that replaced hysteria with something else. Then we would debate about how to interpret my own story. "Hysteria" and phrases like "I love you" are analogues of bombs—they require interpretation because they produce effects that are meaningful, but whose specific meaning is up for grabs.[2] We are at stake in how we take them, and in this we discover ourselves in ways that might surprise us, disturb us. We might even terrify ourselves: "Do I really love her?!" Or "She has skin and it is death!"

Bombs of pure form go off all the time, not only when death and dry skin get stuck together, but when I linked one death with another; ramifying those explosions into a particular abstract form—which I called *hysteria*. I made my own bomb with my story and my described memories.

A political bomb, like a moral bomb, is that because it is recognized as that. But on the other hand, such bombs just happen. We cannot decide that they will have the catastrophic effect we might want (as horrible as that sounds); we cannot build the meaning of the bomb into the bomb. So in recognizing a political bomb or a moral bomb—in being affected by its conceptual force—we are exposed in its happening as people who can be so affected. This is again a bit like Kant's account of aesthetic judgments. But the conduit of force here is not the relation between concept and particular, as with Kant, but between accident and necessity.

It is possible that the only necessity really at issue with these bombs is that of death, or maybe the necessary analogy between nonsense and death. I have been implying that all political bombs and moral bombs imitate corpses because they are versions of death. Any death is accidental—a combination of contingent factors, choices made, actions of others, chance effects and events—that when gathered in a fateful moment produce a death. The *possibility* of that death, however, is necessary. It is the form of the death that is accidental. To recognize one of these bombs—to recognize their pigeon logic—is partly to imitate that logic in oneself. This happens to Winnie Verloc. The sense of her life disintegrates and leaves a man before her who claims to be her husband. He is to her only an accident of a contract, and not a person who should be loved for himself. She sees him as the pigeon sees Alice, but with more devastating effects, partly because there are times and circumstances in which one cannot go on unless things make sense. Verloc is all that is left of the contract of her life—and he is a bit of nonsense: an irritating noise trying to be music. Alice is a hero because she is able to go on despite things not making sense; if she had lived most of her life in Wonderland, she would not have been able to do that. She might have taken to ambushing the Queen of Hearts or kidnapping knaves and cutting them in half.

In the Horrorland world of *The Secret Agent*, life follows the vectors of Vladimir's theory of terrorism: the accidents of life turn into necessities and then those necessities are attacked and destroyed. Political and moral bombs are necessities that destroy. Literature sometimes mimics such bombs: it too turns accidents into necessities in the way my friend's skin was turned into death. Literature lacks the chemistry to explode. But it redescribes the chemistry of bombs that do explode and extends that chemistry into the concepts of sense and nonsense, and thus into us.

When we are overmastered by a surprising necessary nonsense, we are victims of moral or political bombs. If the nonsense is an external threat, we might turn into pigeon terrorists. If we find that we, ourselves, are that necessary nonsense, if we have gotten ourselves wrong in some profound way, then we may pigeon ourselves into panic or paralysis.

Politics may just be the ways we describe our disharmony with each other in such a way as to inherit or imagine ourselves as secret agents for what we can only discover when it is too late to redeem our disappointments and misunderstandings.

I think the prime motive for literature is that we get ourselves wrong in profound ways: we pigeon ourselves by accident and in anxiety. And the hope literature offers is that we can learn how to forgive ourselves for our mistakes before we blow ourselves up.

7

Crucifixion Can Seem Like Standing in Air

My friend's skin by some accident had dried into engraved swirls and a senescent surface, as if he had been powdered by death. I had no idea he would die when I noticed the wrongness of his skin, but afterward, the look of his skin spoke *Death*. His skin had become a poem that I could read, but also that held me beyond my choice. Written poems can speak *Death*, as well. For me, the best example of such a poem is T. S. Eliot's *The Waste Land*.

All interpretations require constraints. When I read *The Waste Land*, I am constrained by an analogy—that nonsense is like the dead and the dead are like nonsense. *The Waste Land* is infused with this analogy. It pivots on the dead. Consequently, I do not read the sense of the poem; I read its nonsense. And when I read its nonsense, I read my fate with death. Which means that in *The Waste Land*, death and the dead get correlat*ed with the failing of sense.* When we stumble over nonsense, we stumble over corpses and dead things.

The Waste Land is filled with dead things: "[T]he dead tree," "I was neither/living nor dead, and I knew nothing," "Lilacs out of the dead land," "Out of this stony rubbish," "Are you alive, or not?," "Phlebas... a fortnight dead," "With a dead sound... that corpse," "I had not thought death had undone so many." This landscape of the dead, this land of waste and of the wasted, does not make a history. The names do not "stand up alone," as the Apache say of placenames that mark the landscape with story.[1] Nor does the poem of these dead make an elegy. There is bitterness at loss, but not grieving. The wasteland is a place between. *The Waste Land* reveals the border between the living and the dead, a place where half-dead overlap with the already dead. Whatever we find in such a land of shifting forms and distress, we must discover. And so, we must ask: How should we read this poem of moral shock? How should we understand a land scared and scaring for those who live in it, its voices and descriptions retrospectively revealing the shocks and moral bombs that have left it in ruins? It is a Wonderland: as if Alice had never escaped back home, and instead had become a terrorist of satire, fighting against those who would attempt to mock her, to dismiss her, to take her to be a snake as the mother pigeon does. How should we read such a poem of catastrophe and disruption?

If being half-dead correlates with half-sense, then reading *The Waste Land*, and asking after its dead, requires that we read how it loses sense, how it fails to mean, even how things—the poem and the things represented within it—do not mean. I ask after its nonsense because I am asking about the dead (its dead and my own). The dead will not answer our inquiries. So we must speak for them. There is more than one way of doing that. I attempt it through impersonation, as if its words were our own. This requires that we discover how it targets us, how it claims us. To impersonate *The Waste Land*—the poem and the language-world it shows—we must learn to read its unintelligibility, its failures of sense, as our own dying, so that our response to our reading (to the poem) becomes a moral test that drives us out of the poem and back into our lives. This is how I find myself dying, the world dead, and my hopes shrinking. If we live as Mad Hatters, if we find that parodies of love replace the hope of love, if our days are tea parties or factitious trials, then the dance of such nonsense shows itself as a dance of death.

I understand poems to be events of form whose senses, no matter how obscure and partial, hold me despite what I think or want. Poems must be discovered, not just made. In this chapter, I will show how we might discover *The Waste Land*. What I offer is a kind of philosophical confession that highlights certain powers of the poem. I begin this confession with the following admission: I read *The Waste Land* such that it will crucify me. In what follows I will explain what I mean by this, and in so doing demonstrate a new way of reading the poem that traces its logical possibilities and its emotional claims.

* * *

Before the dead are dead, they were something else; not themselves. They were us, living and thus dying. But what is dying? One of Eliot's answers is "Death by Water," a title of the section of the poem that introduces Phlebas dead. But to ask what this dying is is to ask "what dies?"

> Phlebas the Phoenician, a fortnight dead,
> <u>Forgot</u> the cry of gulls, and the deep sea swell
> And the profit and loss.
>   A current under the sea

<u>Picked</u> his bones in whispers. As he <u>rose and fell</u>
He <u>passed</u> the stages of his age and youth
<u>Entering</u> the whirlpool.
               Gentile or Jew
O you who <u>turn</u> the wheel and look to windward,
<u>Consider</u> Phlebas, who was once handsome and tall as you.
(underlines added)

What is the dead Phlebas such that I could be him? The Phlebas passage describes a progressive generalization and disintegration of Phlebas as a *person* into Phlebas the *bare name* (the minimum Phlebas), marking *the limit of his being something*. A name names a particular person, but if the name I know is nothing but a name, then that name becomes a bare marker of a person, a kind of *generalized pronoun* that says "This was human." Phlebas as dead is mere pronoun.

This mode of generalization allows Phlebas to stand for us—where this "us" is given meaning by this possibility of taking Phlebas as our representative. Thus, this kind of generalization could itself be described as the pronominalization of the name "Phlebas" and in a similar way of the lyric fragment "Death by Water." In reading this passage we follow the loss of Phlebas, a process by which what he is is simplified such that he becomes, as a particular "he," nothing but a name. What does this mean? To answer that, we must read ourselves into Phlebas.

We can enter this water-passage and pursue Phlebas through its verbs. The first verb we meet is "forgot": Phlebas forgot. What is the subject of this verb? Straightforwardly it is "Phlebas the Phoenician." But he is dead. Recalling a question Wittgenstein asks about Mr. N. N. in *Philosophical Investigations*, we can ask: Whom do we refer to when we refer to Phlebas when he is dead? (§40). This is a logical problem of reference for Wittgenstein; it is not quite that for Eliot, but it is closely related. "Phlebas the Phoenician, a fortnight dead/ forgot…" picks out the Phlebas that is dead and thus the Phlebas when he was not yet dead (and thus still a person and not a corpse) and also his being dead for a fortnight. This last is a description of the person of Phlebas, who is no more, relative to the body that was once his. We are on the edge of a riddle: What is Phlebas when he's not alive? Phlebas cannot forget, being now no more. The use of "forget," therefore, further describes what it means for him to be dead relative to what we, who are still living, understand him to be. This verb ("forgot") and any statement about what it would mean for him to be dead personifies Phlebas. One does not notice this at first since Phlebas would already seem to be a person, but that is just what he is not since *he* is not anymore. Phlebas acts, but acts against himself by forgetting himself, his living. He remains Phlebas to us, but he has forgotten *that he is Phlebas to anyone.*

So how could anyone know that Phlebas forgot? The answer: by personifying the dead and using forgetfulness as an analogical description of the meaning of death. Phlebas is reanimated just enough so that the loss of the world is his loss. In this loss of memory Phlebas, the Phoenician trader, loses the predicative use of "loss" in relation to "profit," as well as losing any sense of the sea that contains him, that moves him. The sea *picked* his bones: the sea acts against his body. The sea is animated and personified by "picked," but how does the sea pick at the body? Animals could pick at his body, but the sea cannot, strictly speaking, do that. It lacks the intentionality and the means. The corpse could get torn by rock edges, but that is not to pick at a body. The phrase "the sea picked his bones," therefore, personifies the sea into something that could pick at poor Phlebas. The peristalsis of profit and loss that he forgot is picked up in the next stanza in his own rising and falling, which also mimics the "deep sea swell." Phlebas, as Phlebas, is now nested not within his body but in this periodicity. "As he *rose and fell*" who Phlebas is (as the name "Phlebas") is reduced to that which "*passed*" the stages of his life: Phlebas passing dioramas of his life when he was sixteen and eight, and so on. This parable or drama separates who Phlebas is as Phlebas from the psychological content, his memories, that might describe his life. Phlebas does not act, even through the negation of his forgetting, but becomes coextensive with a particular temporal series: "He passed the stages of his age and youth/ Entering the whirlpool."

Phlebas' death mimics the life the Sibyl in the epigraph suffers and enacts the death she yearns for. The purity of the burning, the transcendent promise of "O Lord Thou pluckest me out" that closes "The Fire Sermon," the section of the poem that precedes Phlebas' drowning, opens with the breaking of the "river's tent": an inundation that at this point in the poem seems to lead to a transformative purification. Phlebas exemplifies this transformation and he is a mock of it. Beneath the absence of the "empty bottles, sandwich papers,/ Silk handkerchiefs, cardboard boxes, cigarette boxes, cigarette ends/ Or other testimony of summer nights" Phlebas passes his life (this "passing" is not him living). Nested in world-time and passed through his end to his beginning, Phlebas enters, and is further nested within at least an image or symbol of absolute movement: "the whirlpool." To enter the whirlpool as if the subject of an episode of *This Is Your Life!* means to enter "the womb of the sea." Phlebas enters the whirlpool after he has passed his life in reverse ("the stages of his age and youth"): thus one is prompted to ask "What enters this whirlpool?" The bare identity that is Phlebas? But what could that be? This parable, however, has always been directed at us, who remain and read, and whatever unity of opposites this whirling might seem to suggest, it just means that what is left us is a name, Phlebas, and his loss. Phlebas transformed has become mere name.

These waters do not speak, nor can Phlebas. We can follow Phlebas to the edge of the whirlpool but not into it. We are not dead and have not forgot; we are addressed and entreated to "consider":

> Gentile or Jew
> O you who turn the wheel and look to windward,
> Consider Phlebas, who was once handsome and tall as you.

Phlebas, who is now dead but was once like you, marks, as does anyone we could name, the limit that is our mortality and our finitude. Does this force us into an existential crisis, into dread? I am not yet afraid, but the difficulties of sense and uptake the poem offers frustrate and promise at the same time. But this demand that we, Gentile or Jew, consider Phlebas, forces us to react and to choose.

If we resist our inclusion within the initial two categories of Gentile or Jew, are we immune from the dread of the vision? If we can read the symbolic links that structure the poem with mythic force, then are we not already reading as Gentile or Jew, as a function even of our difference from these faiths? In fact, the particularity of the equation "either G or J is like P who died" forces us to understand this, regardless of whether we hear the poem as addressed to us, as an equation describing human kind: we who forget, remember, and die. Whoever we are, we are addressed. But this ritual and its obscurity make it impossible for us to read this from within, as if we, ourselves, made this claim about Phlebas. *We are necessarily described by the poem, in words that can never quite be ours.*[2]

Thus, I am returned to my earlier question: What is the dead Phlebas such that I could be him? "Death by Water" shows us the answer. As I commented above, it describes a progressive generalization and disintegration of Phlebas as a *person* into Phlebas the *bare name* (the minimum Phlebas). This is all Phlebas is and all I know about him. His name becomes a category marker, as I argued above: a *generalized pronoun* that says "This was human."

Phlebas as dead is mere pronoun, a pronoun that is one we can use to speak of ourselves. This is a way of seeing the dead as pronouns—as not objects against us, but as forms that we can use to talk about ourselves—in first person (I, we) or about others (you, he, she). That we can use pronouns means that we can speak for each other, stand in for each other. What I am suggesting is that *The Waste*

Land is filled with pronouns: that names (like "Phlebas"), allusions, fragments, and characters all become kinds of pronouns because they approach the limit between person and corpse. Let me elaborate slightly to makes this claim clearer.

Pronouns, names, allusions, and fragments all offer targets for impersonation and exemplification. The pronominalization of elements within the poem shows something about the nature of pronouns. That we can use pronouns means simply that we can speak for each other; that we can speak for each other requires that pronouns be able to symbolize us. Pronouns can replace us because we can understand ourselves to be reduced to pronominal particularity and generality: everyone is an I, or can be a we, or can be addressed as a you, picked out as a he, she and it. In *The Waste Land*, things are pronominalized into what can stand for any of us or all of us. Phlebas, as a mere name, is merely anyone. And what is true of Phlebas is true of all the names and phrases, situations and objects in the poem. Eliot is circumscribing our humanity not in biological or theological terms, but internally, from within our ways of making ourselves visible to ourselves by means of words, and thus by means of logic and grammar.

What this means is that *The Waste Land* highlights our language into what we might call a subjunctive mode through which we find ourselves in this language. Any fragment of the poem would not only count as a voice but would count as a set of interpretative possibilities that are themselves open in the way a pronoun "I" or "we" is. In other words, to understand the fragments of the poem as meaningful in relation to each other and in relation to ourselves or the world is to take them as subjunctive statements about ourselves ("I may be this… ") or the world. This need not entail anything like an imaginary mode or any other psychological or social mode construed as existing somewhere or somehow. We do not learn something new about the world or even about ourselves by reading the poem. The stakes are not knowledge or understanding. Reading the poem is an act that is shown by how the content of what we read rests against us in the way our dead do. This sounds obscure, I know. I will attempt to make it less so in what follows.

The dead, the narrative voices, the lyric I or "I"s, the quotations, if they are subjunctive in the way that pronouns are, require us to describe how we accept or refuse the possibilities and masks they all offer. It is the grip, attraction, refusal, and disgust of taking *other* lives, fictions, and voices as our own that is left of our world in *The Waste Land*. This leaves the poem itself, as a kind of pronoun, and leaves our lives leaning against the subjunctive promises we use to give it content. Our lives are not empty, and this is no argument for nihilism. It is rather a sketch of the outline of what we have left if we are mostly pronouns attached to memories and words that leave us facing different directions, on different roads constrained by our patience and by what the world is not, by what we are not.

In reading the simplification and consequent generalization of Phlebas and situating that process with the general indeterminacy of pronouns and with the disjunctive quality of phrases and scenes in *The Waste Land*, I have been describing ways in which the poem pressures sense into nonsense. And what do we read, if we read the poem's nonsense? Not disguised sense and not simply noise. We can certainly read *The Waste Land*, as many have, as a complex objectification of an analogy between the conditions of the social world and the disposition of a person. Thus, we can read and reveal the poem as both an expression of an individual attitude and a description of a situation. The analogy between person and situation leaves a residue, the residue of what is left under the attack of anxiety and despair modeled by the nonsense of the poem. This residue is the pronoun. Thus, I read the poem as a parable of our human reduction to pronominal surrogacy, as if we could live in such a condition of displaced orientation, as if our form has become what we might recognize as a mere pronoun, mere and yet uniquely human.

The cacophony of fragments and voices in the poem challenge our sense of things (whatever that sense might be). If we want to make sense of this plurality of voices, their unstable and incoherent relationship to each other, and the contingent sense of the poem's narratives, we can unify these voices under some concept of a meta-consciousness, modeled on God speaking with His "I." Or, instead, we can read by either accepting or rejecting the implicit "we" expressed as these voices. Reading the poem in this second way becomes a battle over this "we." Is it us? Do we want to be included? And so on. But it is not the particularity of this "we" that matters, as if it were just a question of being in the right or wrong group. The threat of death and the indeterminacy of reference mean that it is the ordinary sense of "we" that is at stake. Making sense of this "we"— inhabiting it or not—proceeds through describing a limit to it. Such a limit is at least analogous to that which would distinguish animals, humans, and angels or that which would distinguish the animate and the inanimate. In this case, however, no description or definition will stabilize our use of the designation of or, more importantly, our understanding of the criteria for accepting or rejecting the offer of this "we."

The generalization of pronouns, names, and fragments in the poem marks one "we" against another, where this means "we dead," "we not only human persons," "we inanimate things," "we neither dying nor living," and "we dying with patience." This is one source of the insidious power of the poem: the effect of the poem as being addressed necessarily to you: to read any "we" as both an affront *and* as an obvious and simple word is near impossible to resist, even if we reject the poem.

The Waste Land often seems like mad hatter nonsense. Alice, at one point, listens puzzled to the Hatter's explanation of why his watch tells the day of the month but not what o'clock it is. The narrator explains her puzzlement: "The Hatter's remark seemed to have no meaning in it, and yet it was certainly English." In *The Waste Land* we understand most of the sentences and phrases. If we do not, we can look-up certain words or follow Eliot's notes to a source which we can translate or in relation to which we can situate the fragment found in the poem. We can often enter into partial narratives and scenes. We might recognize passages as conversations someone might have. But we do not understand what any of these stories might mean in relation to any other story or fragment. The general indeterminacy of pronouns, the obscurity of names, the vague symbolic import of characters and specific allusions means that in spite of understanding the words, we do not understand how or what they might mean in relation to each other. We do, however, understand what the sentences, phrases, and, in general, words say, at least as part of the fiction of the persons and voices that seem to speak, comment, and tell their stories within the poem.

Pronouns and names are markers of persons. The indeterminacy of pronouns and names in the poem does not undermine the sense of these pronouns and names as identifying or expressing what we would fictionally take as persons, but it does force us to question what is expressed by these pronouns and names in relation to each other. Any "I" within the poem can still be taken to have the ability to say "I said..." or "I believe...." Consequently, the full range of sense and import of "I" and other pronouns remains, but what is expressed by belief, in saying, in doubting, and so on and what kind of who is believing, saying, doubting, etc. becomes unclear. The retention of person-talk, of pronouns, names, and intentional vocabulary protects the idea of persons without giving it any stable content that could be understood as picturing consciousness or subjectivity.[3] As a consequence, the indeterminacy of pronouns and names in the poem does not undermine our sense of person (personhood) but exaggerates it into abstraction. An example. The emptiness and the midden heap of modern life would seem to be answered within the poem by a poetic ritual ventriloquism:

> By the waters of Leman, I sat down and wept...
> Sweet Thames, run softly till I end my song,
> Sweet Thames, run softly, for I speak not loud or long.

The emotional resonance of these three lines with each other helps gather the waters into one image and the three I's into one I. But we can push the other way, and mark allusions and gestures as forces of disjunction. Psalm 137 ("I sat down and wept..."), Lake Geneva (or in French *Leman*) where Eliot convalesced and wrote this section of the poem, and the archaic noun "Leman" (lover) would disjoin a singular I into three. Conflation and dissonance abide together. Such abiding might suggest that three I's make a we—but I think the effect is somewhat different. The singular I and the multiple I's, like the conflation of these waters into the same river (of life and place) by which we cry and sing, generalize the I into what it already is: a particularity that anyone can say.[4] But why go through this extra effort to foreground the "I" as somehow more than just any particular I? The point is not to invoke God, the ultimate I: the I that sat down and sang, and spoke not loud or long is neither God nor Christ nor the Holy Spirit.[5]

What is this generalized I, then? Who is a generalized I? Either it is just anyone—like any normal first person I—or it is what? A generalized *I* would just be an I before anyone has used it, a grammatical and logical potential, waiting for someone, for anyone to take it up. Eliot in this way has situated us within logical possibility.

My questions about this generalized *I* are dramatized numerous times within the poem, quite clearly in the lines that include some verses from Wagner's *Tristan und Isolde*:

I will show you fear in a handful of dust.

Frisch weht der Wind
Der Heimat zu
Mein Irisch Kind,
Wo weilest du?

These last verses are part of the song a sailor sings to a girl he has been forced to leave behind. Isolde, mistakenly or not, interprets them to be about her: "Who dares to mock me?" She imagines she is the "du" sung to. Asking "where dwelleth you?" to a woman figured as nothing but a pronoun in a boat, even if we follow or care about this allusion, cannot mean in the way it might mean if we heard the opera or if I asked you, "where do *you* live?." One can construct various kinds of allegories in order to answer the indeterminacy of this "you" and to compensate for the loss of the conversational sense of words and sentences. We might say, for example, that we are all like this woman, or that the role of women in the poem figures them as romantic temptresses and as frustratingly distant and vicious. We construct an interpretation so that we can identify with or reject this "du" or the implied "we" that could speak or mean these words as something. We provide a reason and context (a story) within which these phrases mean something. We attempt to turn poetry into conversation.

Isolde's mistake and the ambiguity of reference in the sailor's song are increased into a principled indeterminacy by being quoted. In trying to provide a justification for the quotation one must redescribe the quotation relative to some meta-description of the poem, attach it to a theme, to a particular "I," as part of a specific kind of poetic world, so that the quotation becomes exemplary. Our situation in reading *The Waste Land*, therefore, resembles Isolde's. She is our surrogate, and we might imagine ourselves as hers. We have been reduced to pronouns together.

Pronouns mimic the dead; particularized by their abstraction into corpses and names. A name of someone of whom we know nothing and who does not exist is a marker of human particularity like anyone's use of "I." We use them because we humans are all joined together, even in our discomfort in being so enjoined. In the poem the "I" we mistake as general and particular is all of us living and dying or it is someone already dead.

Names and memorials and other ways of marking the land intern the dead into the world in which we live. Aeneas' companion Palinurus died near the Italian coast; the sibyl consoled him, telling him that the place of his death now bears his name (VI.490–505). This kind of story is often repeated. But this is not how the dead are invoked or evoked in *The Waste Land*. The land(s) in the poem lack the particularity that would allow names to reveal the history of a place. There are places in the poem that we can identify in some gestural way—the Thames, Lake Geneva, London—but that is all. The landscape has become generalized.

> Here is not water but only rock
> Rock and no water and the sandy road
> The road winding above among the mountains
> Which are the mountains of rock without water

The "here" of rock is framed by the idea of absent water. If I said "here is a bit of obsidian," I would be using "here" to point to a particular rock. But the "here" in "Here is not water..." has lost the specificity of such pointing. "Here" in this case is just where we are. But where is that? As Kenner observes, the particulars in Eliot's poetry (unlike in Pound's *Cantos*) are not places you could find if you could travel to the right spot.

This "here" is not our here, nor anyone's "here." The scope and possibility of "here" in this passage reveal a similar kind of generalizing force as the pronominalization of Phlebas, adumbrated in the subjunctive dripping of absent water as silent music.

The music of the lines in "What the Thunder Said" gives us a bare description of a place. In its simplification of sense and in the music of water that is absent, we are given a kind of insistent *here*: sense becomes completely subordinate to reference, but the referent *is a here that is nowhere*. The place cannot be identified as a specific place in the world, but it can be taken up and imagined as *the form*, abstracted and simplified, of specificity—the landscape becoming a demonstrative pronoun, indeterminate between "it" and "I." Phlebas and the land of *here* are corpses, and corpses have the form of pronouns; subjunctive forms that parody us. Corpses parody living persons, just as nonsense parodies sense. One is an analogue for the other: the dead for the living, nonsense for sense.

I read *The Waste Land* as an inverted parody of the land that would be the garden in which love might be found. It is a parody of a garden just as a corpse is a parody of a living person. It is land that has yet to gain a name, and so is named as waste. If the wasteland is ours, if the words of *The Waste Land* can be ours, then we are ourselves *land*, waiting for the name we will gain by our deaths.

In *The Waste Land* people get simplified, as if they were always only pronouns filled with dread and memories. To read the poem we must get simplified too, crucified into half-sense and nonsense, to find ourselves at the limit between person and corpse. Crucifixion is a painful simplification; when crucified I become the gasp of breathing, of enduring one moment of life to another. Similarly, what I grasp as I read *The Waste Land* is everything becoming mere pronoun, a mere Phlebas, a land waiting.

The Waste Land as I read it is a *Crucifixion Standing in Air*. Why standing in air? Because in the poem for human beings it is parody all the way down. We are standing on Phlebas, but where is he?

We have to remember that crucifixion can seem like standing in air. Dangling and dying toward the earth is also, at least once, a rising from the earth. Such was Christ. In *The Waste Land*, we are buried in earth, burning in fire, drowning in water. The air at times carries maternal lamentation, and at others hangs with towers out of which voices carry. What Karl Barth takes as "the positive relation between God and man," Eliot takes as the demand the world makes on us, asking what Barth asserts: "The righteousness of God is our standing-place in the air—that is to say, where there is no human possibility of standing—whose foundations are laid by God Himself and supported by Him only."[6] Whether we put culture, or orthodoxy, or ritual, or belief beneath us to hide this standing in air, and whether or not we think Eliot did this, *The Waste Land* shows in its own difficulty that we need to put something beneath us and that nothing we put will be fully adequate.

How do I stand amidst indifference, with my life a parody of other lives? The same way we all stand in this poem, understand it as describing us, take it as our words. We simply try to continue standing, describing, and speaking with patience and with defiance. Patience is a virtue of reading. Defiance we discover in ourselves. Our defiance will cost us. We discover it like land named for the dead. The land we discover with patience and accept with defiance is named for us, or it would be if we could discover it. Poetry might be a spyglass through which we look for that land, or it might be the mast from which we look.

8

Does Poetry Exist?

Poems exist as oddities of particularity and dispersion. Poems exist, but poetry does not, except as a contingent way of gathering together poems as poetry. "Poetry" is a label of convenience. Poems, however, are kinds of things, even if they are not a kind of thing. They *are* the kinds of things we call poems, but they are only contingently and by convenience called poetry. Poems do not have a nature or an essential form. Because they lack any essential form, they are radically dependent on our ideas of what we call poetry. This does not mean, however, that poems can be anything we so categorize. They are limited by their dependence on our ideas about them, such that to read a poem is also to read a concept of poetry. In this chapter, I will explain how we can read the concept of a poem by reading a poem, and why we should. In order to establish this claim, I will investigate what kinds of things poems are and the kind of thing poetry is not.

I realize that my claim that we read the kind of thing poems are when we read a poem is odd and unclear. Let me begin clarifying it by looking at part of a so-called poem by Jackson MacLow called *Words nd Ends from Ez* (1989) that I think is not a poem at all.

> En nZe eaRing ory Arms,
> Pallor pOn laUghtered lain oureD Ent
> aZure teR
>
> un-
> tAwny Pping cOme d oUt r wiNg-
> joints,
> preaD Et aZzle.
>
> spring-
> water,
> ool A P

The poem is constructed from Pound's *Cantos* by means of a set of arbitrary rules, which MacLow calls the "diastic chance selection method." I dislike this text. It is not poetry. I say this last for two reasons. First, this is not a string of words, but a string of marks having a passing resemblance to words. Second, if these are not words, then all the text can do is demonstrate the consequences of the "diastic chance selection method." If in being made the text exemplifies an idea of poetry, then I would take it as a poem, despite its triviality. This can seem overly fastidious. The text exemplifies the technique by which it was produced. That technique might exemplify a particular idea of poetry, but the text, without further redescription, does not. In the face of its difficulty, we might be prompted to discover the technique by which the text was made (we could decode it), and then we might invent or discover a justification for the use of that technique. This might even be interesting, but it is nothing we read through the text. It would be a theory justifying a technique—and that is where the poem would be, if there were one. A statement of the technique relative to its justification (regardless of whether the justification makes any sense) would characterize the technique as a certain kind of thing. This would require that in grasping the technique as that special thing, not simply as a set of instructions, we would be tempted to ascribe meaning to it. To take a technique as a kind of object—and this is neither the doing of it nor the talk about it, but the idea of it as a special site of meaning—requires that the technique be dependent on the theories justifying it. Such justificatory theories could be an aesthetic, or a description of poetry as a kind of thing. Of course, one could also take the pseudo-words of the so-called poem as prompts to develop one's own poem, which would be to work toward the same kind of thing that the technique might be, if it is taken not as a set of instructions but an idea requiring justification. But regardless, these strings of letters are not a poem. If a poem is a person and a bad poem is a carving of a person in a wooden log, then these lines are just a wooden log in rather bad repair. (If you accept a distinction between verse and poetry, and if verse is mechanical, a question purely of form, then this is an example of verse not of a poem.)

    I want to be able to say that certain objects can be poems and others not, while at the same time refusing any general definition of what poems are. Since I am saying a poem has to have a certain dependence on the idea of poetry, won't that count as a *de facto* definition? It does not. Poems have this dependence because they have no essential form or determinate nature. I will suggest that sentences and fictions do have such a determinate nature. Poems are different. They have contingent relations with each other.

Poems are kinds of things in absentia, or rather they are secondary things, things dependent on the idea of the kind of thing poetry is. The important question here is: In what way is a poem dependent on the concept of poetry?

We might answer the question simply, as if it were like needing to have the concept of *stereo* in order to recognize a stereo. There is something to this. The problem, however, is not one of simply recognizing and understanding what a poem is, but of constituting something as a poem. At the same time, it would be too much to claim that a poem is nothing but the idea of poetry it exemplifies. Poems can grip us seemingly as poems even if we have only a vague and inchoate idea of poetry.

I am held here by two ideas. A poem is something. It is that something only relative to its radical dependence on an idea of poetry, but it is not reducible to that idea. So what exactly is the relation between a poem and the idea of poetry?

* * *

I originally presented this argument at an unusually interesting conference on reading poetry, advertised as an attempt to recover some trans-historical thing called Poetry, and also to deny various attempts to reduce the study of poetry to the study of culture. My discussion of poetry seems to fit uncomfortably with the précis of that conference. So, then and now, I want to re-establish my credentials for being on the side of poems.

I applaud what I take to be the central resistance expressed in the précis of that conference: a refusal of the now rampant and militant cultural and psychological reductionism and a rejection of the idea that poetry is nothing more than "a name for a changeable set of desires and cultural ambitions."[1] This challenge to poetry, often tied to both a desire for political relevance and a disgruntlement with interpretation, represents an attempt to reduce poetry to nothing but the conditions or motives for its production. These conditions and motives are an amalgam of psychological theories and ideological or cultural causes. The reduction of poem to context is often hidden, as in New Historicism, by a tendency to continue to interpret poems as if simply looking at evidence. But the texts interpreted by such historicists are linked to the cultural context in strong and linear ways such that one can pretend to read the culture straight off the poem because the poem is an expression of that culture. The poem can be read as the culture saying something, and the culture is itself organized as a kind of mind, with a political unconscious or a swarming circulation of ideas. The link between the poem and its context is reductive because the culture is expressed as the conditions of possibility of the poem, and the poem is nothing more than such conditions. Such a reduction is confused. If I am to drive my car, the motor must be running. That is a necessary condition in order for me to drive. But if the motor is running, I am not yet driving. That is a further action.[2]

The claim that everything is culturally determined and historically bound is part of a general defense of ideological relativism. The historicist position, like all strong forms of relativism, is confused. The idea here is that historical circumstances are contingent, such that your circumstances are different than mine, and that is a merely arbitrary fact. But our being bound to these circumstances is not contingent; we are determined by those circumstances. If it is true that every perspective is historically, that is, culturally and contingently determined, then what choice do we have but to do what we do? Why should we be responsible to some particular idea of our necessary historical contingency? If we must judge the contingency, then we must judge our own contingent entanglement relative to our prejudices or we must judge such entanglements relative to some further idea of what is good. And any such judgment would be an evaluation that, even if historically informed, would not be simply an expression of historical forces. It would be a judgment relative to an idea of the good. Regardless of the content of the idea, the judgment itself is an individual act relative to criteria, and as such would be an ahistorical act. If we can make judgments, we are not merely historically determined. That alone is enough to show that we do have a perspective on our circumstantial entanglement. The decisive role of judgment is evident in cultural studies itself. Its struggles are less over historical, aesthetic, or philosophical positions than over ideologically inflected moralisms and various ideological projects. The vagaries of reputation, endemic to academic and literary life, as Samuel Johnson commented long ago, are now being combined with coterie struggles to build academic sinecures and moral good feeling for those who join the club at the expense of education and thought.

I can now make a general historiographical point. There are certainly continuities in the practices of poetry and reading, and these have a place in a culture and a relation to historical situations and conditions as well as to events and people. Those continuities matter and our understanding of them will be affected by the historical and cultural contingencies of which we are a part. We can even argue that poetry is determined as a practice by such contingencies, but it does not follow from this that our claims about poems must be and necessarily are about those cultural historical conditions. I can make claims about poems and I can make claims about cultural conditions. It is only when we reduce poems to their so-called conditions that we then imagine we can only make claims about culture or history, and in effect dissolve the poem into those conditions. Of course, this is the goal of the reduction. Such reductionism is both fallacious and nonsensical. It is fallacious because as a matter of fact we can make claims and observations about poems and poetry that are not de facto claims about the culture, even if they are shaped by our cultural situation. The reduction is nonsensical because conditions, in order to do their conditioning work, are not the same thing as that which they condition, or else they would not be conditions.

Generally, I think literary history, far from being a great sociological enterprise, is a way of telling stories about literature and its motivations and methods. When literary histories try to become cultural histories, they sound more like just-so-stories than historical explanations. In any case, the claim that all is historical is not an historical claim, but a philosophical credo. I do not share it.

The précis of the conference mentions a group of stalwart resistance fighters against this historically disguised ideological relativism—we happy few; there were eight of us. How are we opposed? While I am opposed to historicist reductionism, as I have already said, I do not believe that we should posit a non-historical, non-contingent entity called poetry to block the reduction of poems into desires and ambitions, cultural or otherwise. So I am prompted to ask: Why the appeal in the précis to poetry as a whole, as if that were the best way to resist reductionist historicism? It is, I think, a reasonable appeal. I am sympathetic to it, even if I do not believe in it. One can construe poetry as a contingent whole, for various purposes, defined by various interests, influences, and localized continuities in aesthetic practices and beliefs. But I do not think that such continuities point to some stable kind of thing called poetry.

I want to note, however, something implied in the précis of the conference that I think is both true and important: the kind of thing you think a poem is will determine in various ways what you do with it, how you make sense of it. This is a simple point. You respond differently to a knock on your door than you do to the knocking in your car engine. How we interpret things always depends on what kind of thing it is. But there is a further point with poetry. Poems are odd, funny kinds of things—and that is both their danger and their promise, and a further reason for the dependence of our interpretations on our judgments about the kind of thing a poem is.

* * *

What is a poem? It seems to be made of words—but words are things that are identifiable and have import as parts of phrases and sentences, even if those are radically diminished or distorted in a particular poem. So to get a sense of what a poem is, we have to understand something of what words, phrases, and sentences are. At this point, I return to the argument I made about this in Chapter 3.

A poem consists of a determinate set of words—although more properly a set of phrases, even if only implied—in a certain order. This is what is visibly manifest as the poem, although this is misleading. A word is manifest as marks or sounds, but it is not simply these. A word is a set of such marks, normatively constrained, with which sentences and phrases are made, or by which we can say things and by means of which we can understand things. What we understand and say range from thoughts and intentions to possibilities and states of affairs.[3]

The so-called materiality of language, its physical form, is a misnomer when understood as being constitutive of language: there is no reductive fundament of language, nor are the manifest forms of language anything but contingently material. Our grasping of anything requires that something be manifest somehow. The thoughts in my head are also manifest to me in normatively constrained ways, dependent, although not directly, on the interpersonal and generally matter-constituted means of saying, seeing, and interacting. But always much is implied—and implication *per se* is not made of atoms or shape. Language is nothing without the aspects we gesture toward with the words "meaning" and "thought." The materiality of language is simply the sensory means, the tokens organized as words and sentences, of manifesting those norms, intentional structures, implications, possibilities, meanings, and thoughts we say and grasp. If we had some other kind of sensory mode, language could take some other form.

Language is not essentially anything that does not include conceptual norms, intentional structures, meanings, and so on. All these are themselves normatively constrained patterns of manifest form and relations. We have to grasp them, so they must be manifest in some way. They define our expectations at the very least. We can play with both the conceptual aspects and the means and modes of manifestation relative to the contingent aspects of each. We manipulate the means and modes of manifestation: sounds, patterns of articulation, and orthographic form. The means of conceptual play would include equivocation, confusion, parallels, puns, and so on. Of course, to play with one list is to play in some sense with the other. But even with these two lists, you can see that the play with manifest form is more contingent, and thus more open-ended, less significant, because by definition less meaningful, since the register of that play must take place relative to the conceptual aspects of language. But the play with form disregards that—unless one is using some further norms to organize that play. So one might find that penultimate words in a poetic line are deemphasized relative to the ending word, or that rhymes tend to emphasize (especially with training) connections between words as opposed to differences, although there is no reason that one couldn't be trained to reverse this tendency.

These kinds of play characterize poetry. One could even describe a typology that would span from form-centered play to conceptual or meaning-centered play. In each case, aspects of the other would be affected and effected. The marks of language without the possibility of meaning are not language, and the putative meanings that we grasp are neither meaningful nor linguistic without some means of manifestation. Poems are kinds of things that develop the oddness of the relation between the manifest forms of words, phrases, and sentences (relative to whatever and however these all mean) into a further abstraction of these elements, and in so doing produce feelings of meaningfulness.

There is a lot more to say about words and sentences that would be relevant. My attention, however, must remain general. I have highlighted a simple fact that words are not what they are, nor are sentences and phrases, if they are not individuated and understood relative to those semantic and conceptual aspects by means of which we grasp them. On the other hand, the meanings, thoughts, implications, concepts that we take up or understand must be manifest somehow, and the modes of such manifestation are contingent but determinate and can be manipulated in various ways. One kind of manipulation is poetry.

* * *

Poems, as commonly understood, are language things, developing and relying on the relation between manifest form and conceptual sense that defines language. If poems are like port and language is like wine, how are they both like and unlike other kinds of alcohol, let alone milk, water, and hair tonic? Or is the question of kinds here better a comparison of wines with gardening, traffic laws, and a day?

Poems would seem not to be like natural kinds, like water or wood.[4] Natural kinds are naturally occurring things the particularity of which is dictated by the conditions described by science. Their nature is determinate, at least in theory. So water is. Water just is that, although in practice one might have difficulties in identifying some cases of it. But the resolution of these difficulties presupposes the natural kind status of water. Water, while necessarily defined as, might be combined in some puddle with other chemicals and liquids. Is the puddle water? We might decide by taste or by stipulation the ratio of to iron-oxide and oil in order for the puddle to still count as water. We also might decide the issue by trying to get our dog to drink it. We do not, however, question the natural kind status of water as a determinate substance. We have no reason for such confidence when dealing with poems and poetry (nor do we have any adequate or reliable empirical tests to determine if a poem is a poem).

If a poem is not a natural kind, maybe it is a kind of thing like a chair: an object of use. A chair is defined by its function relative to specific sets of forms, aspects of which are contingent, and aspects of which are necessary for it to be used as a chair. When we want to cast poems or art as like chairs or such like-objects, we ascribe functions to art, including the function of having no function. Such functions are stipulations. There is no non-tendentious way to establish a link between the posited function and the thing the poem is. The appeal to function is so metaphoric that it is not clear what it is explaining: it is a theory of poetry, not a description of poems.

If poems are neither natural kinds nor objects of use, are they logical kinds? A logical kind is very loosely a conceptual form that necessarily has that form. The logical operators "or" and "and" are logical kinds, in the sense that they can be defined necessarily and sufficiently by their description using a truth table. It is not the role of truth tables that matters so much as the determinate description possible by means of them, such that what something is by necessity is sufficient for it to be that thing. The more useful example of a logical kind relative to poetry, though it is controversial to say it is such a kind, is fiction.

A standard description of a fiction would be the following: a fiction is a story or sentence or whatever from which we should not infer in any straightforward way, by virtue of what is said or asserted or claimed, anything about the author or the world.[5] It may express the beliefs of the author, but we cannot conclude that from the fiction in the way we might if someone said to us amidst our everyday lives "*I believe in leprechauns*." Nor should we infer something of current or past states of affairs from a fiction in the way we would if someone said, "*Gaius Gracchus' son committed suicide when he learned that his father had been killed.*" This might be false, but it is not fictional by virtue of that. A fiction can in this sense be neither true nor false. Utilizing other information and setting the fiction in context, we can use it to help confirm or trace aspects of a cultural or historical situation. This is to use the fiction, not to read it as a fiction. In order to use it to make such confirmations or inferences requires that we normalize aspects of the fiction relative to our understanding of evidence and relative to the logic and constraints of non-fictional statements and stories. A non-fictional statement need not be true or undistorted, but it can be evaluated relative to what is the case, and thus can be false, even if only potentially. Thus, it is necessary, when we understand a fiction, that we understand that certain inferences about the author and the world are not permissible or are nonsensical. Thus, what is *necessary* for a fiction to be a fiction—that straightforward inferences to author and world are blocked—is also *sufficient* for it to be a fiction.

But fictions need not be art. The logical form of fiction does not tell us how a fiction means, but how it cannot mean. Although poetry lacks such a specific form, it in general mimics in its peculiar generality the logical form of fiction. The logical form of fiction, by limiting how it can be about something and what we can infer from it, prompts our interpretation of and reasoning about it.

How is a fiction different from a lie or a myth? A lie is a fiction for the liar—he doesn't think what he says is true of the world—and he is saying it in such a way so as to get someone to take it as true. Thus, the hearer understands the lie as a statement, and when he discovers it is a lie, he understands it as a false. The liar is making a false statement about the world, but because he is lying, he is disguising that fact and thus treating, although disingenuously, the statement as a fiction that he knows and others do not. A fiction, therefore, is not a lie.

A myth is a more complicated exercise of storytelling and belief. For those who understand myths as true in some supernatural way, not simply true of our human condition or thematically true, a myth is not a fiction. If we take the myth as true of us without the appeal to supernatural content or warrant, then it is just a fiction, regardless of what we call it. As I have said, the minimal description of a fiction as blocking certain inferences defines what fiction is both necessarily and sufficiently. And this is only to say that it is a logical kind. It is a kind of thing or linguistic possibility that accompanies our ability to talk about the world in true and false ways, as long as we can reflectively evaluate those ways of speaking or writing. If we can quote ourselves and others, if we can logically frame words and their sense, then we can tell fictions. And what fictions are, even if they are not recognized as such, is necessarily defined by the logical possibilities of language.

There is something important to note in this last set of claims. Fictions, I would argue, are not said by anyone, but are as if quoted. In their very possibility, our saying something is split from our meaning it. Fictions can be used to communicate. I can have many purposes in telling you a fiction, but the fiction *per se* is not such a communicative act. It has possible content and certainly must have sense, but its sense is parasitic on our taking up a complex and often shifting position relative to it in order to get what is said to have the sense of a statement. And anyway, I can tell you a story, even a true story, and have no idea what it means: its significance, portents, point, or value. In such cases, the difference between a true story and fictional story is important, for what you infer from it about me and the world will be determined by whether it is true or false on the one hand, or fictional on the other. Of course, I could tell either kind of story for the same purpose—to scare you, for example—but that would be my intention in telling the story, not the meaning of the story.

My desire to scare you does not produce a quasi-quotational framework but a further way of normalizing the fiction relative to how I mean it and intend you take it. Think of how when viewing a frightening film scene with children, we reassure them by saying that it is not real—only a story. By saying that, we alter what they can infer about the relation between the story, the scene, and their world. It is less reassuring to say: "this is not happening now." That is not reassuring because it can then seem as if it were only a contingent fact that it isn't happening now. To say the story is a fiction is to say that it is logically not the case that this ever happened. Maybe it could have, but this story is a fiction, not a true or false account of something past.

Poems can be fictions, but they need not be. Poems can look like fictions because they can seem generalized beyond any particular communicative act or context. This generalization can be accomplished by ambiguity, indeterminate pronouns, vague references, obscurity, or (and) excessive particularity. All these devices can create a seeming logical distance between the poem and what we might take as a state of affairs or a thought or a determinate and meaningful expression. The formalization of phrases into a poem, into an interconnected set of phrases fitted with a sense of what a poem or an idea of poetry is, encourages us to be suspicious that the poet needn't quite be the speaker. One can wonder who says a poem and how to take it, and thus poems can imitate the logical form of fictions.

The relation of the concept of fiction to particular fictions is not like that between the concept of poetry and poems. I do not need to rely on any ideas about fictions in order to recognize a particular fiction as a fiction. I just have to know what fictions are. A fiction is a certain kind of thing; to take it as a fiction is to recognize what might be called properties of it. But these are not properties we recognize if we do not understand what a fiction is. We either know what a fiction is or we don't. But this is not true for poems. We often do appeal to or argue for a set of necessary properties in our attempts to define what a poem is. Various properties of a poem will not tell us what a poem is without having a theory about such properties, and knowing those properties does not determine what a poem is. Recognizing a poem is either something we need not worry about or something we can worry over without end.

We can try to define poems simply by formal elements like rhyme or meter (although what meter means will depend on the language in question), but this will be tendentious and leave out lots of so-called poetry. We rely on an idea of what poetry is in order to define what a poem is, and we utilize these ideas to determine whether a text is a poem. This idea of poetry defines what we do with it. I will give an uncontroversial example. Helen Vendler claims that "'poetry' is the construction by consciousness of an apprehensible world."[6] Everyone, Vendler believes, constructs the world out of his or her apprehensions; poets are conscious about this construction and display it as poetry. This means that when we read poetry, we read this constructed apprehension and we make claims about this construction, especially about how that construction and apprehension are realized through language such that a similar sense of apprehension is produced in us when we read a poem. How Vendler reads a poem is dependent on her idea of poetry. The work of art, for Vendler, is as a consequence hardly an object at all.

Vendler demonstrates through her particular aesthetics what is more generally true. No poem can be a simple object if it is made of language. But neither is it a logical kind like a fiction, since there is always a question not just about whether it is a poem, but about what a poem is such that this could be such a thing. And that question has no definitive answer as it does in the case of fiction. To fail to recognize a fiction is a failure of logic and linguistic competence. Not to know what a poem is *per se,* given the polemics of poetry, is either a failure or a display of taste.[7]

The strangeness of the relation between poem and idea of poetry can be suggested by analogy, using a thought experiment. Imagine that our access to other people's feelings were simplified into a single, one way conduit. Imagine that the only way for you to discover how I felt about you would be for me to tell you. If so, then your grasp of my feelings would be dependent on my telling you. If Fred said, however, that he understood someone else's feelings by looking at the stars, you would say (because the only way feelings could be known is by someone telling you): "Fred, you are just making noises." Poetry is dependent on the idea of poetry in the way that grasping the feelings of others, in this story, is dependent on people telling you what their feelings are. How could you tell the difference in this world between a feeling someone actually has and their just making it up with words? You couldn't. So for you, other people's feelings would have no determinate nature. We could still take those feelings to be like our own feelings, but the feelings of others, because they could only be expressed in one way, would always be suspect. We would always suspect these feelings because of their radical dependence on their means of expression. So true feelings and false feelings would be like poems and not-poems. You couldn't tell the difference just by hearing them described. You would start to think about the relation between how the feelings are expressed and the nature of those feelings—and you would explore that relation relative to your own feelings and the limited relation you have to other people's feelings. In this analogy, the words are like the ideas of poetry; without them there is no poem, no feelings, to recognize. But the feelings are not just the words by means of which they are expressed; the poem is not just the idea of poetry on which it is dependent. Poems should not be reduced to the idea of poetry they might exemplify, and yet no poem is separate from such an idea. We have a hard time understanding such a relationship. We constantly want to reduce one to the other: everything to context or everything to text.

Poems are analogous to sleep in the way that poetry is analogous to death. This is a more complicated analogy—it is based on the sense that our relation to sleep is analogous to our relation to death. There is too much to say about this here. I will only gesture. I would call sleep and death asymmetric analogues. We can pretend to be asleep as we can pretend to be dead, but we cannot pretend to be awake when asleep nor pretend to be alive when dead. This asymmetric relation between us and sleep and death points to the way sleep and death undo us. Sleep and death for human beings are not things we have relations to but things that we in some sense are. But that is the oddness. When I am asleep I am not awake, and when I am dead I am not alive. Thus, sleep and death have claims on me, a relation to me by virtue of their power to deny me, to remove me in their particular ways. Sleep and death are themselves analogues for each other given this odd power they have on us. I am suggesting that poems have a relation to poetry in the way sleep has a relation to death. The strangely known things of poems and sleep show us something of the greater unknowns of poetry and death. Our stories about death are often based on our stories about sleep; both are states of losing ourselves. Death is something we can't know and sleep is something we imagine we should know; we are gone in sleep and yet our sleep has an intimacy with us that lets us imagine that it is a state of expressiveness, as in our dreams or our inspirations. Still sleep is something in this world that seems to point to the death that is beyond us. Sleep is a limit to our consciousness, and death to our being anything as persons. So death has fundamental ontological scope, while sleep seems to limit just our seeing or knowing of ourselves. But our knowing and our being are entwined. Poetry like death is that which we can only know by analogy—by examples—but it has a scope beyond all our examples. Poetry claims poems as surrogates for itself, although it can only show itself through such examples. Poems are like sleep in that they point beyond what they are but hold us nevertheless as surrogates for poetry. And yet still this surrogate poetry, like death, is like nothing much at all, or nothing but a hodgepodge of beliefs and hopes that we collect into an idea in order that we have a target to talk about.

My argument has been that poems are radically dependent on ideas of poetry and that they do not constitute a particular kind of thing. There is no poetry as a whole, but also no dissolution of poems into a cultural matrix. Poems are something, but what is not clear. I seemingly want to have my cake and eat it too. Kind of.

When we eat a cake, we do not simultaneously eat the concept of a cake. We eat the cake made of flour, sugar, and eggs. We do not eat the concept; we don't eat concepts. I am suggesting, however, that when we analogously eat poems, we also eat the concept of a poem. It is not just that a particular poem is dependent on the concept of a poem in a particularly intimate way, but that poems are funny kinds of things that are always concepts of poems and never just poems. Hence there is always an idea of poetry as such being expressed in a particular poem.

* * *

We can plagiarize a poem, but we cannot forge it. (Wolheim in *Art and Its Object* makes a similar observation.) The poem is not particularized as an object, but at best is a set of words, and thus it is a type relative to whatever particular tokening we might find and read in a book. A poem is already a type or a concept. But if it is an example of the concept of poetry and that concept is given as the poem, and not as some further idea, then it is a type of a type as well. One might call this a dual aspect (like the famous duck-rabbit picture)—we see a poem or we see the poem as an example of an idea of poetry. But this is to assume we can apply the concept of a poem to a poem, given that the poem is one thing and the poetry another. This is to imagine a poem is like an object, like a chair. We can have numerous and unexceptionable examples of the concept of chair. I am arguing, however, that we cannot have unexceptionable examples of a poem; all examples of poems are exceptionable.

Poetry is a contingent concept and poems have a claim on us separate from our particular beliefs in poetry, but in that claim we can always discover some constitutive notion or idea of poetry, and that idea will help differentiate poems from non-poems.

I argued in a previous chapter, that a poem has an analogical relationship with its words (it is not equivalent to them, it is similar to them). But when one attempts to take the words of a poem as equivalent to or constitutive of the poem, then those words become analogical with our ordinary language. Either the poem is analogical or its words are (and if its words are, since these are taken in this case to be what the poem is, then the poem is also analogically related to ordinary language).

A poem reveals the kind of poetry it is. A poem is not, however, a mere illustration of the kind of poetry it is—it is a particularity that is also a kind. But like an example of an example, it must be an example of something besides itself if it is to be recognized also as an example of an example. (In other words, there can be no example of an example that is not also an example of something else—a bar of soap, a patch of red). A poem is a poem relative to some particular ideas of poetry, and without those ideas it is no poem, but those ideas are also not sufficient for it be a poem. A poem has a claim on us, a force—it happens to us, and in that happening we have to discover what ideas of poetry are revealed in that poem. That a poem is a kind of thing that reveals and does not just illustrate a particular idea of poetry means that a poem is a further kind of analogy.

Poetry is dependent on the examples of poems, and yet those examples are examples of poetry only if understood as that relative to our ideas of poetry. But again, we are not just trying to recognize poems but to make poems or read poems such that they are poetry. The kinds of properties we might ascribe to poetry—the expression of a certain attention, a certain concern for the sounds of language, a sense of resonance or extravagance of meaning or suggestion—are all real enough, but hardly qualities in any ordinary sense. They are tied to other nebulous somethings, like the meanings of phrases and sentences, the significances of actions and statements, the power of feelings and emotions. Poetry would seem to be something, but maybe just a hodgepodge, a packaging of the effects and properties of language, emotion, and perception. Beyond that contingent description, poetry is a something that is always bound to our analogies for it. Poems are nothing separate from the analogies that enable us to recognize them. "Poetry" is simply the name we give to these analogies.

9

Where Are Love and Death?

Although *The Waste Land's* dynamic configuration of revelation and parody is specific to it, poems as a general species suffer some such configuration of promise, if not always of revelation, and of parody. A poem, as a written target or as a crystallization of form amidst our day, as beauty, or love, or death, or attention, or fear, is an unstable site of revelation and parody. As such a site, it provides a crux for our attention and investment, and for our shock and alienation.

Poems are events that claim us with the force of necessity, seeming necessities of form emerging, sometimes built from contingencies of situation and pattern. Such a configuration of seeming necessity and contingency in the particularities of form makes poems unstable. No element or aspect of a poem gives it the claim of necessity. It can at any time, like romantic love, shift back into contingency. And so Emerson describes youthful love in a way that also describes the motive and form of many poems: "affection contrived to give a witchcraft surpassing the deep attraction of its own truth to a parcel of accidental and trivial circumstance" ("Love," 330). A condition of erotic intensity, fueled by desire or hope or fantasy, allows the accidental and trivial to gather that intensity as their own, the world of the moment dawning, revealed in an immediate recognition. Emerson confesses, almost reluctantly, that the permanence of such moments monument our memories with our essential histories.[1]

T. J. Clark, in his diary explorations of Poussin's "Landscape with a Calm," puzzles through a similar visceral sense of revelatory permanence, not fueled by the witchcraft of affection, but rather by a discovery of form in the details of painting:

> Aren't there plenty of moments in life that, whether they last or not, have enough of permanence about them to stand for things as they are, things as the mind

conceives them—and not just to stand for them notionally, but have them be visible on their face?

(16)

Some moments in life "have… [a] permanence about them," whether they persist or not. These moments are close relatives of the hyperreal circumstances of witchcraft Emerson describes. Clark does not psychologize the causes behind these moments in life; he generalizes them—they have many sources and causes—and he places them at the intersection between how things are and how the mind conceives (recognizes) these same things. Such moments make poems.

Poussin, in "Landscape with a Calm," fits details of movement with details of stillness, producing a scene of harmonious tension, dashes of action and weather in counterpoint with calm. He constructs an order of tautness. Is this harmonious tension, the calm in "Landscape with a Calm," a momentary pause in the dynamic of time or a revelation of the underlying order of things? Do his paintings *achieve* a harmony or *discover* it? A harmony *constructed* or a harmony *revealed*? Both, I would like to say. But what is an achieved revelation? A revelation of what? And if made, then how is it a revelation, since that would be a discovery?

Clark hints at an answer: Poussin relies on what we also know, that some moments have enough permanence (what is enough?) to stand not just notionally (as symbols) for how things are, but, instead, these moments make "visible on their face" what they stand for. The details of a moment, configured into a whole, show the order of things in the particularities of an expression. Love and death are revealed in similar ways, or rather as similarly visible—the face of my beloved, for example, revealed as the face of love. My goal in this chapter is to show that such revelations are not fantasies, but are what they seem to be—revelations of the face of what is not visible in any other way. These are the faces of poems.

* * *

A gesture of love manifests love by expressing it.[2] My love and care can be expressed and enacted through a gesture. Love can be given by the gesture; the gesture counts as evidence of my love, and thus it can be an example of love. We have to grasp the love shown by such a gesture; it need not be obvious. Such gestures fit with the complexity of our interactions and emotions. And this is true of how any gesture might reveal aspects of me—my character, feelings, attitudes, desires, and so on. Such gestures are part of a broader set of behaviors and make sense relative to various complex parameters and judgments. The face of love fits with this complex gathering into form that allows a gesture to reveal character.³

A gesture simplifies a complexity of significance into a movement. I express care for my child through a gesture of comfort. My care is expressed through that gesture (as is comfort). My care is also part of that gesture (the gesture of care by which I comfort my child). It is not only *that* I am offering comfort, but how I offer it—not simply my movements, but my facial expressions, what I say and what I do not say, and so on. Those qualities are not just expressed; they partially constitute what my comforting is, and thus what my care is. My gesture matters and means as my care: it is both ends and means.

Love is a natural simplification that complicates my world. Love is not a gesture, but it is like a gesture. A gesture of love is like but not the same as the pigeoning of someone into parody, their simplification into something that only means relative to me. We do this to people we say we love, but that is not love.

But I am anxious. Expressions of love are very close to parody. I want to show how love is visible and not as a parody. I want to show that love stands forth in the faces of those we love. That is what I will try to do in what follows.

* * *

When I claim, as I do, that love is manifest in the faces of those I love, I might be acting the pigeon, parodying the faces of those I love into a fantastic hope of Love made visible. And if, as I also claim, this love manifests in those we love in the same way that death becomes visible in the corpses that parody the living, I seem to be insisting on a horror. As if the death that was revealed in the dry skin of my friend mimicked the love now revealed as the faces of my children.

How awful!

Can I really say that seeing the face of my child that I love is akin to seeing death in the skin of my soon-to-be-dead friend? His skin meant death, spoke death, was death; naturally, this sounds like metaphoric extravagance, projection, or mere correlation. But what else *can* death be? It is, after all, nothing *per se*. There are the dead, who were once living. We can remember the once living. There is dying, which is not yet death. Death cannot be a state, for there is nothing that can be in that state. Death does happen. But what is that? The death that happens is a cessation of life; so the happening of death is the happening of an ending, of a stopping. Death is the happening of life no longer happening. The death seen in my friend's skin is not a something like a stop sign, nor an act of communication, nor even like things more nebulous in their ontological status—the two-bodies of a king or prime numbers (although it would be closest to this last, or it might be like numbers *per se*). Death is a manifestation of what cannot be shown except through such manifestations. Death is like a word that has lost its sense but reminds us of the sense it had. It almost sounds like the word it was, but not quite. We grasp a word within our understanding of language, like we can grasp a face within our apprehensive capacities as human beings. Death is grasped as a lack, which we populate with ghosts and dreams, attenuated forms of life. If life is sense, death is nonsense.

We live dying. When dying, we know death approaches; seeing the dead, we can know, although we will try to blunt our awareness, that we will be as they are someday. The dead are not simply inanimate; we recognize them relative to what they were, that they were once alive and are no longer. The dead are what they are relative to their history. We do not grasp them simply relative to what they now are. The dead are already dead, and so death is not there but is figured in them.

But for all our fear, and even with the biological inevitability of death, there is no death that we can see. The dead are not death; dying is not death, since it has not happened; the moment of death is death only because it is when dying meets being dead; when it happens, it is already past. Death describes a limit, but it is nowhere present in this world. Death is real, and yet nowhere; it happens, but there is no when in which it happens, but as a mark of convenience. Like the meaning of a sentence, death must be manifest somehow, but none of the means of its manifestation are what it is, and yet they give the evidence for and force of what it is. If it is not something in itself, it might as well be; if it is something, we only meet its consequences.

We see death, as opposed to the dead, by catachresis—the skin becoming the form of something that is never manifest as what it is, but always by some surrogate. Death's dependence on the dead as a means of its manifestation does not mean that death is the same as the dead. We cannot get to it without the other. There may be nothing to get to except the limit of life: death is not something in the way a palm tree is something, or even in the way a thought is something (even the thought of death). While dying is our biological inheritance and the dead are physical things, death is not a physical anything; it is a conceptual limit like that between necessity and contingency.

Love, like Death, manifests in its examples, although love is less a limit than a meaningfulness the possibilities of which we have to discover. And so, I see love in the face of those I love. John Donne sees love in this way, too. He describes love as incarnate in the face of his beloved:

> But since my soul, whose child love is,
> > Takes limbs of flesh, and else could nothing do,
> > > More subtle than the parent is
> Love must not be, but take a body too;
> And therefore what thou wert, and who,
> > I bid Love ask, and now
> That it assume thy body, I allow,
> And fix itself in thy lip, eye, and brow.
> > > "Aire and Angells"

Donne says: just as the soul inter-animates our flesh, Love assumes the body of the beloved, becomes fixed *as* her lip, eye, and brow (not *in* her lip, eye, and brow). Is this fantasy and projection? An appeal to a transcendent Neo-platonic form of love come to roost in human form? A mere figuration and seduction? If the sense of Donne's figuration depends on Neo-platonic metaphysics, or even simply an ideology of love as a transcendent form or concept, then the poem amounts to very little, except as an exercise in metaphysical posturing or a confession of hope. And if projection or conceit, it is a mere means to an end: a rhetorical game. I leave aside Donne's beliefs and purposes, or rather I subsume his in mine, since I would reject all three of these options. The love that incarnates as the beloved is not fantasy, not a transcendent metaphysical form, not rhetorical seduction, but is an actual fact: the faces of those whom we love reveal Love.

Love describes a necessary flinching of our heart—not a flinching away, but a flinching toward. It happens. Love is not a choice, even if it can be part of our deliberations. Love happens. Is that all? I can feel a love that I take as part of me, but my sense of it is that it is greater than me. I am surprised by it, taken by it, shattered and overwhelmed by it, but not really by love itself: rather by the way the persons I love carry with them, whatever they might say or do, my life, the scope and intimacy of how I can be and live as myself. This need not be and usually is not conscious. To love someone is to find that the love you have is a love that holds you elsewhere; it is greater than you—with limits and effects that are unexpected.

If this is the case, then love is *not* something I simply manifest in what I do since I am framed by it as well and since it includes necessarily and in particular the person (or thing) that I love. And thus, the love shown is not simply an expression of my love, but of the love I discover; the love I discover is for the person I love, who therefore shows that love. The primary site of that showing is in what most fully reveals that person—which is their face.

This is what I see.

Love, however, is not just something that happens to me, it is something out of which I act, and in that action, I express love. How I relate to the people I love in my actions of love shows that love is relational, and that I have a special relation to those people by virtue of the role love plays in my actions.

Love cannot simply be a mental state, since such states are so changeable and do not capture the sense of commitment and attachment that characterizes love. At a minimum, therefore, we can say that love is a particular disposition, and that such a disposition constitutes in some critical way the person who loves.

The disposition of love is defined in some constitutive way by that which is loved. This is part of love's relational character. By looking briefly at the intentional structure of love, its aboutness, how love as a disposition is *for* and *about* someone or something, we can see more fully how love is partially constituted by its targets. It is because it is partially constituted by, for example, the person I love, that that person's face can reveal love.

What role does love play in what we do?

When we act to achieve particular ends, our actions are purposive. But this is not the only way we can act with a purpose. The ends for which we act can be understood as taking two forms: (1) an end can be understood as a goal—a target—which we attempt to accomplish or effectuate and (2) an end can be something for the sake of which we do something. In this second case, I might do something, for example, for the sake of someone or for the sake of love.[4] Aquinas, for example, insists that we act not only to achieve particular goals, but we also act fundamentally for the sake of something that is already the case. We act for the sake of God, or for the sake of our love of God, but in so doing we do not achieve (or make) God, nor do we accomplish our love. We love God and so we act in light of that love, for the sake of that love (or at least we should).

We need not accept Thomist theology in order to see that we do not only act to achieve ends. If my goal is to make a profit, I will act in certain ways. I might find it practical in such dealings to act in a trustworthy fashion, to refuse to betray confidences, or to cheat or take unfair advantage, and so on. If I remain trustworthy for such reasons, then my trustworthiness acts as a means to my practical ends. But if, instead, I feel myself to be trustworthy, because I value certain kinds of behavior, and because I assume that to be trustworthy is itself worthy and is simply the way to act, then when faced with an opportunity to cheat, I would refuse for the sake of the virtue of trustworthiness, not because of some practical benefit. Because I am choosing to deal fairly with someone, I am *being* trustworthy not for my sake, but for the sake of the person I am dealing with. This is what my virtue of trustworthiness means; it is not for me, but for others. My actions represent an example of trustworthiness. I am confirming my trustworthiness, re-accomplishing it, if you like, and I do so by acting for the sake of someone else, not for the sake of an end.[5]

Another example more to the point will make the distinction clearer. I act in such a way as to care for my children—I make dinner. But I also do this for their sake, and also for the sake of my love. If I imagine that I do it in order to accomplish my love, as a kind of goal, then I would achieve my love and then, as a secondary effect, feed my children. I would not be showing my love, I would be accomplishing it as an end. But if the point was merely to show or accomplish my love, how would I be loving my children? It would be a mere game of display. To frame my actions in this way would be to take my children as means of manifesting love. This would be pernicious. I want to say instead that I act for the sake of my children—and they are who I love.

And this love is a noncontingent fact. What is required of me as their parent, in any particular situation, is subject to many questions of practical reasoning. I might fail in various ways to do what is right and best—but that need not mean I have failed in my love for them (although it could mean that). And thus, the love for the sake of which I act *need* not have any normative role in my actual reasoning about some action; my love is a necessary frame relative to which my actions make sense. Should we say that my love is one motive among others for some action, the reasons for which are justified relative to more specific factors— like ingredients in the pantry, time available, state of hunger and tiredness, and so on? This would be a mistake.

My tiredness and even my forgetfulness (God forbid) would be failures, but temporary. I do not say: "Oh, kids, I forgot to feed you because my love for you vanished for a while." If I forgot enough, you might conclude—"he does not love his children." That conclusion, however, would be a condemnation, not an excuse. My love does not play the same role in my actions as does my tiredness or wakefulness.

My love is a frame by means of which my actions make sense as the actions they are. My actions make sense relative to the love that defines *a priori*, as it were, my possible actions relative to my necessary relationship with my children. If we understand love in this sense, then it is misleading to say love is a goal motivating my actions.

If love has happened to me, already an indication that love is something greater than myself, as I have argued, then when I act for the sake of my children, I do not act to accomplish my love, I act and in so doing manifest my love. With my children, the love I show furthers the form and goodness of our relationship. (Acts of love express my love, but fundamentally they are my love. In this way, an act of love mimes the logical form of a gesture).

When I act out of love for my children (or anyone else) I act for their sake, and in so doing manifest love. The love is not achieved in the action, since it preexists my acting. That love defines the relation I have with my children, and thus is the frame within which I take care of my children. My children might see my actions as the face of love, but, for me, those actions are what I do for them as people. My children for me, however, are the face of love because I act for their sake, and that just is to love them. The face of love, in this sense, shows forth in how I see my children within the light of love.

My children are visible within my love as a preexistent frame relative to which my actions make sense and mean as actions of love. If love is not a simple motive, but is instead something like a frame, within which I act for the sake of those I love, then those I love, in my stance toward them and in how I see them, manifest, whether I know it or not, the frame of that love. The intelligibility of my actions relative to my children assumes and relies on the love that organizes my ways of being with them. I see them as part of that intelligibility. They make a sense not only as the particular persons they are, but as primary people for the sake of whom I act in a way that comprehensively defines my life. In playing that role for me they in effect reveal the intelligibility by which I see them. That intelligibility is love. That revelation is the face of love.

When we act toward a goal and accomplish that goal, then we effect something by means of our causal agency. We make something. So I accomplish these words as I write; I am the agent and these words are the effects. When I act for the sake of something, on the other hand, I am not accomplishing what is not the case, but manifesting what is already the case. What I manifest, however, is not visible unless I act for the sake of that thing, for the sake of love, for example. Love manifest is love recognized, which is to say: we recognize love, we do not make it like we make a cake. Love made is love pretended.

When we extend this idea of recognition to our understanding of language we find some ambiguities. I make these words by writing them, but the meaningfulness of what I write is manifest in the writing in the way that a person is manifest in their face and love is manifest in my children. Does that mean that the meaningfulness of what I write preexists what I write? When I understand a sentence, I do not make my understanding; I simply recognize what the sentence means. Does the meaning preexist my understanding? In a way it does, since the words are the means by which I grasp a thought, and since the thought is not the marks, we naturally imagine the thought has to be somewhere else. In the case of language, the issue is not whether the meaning is causally prior (prior in time to my speaking), but logically prior. With ordinary language, we can say what we mean in multiple ways, and the justification for any particular sentence rests on what we take it to mean. There are further complexities in this that I need not address now. But it does look like things have a face, in my sense, when something is bodied forth by means of that thing (that word, that face, that gesture) and when what is bodied forth is logically prior to the means by which it is made manifest.

Within the context of these various cases of acting for the sake of which, a poem is not yet an action. We have to make it one by reading or taking it up somehow. And when we do, it may not body forth a meaning in the way an ordinary sentence does. The poem would become more like a face showing a person than a string of words showing a proposition. What the words and clauses of a poem mean would be the further means by which the meaningfulness, that is the face, of the poem would be made manifest. The poem as a whole need not have a meaning in the way an ordinary sentence might.

As always poems are odd, dependent things. The case of love is clearer. What is true of my love for my children would be true for any other kind of love. My children manifest love, just as I do in those acts that I do for the sake of love and for the sake of the person I love. Thus, we meet Donne's notion of love incarnate, without any of his attending metaphysical beliefs.

*　*　*

What is stable with children (or should be) is less so in romantic love. In romance, my heart-felt, desperate expressions of love can turn affected, into pathetic embarrassments. You can feel this kind of slip, if amidst an intense conversation with someone you love at a restaurant, you turn and look at the people at the other tables. One person's tête-a-tête is another's mad hatter's tea party. This can strike one as comic or horrible.

Romantic love is horrible, because you cannot always tell the difference between something mattering to you and your pretending it matters. There is a difference, but it can get lost, and it may not be great enough. In love, I can reach such a state of exhaustion or excitement that I can't tell pretending from feeling. I can't tell you where I am in relation to the feelings to which I know I am committed.

The distinction between appearance and reality fails to be either determinate or stable for those ethical feelings that matter so much—especially love and sympathy. And what is true of these ethical feelings is also true of the beliefs of which they are a part. To be in love is also to believe one is in love. To feel sympathy is to stand toward certain feelings with a particular belief and trust. But this belief is subject to the same uncertainty and shifting aspect as love. I believe x or I believe that I believe x. I can realize the differences between these two ways of believing when I realize I don't believe x anymore. It can disturb and disrupt my sense of myself and the world, because my loss of belief might not matter at all, because I had only believed I believed. The habit of belief need not end in anything but inertia, and when called to the effort of acting on a belief, the habit can fail. Love constrains us and the horror of it is that it is a necessity that we can fail or that can fail us. And we might have to discover that difference as well, when the loss or promise of that love is beyond recovery.

No action or display of putative love or sympathy is decisive in proving that we do love or do have sympathy. No manifestation of these states of feeling provides definitive criteria for the state or condition. Similarly, we can discover that our feelings of love or sympathy have not really been these. This is not simply because no given feeling can provide a foundation for our knowledge of anything, but because what counts as these feelings relative to our self-understanding of our own states and commitments cannot be determined by those same feelings. This is a motive for skepticism—both of other minds and of ourselves. But it need not take those pathological forms, and the question is not just about what exists or what is a particular fact of the matter. The doubt gets its grip because we can feel that things just as they are do not mean in the ways that would seem essential or in ways that we had at first thought.[6]

Romantic love is built and relies on the fact of some reciprocation (if it is not simply projection)—it is shared through that building. Love for children is different. They live and grow within the context of a parent's love, and thus the love revealed as the child's face is not part of a built structure of reciprocal love (it can be, but this is not essential). The love shown in the face of my child is not her love for me, although that can be expressed, nor simply my feelings of love for her, although that can and should be expressed, but it is what is shown by her particularity within the frame of my continual love, regardless of how I understand the psychology of that love. The face of my child does not simply show me my child, but her face reveals the love by which I see her in her particularity. She is the contingent person she is, and I see those contingencies in her changes, her growth, the dynamism of her life. With my child, my love, which is not simply a feeling, but a commitment of care, a meaningfulness and significance that I can only discover since it is always greater than me, describes a sense of necessity that gathers in the child's particularity for me. The child's particularity should always be recognized as a manifestation of what our love is for them. Our love for our children should not turn parodic, and, if it does, this only confesses our failure.

* * *

We give love a linguistic form in order to remember, explain, commemorate, excuse, clarify, condemn, praise, share, confirm, or believe something about it, about ourselves, or about those whom we love. "I love you" is a poem because of the complexity it gathers in its simple form, because of how we meet its words as if they carried someone with them—to which we can respond and react with greater force than we might anticipate and understand. Such a phrase is a poem and surrogate for whoever would use it. The surrogacy of the phrase matches the surrogacy of qualities that carry us into the view of others—charm, beauty, sensitivity—as targets for love and hate, and much else.

This produces a challenge for the ethical valence of love.

It is easy to say we love a person, to feel that we do—but neither the saying nor the feeling makes it true. Harry Frankfurt argues that love *per se*, especially the love for our children, is not a love of qualities but a love of a person.[7] This seems correct, but is misleading, since there is no person who is not manifest through their qualities. The difference between associated qualities that might symbolize a person, a gesture, for example, and that person is not easy to separate. We can understand that a person might never make a certain gesture ever again and still be that person, and our love need not diminish, but it will change in its shape and even intensity. That might be a moral failure, as with the mother who can love better her infant child than her adolescent child. Our love should not be contingent, but how it lives for us and in us and is sustained, pursued and held is not static or given simply.

This is especially true of romantic love. The love remembered when I smell her shampoo, even if it is no longer hers or she is no longer here, is not simply a memory. The desire and the care sprung into consciousness is for that smell and what it entails; it moves through that smell toward her that is gone because she manifested her beauty, herself to me through that smell, as that smell, and not just in association with it. She might never even know of this olfactory means I had of sensing (touching) her. Love is not simply an ethical concept, even in its ethical forms as care or respect or goodness. It is assailed by contingencies of psychology and manifest form—words, gestures, and smells. Recognizing her and remembering her is not her; but she has to be manifest somehow—and those means gather her; they are her poem, her surrogates, for me.[8]

Understanding the qualities of the beloved as surrogates for her does not resolve the confusion about how my love for her fits with my love of her qualities. Do we love the person or their qualities? Sometimes when the qualities change or one sees them under a different aspect, the love lessens or leaves. In other cases, regardless of changes, love is love and is unshaken. Are both love? I am not sure that there is a definitive answer. But how love for a person relates to the qualities by which we know them, see them, and love them is what I would call the aesthetic question of love. I call this an aesthetic question because of the centrality of qualities and aspects on which feeling and sense depend. In our literary practices we read aspects, categorize and delimit aspects, and in making art we manipulate aspects, explore and exploit them. If philosophy concerns itself with the kind of thing something is, the study of art concerns the immediacy, force and shifting aspects of things. Philosophy and the study of art each imply the other: an aspect is an aspect of something, and the ambiguity and complexity of these draw up questions about what kinds of things have what kinds of aspects, including the aspects of art itself. Similarly, philosophy depends on determining what is what, given the aspects by which things, from objects *per se* to actions *in situ*, are manifest and grasped.

On the other hand, love, to be love, seems to be for a person, not their qualities; certainly, love for one's children should not diminish or increase because of their accomplishments or qualities of character. And yet we can love those qualities as well. We have to love something and someone, and, to remain with people for the moment, a person may be a person no matter how small, but to be loved as a person requires that he or she be manifest to me in some way. Our loves are not random, although they can seem inexplicable. The qualities of a person constitute that person in some sense, to some degree. We do not simply love a person *tout court*, nor as a bare minimum. And thus, I am stuck with two competing, if not always conflicting, intuitions: (1) love is for something or someone regardless of their qualities (and thus is for the person or the activity or the country) and (2) love depends on and includes qualities of character, type, and aspect.

By necessity, if I love you, and if that love has content, then it is particularized. And any love for which the beloved can be easily replaced with someone else is suspect. But the love for someone is hardly very full if it is only their bare presence or existence that we love. We love the qualities of someone, but we should not love them because of those. Our love for them is for them, but what and who they are is a complex target and enfolds our sense of that person in the ways we value them.

There is an order of development in love. Despite the ideologies of love poets, love lives and advances in time, not in the moment. Loves of the moment are often retrospectively discovered to be obsessions of attraction or pathology. Different kinds of love involve different orders of development. So with my children, I love their person first—they are mine to love, to care for, to protect, to nourish; and as they grow and develop and show and share their qualities of person, their engagements with the world, their personalities and attentions, my love develops through these. We do not value our children because of their virtues, we value their virtues because they are our children and we love them. Our love for our children develops from a love of a person into a love of qualities that are the expression of that person. In romantic love or friendships—in loves that emerge for us amidst our own independence—we know a person first through and relative to their qualities, although these can be nebulous and factitious. From these qualities we may come to love the person, and when we do, our love becomes independent of those qualities, except in so far as they collect or determine that person as who they are for us to love. My love for my children develops from their *person to their character*; my love for my romantic beloved (or friend) develops from their *character to their person*: a chiasmus of kinds of love.

From this chiasmus we can see how the qualities of a person can play different roles in our commitments of love. Such qualities can provide reasons for our love, and as such they characterize either a certain kind of love or a certain stage in love. Those same qualities, once love is established, are the means by which the person we love is manifest to us. The shifting role of qualities alters the aspect by which we see who or what we love. The qualities of my beloved, the means by which she is manifest to me, can become surrogates for her. Any such surrogate would do, because what matters are not those qualities but the who (or what) they show. As a consequence, anything that invokes the love or the beloved becomes a kind of emergence of the beloved. This does not mean that such qualities, the smell of shampoo, for example, are mere subjective associations. Rather they are more like ceremonial invocations, even if only recognized in the passing by of some other woman. I call this ceremonial because the smell of shampoo has become a language that speaks my beloved, but a formal language in which she is consecrated. The smells are notes in a melody I know well. It is not just the subjective associations that attach to the melody, but it is the melody itself that I am hearing. That smell was not associated with my beloved; it was an aspect of her, a surrogate for her. The smell of her shampoo names her, a quality that necessarily and *a posteriori* is her name. Hence when I smell that shampoo, no matter where, I recognize her in that smell.

The smell of her shampoo names her; and I react to that name viscerally with recognition, and desire, like I would if I saw her face. Her face names her, but it is also more than a mere name. It is a means of showing herself to others. Her face is meaningful in all sorts of ways. This does not mean her face, as a name, is some special name. It is a name like any other name. It refers to her, and in that has no meaning. But it is also more than a name, just as the word that names her is more than a name in my love for her. The face of someone I love becomes one of her names. And your face is one of yours.

Her face is her face, but if it also is the face of love, then her face has a face, but a face that is more than just her own. And this is true of my children, too. We make that second face together, in our living with each other and caring for each other. With our children this second face of love is made more or less out of our simple living. In romantic love, this second face is made mutually, and it is a face that reveals love, as if love had a face which we recognize, and through that face we find, describe, reach for that which has that face. Love is not a person. If the face of love is manifest as the face of my beloved, it is not the person of love, or the god of love, or any creature of love that I discover through that face. And the face is various, volatile, changing, and yet it remains a revealed face.

And this is true of poems as well. The poem, in its particularity, names itself, and in its tones, which we find and lose, accentuates and diminishes. It has a face, like all words and sentences do. We grasp their meaning through their shapes and sounds. But a poem in its meaningfulness as more than mere words has a further face, like my beloved has the further face of love. This face of a poem is what we try to articulate in our reading, to describe and recover. It is not clear what it is a further face of, if not of our involvement with it. Every description of the poem is a new name of its already being a name, and in naming it again, we refer to it and we show it. But our description (interpretation) of the poem is not a name in the sense that Russell thought of a name as a description (as if every name were a collapsed description). The description of a poem points to the poem, naming it in a new lexicon, but it also does something else entirely, since a description interprets the poem, gives the poem a face that we read as an aspect of its meaningfulness.

A poem has the particularity of a name, but its face has to be discovered, since it shows in the way that a face can show love. It shows a meaningfulness that has to be found and unfolded. A poem shows a face in gesture. It means like a gesture. It means in the way a face does (which suggests that we might better claim that a poem is meaningful in the way a face is; neither of these might have a meaning). Poems have faces, which is to say that they come together in a wholeness that can seem like a face or a countenance. This is metaphor or analogy, but it is also more than that. Poems are manifest in a way that is like a face: something is manifest and, for convenience, we might call it the countenance of the poem. Those who read well can find that countenance, those who cannot, do not. But I mean the countenance to be more than a convenient catachrestic term. The countenance of a poem is like the face of the beloved seen as manifesting love. One way to make that kind of countenance visible in a poem is through how we read it, through our tone.

Poems are the faces we share.

* * *

A face I love emerges with a particularity and meaningfulness beyond my basic recognition of any human face. The qualities of the face are the same—I can recognize the same face before and after I fall in love. There is no objective difference. But there is a difference.

We might imagine, of course, that the face of someone we love is different simply because we project our feelings onto that person, those feelings altering what we see like a spotlight might illuminate something in greater detail and intensity than ambient light. And there is some truth to this. But this makes what holds us in our love an effect of our love, and thus our love becomes projection, rationalized maybe by what we see in our spotlight of attention. The beloved holds us, not just in her particularity, but within the context and frame of a love that holds me and her. We see each other, she and I, within the context of that love, especially if the love is fully reciprocal. The shared context, however, can emerge as a surprise—and from this we can build a greater intimacy.

But love has to be manifest: the face of my beloved is one of the most profound ways in which who I love is manifest as my love, not simply as an expression or projection of what I feel. Like when I remembered my friend's skin and I saw death, when I see my beloved, I see love. This does not mean that my friend's skin and my beloved are equivalent to death and to love, but rather they are integral to what death and love are. My friend's skin surrogates death, my beloved surrogates love; these are not romantic unities, expressions of some organic ideal of semantic pantheism, but a recognition that love and death are both kinds of things that exist only in their examples.

Just as we hear some sounds as words, we can see a face as an event of recognition, that is, our recognition of love. My beloved *poems* love into my apprehension, just as the dead *poem* death into visibility. When I see my daughters' faces, I see them as a revelation of their particularity within the love I feel for them: their faces each mean more than a face. They bring into focus a brightness that is my own sense of love, of which they exemplify. Their faces mean love.

Faces become poems when the faces of those whom we love speak love. It may be that the only poems that find us in our lives are the faces of our children, but that is enough. My children's faces, in their beauty and grace, really are them. To see their face is for me to necessarily see them, and in that seeing, I see love—not simply mine for them or theirs for me, but my sense of what love is stands revealed.

On the other hand, I do not look like I look. I rediscover this, sometimes by surprise, if I look too long into a mirror; the strangeness emerges like a hidden image. I am nothing like I look; so how I am seen by others is not like how I feel I am. I recognize similarities between myself and my brother and sister, my parents, my grandparents, my children—and yet, the person I see is not me. I don't look at the world in the way the world must look at me. And then I turn my head. For me, it is to the left—but in the mirror—to the right. And in that half angle, as if looking into the corner of the bathroom I see someone that looks like me. It is like a gesture, but it is nothing but the eyes and the sharpness of the lines and planes of my skull and jaw. It is not what I want to look like *per se*, but rather a recognition of me amidst the contingent particularities of the face others see as, for them, necessarily me.

For other people, to my chagrin, I am what they see. My face is me, not in a complete sense, but, rather, a figuration of me. My face reveals me, in some sense, and stands in for me. It is both figure and analogue. But it is an analogue that collects the complexity of the person I am into its form. For me, my face is contingent: a fact I inherit. I may at some point get the face I deserve, but it is never the face I chose. It is an accident. For others, however, my face necessarily fronts the aspect of me by which I am known and recognized. I can be known in other ways, but we face each other necessarily with the faces we have. We can change the particularities of our face, lose qualities and gain others; regardless, whatever face I have is necessarily the face that marks and even expresses me for others. It is, all things being equal, necessary.

I am my face and I am not. My face can parody me, and I can feel that I am as a person a parody of my own face—when, for example, I don't recognize who I am in the way others recognize and describe me. We can seem nothing but qualities, any of which can become a unifying face, a surrogate for all the others, and for whatever greater unity I might be (as a person).

The face of my child manifests *Love* (it does not just show her love), because both she and I are held by some greater sense of love. Love is logically prior to the love that I would see in her face and the love that she would see in my actions of care. There is no love to show but in how that love is manifest as love. All faces within the light of love can show love, but that just means that the face of one beloved is a parody of love relative to the face of another. All other human faces are parodies of my children's faces. Our face is always a parody of another face.

* * *

If my seeing any face is like grasping the contingent necessity of the alphabet, a kind of given, once I have learned it, then I see my daughters' faces as an alphabet that spells "I love you," an expression of my love for them expressed in the fact of their faces. Their faces are poems, events of form that happen, in which I discover a meaningfulness given as the form of that event. Seeing their faces is an event. "I love you" is a poem of this sort. Such poems, construed in this way, reveal our involvement with forms through an ethos of vulnerability and dependence.

Poems, like the faces of those we love, and like our own faces, like our reading of formal strings of particular words into a surprising meaningfulness, mix necessity, and contingency in a particularity of form; in this, poems embody what our lives can feel like—a mix of fate and choice, of inevitability and freedom, and thus of hope.

Our ceremonies with poems must be discovered and made; they are not bound by rules, but by distinctions and awareness, sensitivities and mistrusts. Poems do sometimes alter the world, stall our forgetfulness in our cherishing and attention to a moment, to a possibility. They can do this in their writing and in our reading, entangling whatever we feel and think and see in words, in descriptions. Words can hold something dear still. "Silence is a shape that has passed," Stevens writes toward the end of his life, listening for death, the sun less and less a hope for him. That silence is love too: living well is risking the silence of the passing of you and me. Love is partly the loving of what is gone; that aspect of love would be silence. And yet it is also the shape present, the shapes being present, beckoning or coming, or holding and lifting you up, us up, lifting the world so we can see it clearly for a moment. Being close to someone is a kind of speaking that fills the silence, even if it fills it with what might be a future emptiness.

Poems aspire to love.

A Conclusion in Two Parts

Part I: Odds and Ends

Poems are odd, peculiar things. So odd in fact that we can't answer the question "What is a poem?" until we decide what will count as an answer. This makes the question a riddle.

Compare it, for example, to the following: "Why is a raven like a writing desk?" Answer: for many reasons, for no reason, but, in any case, a raven isn't like a writing desk! The answer we like best for any riddle will be the one we will count as an answer. And that can change. The same for the question which is really a riddle: "What is a poem?."[1]

Time is another such riddle-thing. Lewis Carroll made up a riddle that might be about time. The riddle goes like this:

Often talked of, never seen.
Ever coming, never been.
Daily looked for, never here,
Still approaching, coming near.
Thousands for its visit wait
But alas for their fate,
Tho' they expect me to appear
They will never find me here.
Who/What am I?

The standard answer is tomorrow. But another answer might be the future. Or maybe salvation.[2]

Time the riddle slips in and out of view, even when we measure it (or think we measure it) with an atomic clock, for example. The clock changes in a very regular way. It is a localized example of change. We measure and count the clock's regularity of change. By that counting we correlate the measured change of the clock with the ordered succession of numbers (in some repeating cycle to make it easier and more useful). This succession of numbers is further correlated with other cycles of change, like the cycle of day and night. Where is time in all of these correlated changes? Is time change or does change show time, which is something else? Consequently, "What is time?" is more riddle than question.

Poems are like that. It makes them interesting. But many people don't think much of poems. They think them oddly trivial or trivially odd or simply irrelevant. Time is something we all suffer; fewer people suffer from poems, despite the large number of bad and painful poems published and recited.

Poems have, however, some important qualities that should make them interesting even to people disposed against them (or distracted by other things). One idea we have about poems, for example, is that they are highly particular. Many people, in fact, imagine that they embody a special particularity. They think that poems are equivalent to the words of which they are made. This can seem reasonable since most poems do seem to be made of a particular set of words in a specific order, such that those words and that order just is the poem. This reasonable idea, however, is false. Poems are not equivalent to the words of which they seem to be made.

This failure of equivalence pressures our understanding of particularity. Even if we are not sure what *particulars* are, we have a fair degree of confidence that we know what *particularity* is. If something is something, then it is that particular something. The oddness of poems helps us see that it is not as simple as that. Poems, properly understood, expose how much of our world is made up of things that are neither particular objects nor subjective projections. Why this is has a lot to do with language.

As a consequence, investigating poems leads to investigating various particularities, like poems and sentences, as they modulate into names, nonsense, and parables. My concern has been not with metaphysical ideas (let alone theories) of particularity, but with how we attempt to make particularities using words and fail. We bewitch ourselves with our failures. That bewitchment is revealing, revealing our own human misplacement into the particularities we think we find in poems, but don't. If we look carefully, we will find something else.

A poem is always more than its words. Even if we make its words the criteria for its identification, the poem is more and other than that: its identification is not its identity. If a poem is radically delimited (defined) by its words in their particular order, then it becomes something revealed only through analogy (as a kind of analogical structure). If it is defined by its words, then as a poem it is only analogically related to ordinary language: the poem is displaced out of language, reduced to a faux-name, or transformed into a kind of complex word. Consequently, by attempting to define a poem by its words, we end up not being able to define it really at all.

The very particularity of a poem (defined by its particularity of words) displaces the poem elsewhere than those words. We might attempt to catch this displacement and corral it under the concept of poetry. The appeal to the particular words in their particular order represents a confession that there is no other non-question begging way of defining a poem. Poems are contingent things. What they are is bound with what we think or imagine they are. These thoughts and imaginings vary and have no essential form. A poem is a kind of thing that depends on our ideas about it, such that to read a poem is to read simultaneously the concept of poetry. There is no noncontingent poetry, no natural or logical category that is not a site of contest.

A poem is not simply an example of what a poem is; we take it and treat it as a poem through our ideas of what a poem is, even if these are inchoate and largely unconscious. But if a poem is a mere illustration of an idea of poetry (an illustration, for example, of a technique of making a poem), then there is no poem. An illustration as an illustration is not an example of that which is illustrated (unless it is illustrating an illustration, a second-order thing, since it would have to be an illustration of something else in order to be an example of an illustration). In such a case, the poem is lost in (as) an idea about poetry. Since I hold that there really are poems, if a poem becomes a mere illustration of the technique by which it is made (or of anything else), then the poem disappears and what is left is no poem. Poems are radically dependent on both their particularity and the ideas we have about poems—and it is that radical dual dependency that makes them the odd creatures they are. (If I define a poem in such a way that the poem ceases to exist, I cannot argue that such a definition constitutes the poem—since it constitutes its disappearance. I can argue, however, that given this, there is no such thing as a poem. But if I insist that poems do exist, then I cannot define them as illustrations of the technique by which they are made.) There is no reading a poem that is not also a reading of the kind of thing a poem is.

A poem has no necessary or essential form, let alone nature. What we understand a poem to be is bound to the examples to which we are committed (and our habits and education, prejudice and assumptions). This is not a weakness of poetry, but a strength—it means that what a poem is will reveal our involvement with it and with the means of our taking it up and of it taking us up. Poems reveal us, reveal our involvement with sense-making, with our aspirations toward sense and significance. Poems can show how we, as human beings, have specific and variable relations with our means of sense-making, primarily with our words. If a recurrent concern of the philosophy of language (and of epistemology in some form) is how sentences or propositions relate to states of affairs, then a recurrent revelation of poetry is that we rediscover that we have an intimate but corrigible and shifting relationship with our sentences and thoughts. Poems can allow us to discover that we are intimate with words, that we can allow words to absorb our thoughts and our feelings, that we can lose ourselves to words as we can with gossip and cliché, and that we can also distance ourselves from words, find ourselves in what we see, in how we move, in our refusals of words and sense. Poems can be understood as sites of conflict between how we find and lose sense. This makes poems peculiar.

Where is a poem? In the same neighborhood as beauty. And ugliness. We needn't distinguish these in this case. But where is beauty? In the grace and form of what we call beautiful. Of course. But also, is it not in the eyes of the beholder? Is beauty in the same place or rather in the same no-place that meaning is? The means of saying something, the forms of words as phrases and sentences, are distinct from what is said, what we take up or understand, what we call the meaning of what is said. Still, to ask "Where is the meaning of a sentence?" is close to a riddle or a joke. What do you mean, where is it? It isn't something that can be anywhere. So there are things that are somethings that needn't be anywhere—how like the spirit! Or does that mean that if it is nowhere, it is nothing? Quine thinks this last; Wittgenstein does not, but he posits other somethings to do the work of the meaning that is something but nowhere: he calls them language games and forms of life.[3] But he is nervous about this—for good reason. Not only are the meanings of sentences not in the marks, but they are also not so easily domesticated in talk of systems or wholes given by social norms called games or forms.

The meanings of sentences are not only said; we respond and live amidst the meaningfulness of what we say. So meaning is not nothing, even if we say it is only a way of going on with others, a way of reacting or responding, a game of correlation between noises and actions, a form of expectation and resolution. We can also find that meanings are everything, that the world is made of them, and that marks are only manifestations of these greater meanings. This is to go too far I think; but the possibility remains. All we say about sentences we say about our body and soul. This human tendency may be one reason why poetry, which is a playing with the soul by manipulating the body, or a dancing of the body by the powers of the soul, can matter so much, and why it can turn simple on us. We are always tempted to say we are nothing but the body (only matter or language) or nothing but the spirit (only thoughts, feelings, or symbols).

Poems are particularities that fail to be particular, because they are in some sense not their words. A poem is elsewhere and yet bound to the words by which it is manifest. We human beings are like that too—manifest in our flesh and in what is visible and yet elsewhere and other than that. I am in my face, but not; I am in my words, but not; I am in my gestures, but not. Poems are symptoms of our own particularity and dispersal. If we understand how a poem is particular and how it is not, we will find the mesh by which we catch ourselves in what is like us, but not.

A poem is more than its words and phrases because it is also *analogous* with those words and phrases. A poem is an analogical thing. A poem made of words is a thing built through and as an analogue, built through and as continual comparisons with words and sentences but it is not equivalent with them. A poem is always more than its words, but, if made of words, then it is a logically dependent on those words. It is not expressed through words but is a kind of thing that gives form to possibilities—what I described as being an abstract of its possible senses. This is why there is no poem unless it is read as a poem that has to be made in our reading; but it can only be made through our dependence on it, our being claimed by it. We articulate it by articulating our dependence on it. The word objects others call poems may not be poems for me. Poems are not ready-made things.

Poems are events of form whose senses, no matter how obscure and partial, hold me despite what I think or want. Poems must be discovered not just made. My argument has been that poems are too many places to be any place. Where is a gesture—simply in the movements? Where is a friendship? Simply in what is said between two friends? A poem is nowhere in particular, and many places in general. A poem may be a memory of some place, but we can only find that place nowhere and someplace else. That is where we reside in poetry—no place and someplace else.

Part II: Intonations of Form

In the preceding chapters, I have concentrated on events of form that interrupt us, primarily the revelations of love and death as they find us through words and the forms of everyday life. I have called these events poems.

For example, the skin of my soon-to-be-dead friend gave him a tone that, after his death, became the expression of death. I could see the face of death when I remembered his skin. His skin, however, was not a mere symbol—it was an event, a descriptive event. To see his skin—its lines and color—was to see death, not to be reminded of it. His skin became meaningful in a way very similar to how the sounds of a word become not a syntax of tones but a word, with its potential senses and possible connections. We hear it and apprehend it as a certain kind of thing, the sounds subordinated as constituents of that thing, that word. With my friend's skin and with words, we learn to recognize them (as what they are) when we apprehend them as that; they are poems of recognition and contingent necessity.

To see my friend's skin as death was to apprehend one aspect of him as more than an accident, it revealed a tone of his skin that, while horrific, sounded a tone for existence itself. Whatever I saw became not simply surfaces to see, but surfaces collected into patterns that could be recognized and discovered retrospectively, not as one might read the tracings of particles in a cloud chamber, but as one might find patterns by organizing things by size. I understood his skin as death relative to my own condition of living. I recognized the poem of his skin as a particular intonation within my life, not by choice, but by attention. My reactions were already an intonation, but as I become aware of these reactions; my responsibility for the poem of his skin that had found me increased. I became burdened with caring.

We all see by such intonations of form. I do not see planes and surfaces when I see my children's faces—I see their faces. I do not build a word out of its constituent sounds—I hear that word. If someone mumbles a word, I hear a blur of sound, often still recognizable as a word, but when the sounds clarify as a word, then the sounds have disappeared into the word I grasp. And the same with sentences, although with further complications. I do not hear mere sounds when I grasp a sentence; I understand the sentence (at least as a sentence). A sentence that I grasp and understand is not its sounds. It is always more and other than sounds, a particular proposition (or statement) and a dispersed complexity of meaningfulness. Despite differences, all three—seeing a face, hearing a word, grasping a sentence—happen to us; they are events of form, facilitated in our actions and practices of seeing, hearing, and understanding.

Such events of form recall my initial discoveries about poems: (1) that poems are parodies of necessary forms (of counting, for example) and (2) that poems are expressions of too much by means of very little. The alphabet is a poem because of its contingent or arbitrary, but, once established, seemingly necessary, patterned order. "I love you" is a poem because it confesses the necessity of another human being in a standardized phrase, which bears the sense and implications of that necessity. The phrase seems to express its promise through the inevitability of its form (as a phrase, "I love you" has the particularity of a word with the meaningfulness of a sentence). When we apprehend the alphabet or "I love you" with the seeming force of necessity, when the forms seem to carry what they say, we are taken up by these forms as much as we take them up. Thus we experience a poem as an event. Poems are revelations of tone. Such revelations are moral interruptions.

Everyday poems, often dependent on words but not constituted by them, emerge through forms that both claim us and suggest, or seem to reveal, a meaningfulness that we may not understand. The baleful domestication of poems within the classroom and the very tradition of written poems masks the everyday ground of poems in our lives, and thus makes it appear as if written poems were the primary analogue relative to which everyday poems, as I call them, should be compared. This book has been written out of an inverse understanding: written poems are analogous to the more primary everyday poems we discover as forms that claim us.

When I am claimed by a poem, I confess my need for what I might not understand. A poem is a promise provoked by my need for it, which is what I discover when it claims me. The meaningfulness of such events of form, whether they are made of words or not, expresses a kind of hope.

The meaningfulness of a poem is akin to the way hope infuses and animates our living and our lives. Hope matters in the way that Samuel Johnson identifies with his usual clarity: "The natural flights of the human mind are not from pleasure to pleasure, but from hope to hope" (84).[4] Thus, our end is deferred by the always ahead in-between stations of hope. This kind of hope is like the hope that draws us through a story, produces in us the desire to reach a resolution in a plot. It is like the hope that attracts us to the melodies of phrases and images in poems. We want such hope to calm our agitation. It is the hope that the world is more and better than it seems. Imagination is a species of hope. And so is poetry.

A poem can seem very present in its visceral qualities, its particularities of words and of forms. But the promise of meaningfulness that gives poems their claim on us, that prompts us to take them up, displaces the poem beyond its particularities and forms in ways that disperse its thereness into an elsewhereness. And then maybe we chase the poem—or it chases us. The poem ships away, but its words remain, in the way Walcott describes figures in Watteau: as "the hollow at the heart of all embarkations" ("Watteau"). If we fill up the hollow poem, we hollow ourselves, for we embark pirated by the poem: we are taken away from ourselves through the words of another. And why? A poem makes us hollow with hope.

My losses and commitments matter too much to me just to write them out as something to share, even with friends. The descriptive sling in which I can save some of what matters, even when obscure, makes what is most personal more than just mine. What is a story to you now in my telling, was to me then living people, a world too full and too taut with significance to reduce to a story made of words. But still I write these words. Each sentence that brings forward the past can bring with it meanings and hopes that confound the present. Our losses and failures can unsettle our world, terrorizing the confidence perched on our shoulder into silence: that bird can no longer tell us that whatever is in front of us is ours. But hoping is not hopeless. Love can flourish if it is not deformed and degraded into mere wanting: projected desire, fantasies of selfish concern, disguised self-love.

Love happens, as do poems, when we can find, by chance and sometimes half-merit, a chorus with another to sing of a love greater than us all. Love is an interruption of life, spoken as a promise and achieved after the fact, but never transparently, with certainty, or even in memory. It is alive with vulnerability.

> I look for the way
> things will turn
> out spiraling from a center,
> the shape
> things take to come forth in
> …
> not so much looking for the shape
> as being available
> to any shape that may be
> summoning itself
> through me
> from the self not mine but ours.
> ("Poetics," Ammons)

"Summoning itself/ through me/ from the self not mine but ours"; this is one way to find oneself recognized. There are others.

Reading is a drama of finding surrogates for ourselves, for what we think we are, only to find the surrogates overwhelming us, haunting us, failing, fossilizing, disappearing, or replacing us. Whether we acknowledge it or not, we are intersubjective when we read. Scaled by our reading, we cannot climb ourselves until we are laid against someone or something else. We must have a place to climb to and a reason.

A poem targets me if I react to it. It doesn't mirror my feelings, I mirror it—or rather, to rewrite Keats slightly, the poem is true not when it illustrates my life, but when I illustrate it. An illustration is parasitic on that which it would illustrate—so, to treat a work of art as an illustration of my life is to absorb it in my concerns, to treat it as an example of me (or my thoughts and feelings). But this is a diminished and instrumental relationship with art. Keats inverts this—I recognize the truth in the proverb (the poem) when I take my life as an illustration of it; my life becomes an example of the proverb (the poem), a gift of the poem.

To illustrate how we illustrate poems, we should recall the demands and difficulties of accomplishing a wedding. For a wedding to be accomplished, we must be vulnerable to not only to the person we marry, but to time, change, distress, uncertainty. The accomplishment of a wedding is a retrospective achievement of love and faith. It will have happened after it has happened, and this is part of its secret. If our wedding has been accomplished, then we must discover that. It is not a case simply of finishing the ceremony and signing the documents. It is a binding by legal commitment and poetic grace. We try to bind ourselves, because we can so easily go astray. The need for binding, and thus what we pledge in promise, what afflicts us as love, confesses our vulnerabilities to words, to temptations, to anxieties. A marriage should be founded in love, but it will certainly be infused with politics—care and desire modulating with power and some kind of justice (or injustice). Both love and politics flourish through the promise and constriction provided by forms—forms of attraction and frustration, forms of commitment and freedom. A marriage is a binding of ourselves in certain shared forms of life and responsibility. But as we are bound, we can be unbound. In marriage we can become unbound by misprision and misalliance, by our vulnerability to disharmonies as well as disquiet. This is our all too likely fate in marriage. We resist that fate with hope. That is part of its poetry, not just the insistence on that hope in its forms of promise, but in its attempt to accomplish a *we*.

To be achieved, a wedding must make a chorus, a "we" beyond what we might willingly acknowledge, a "we" that for anyone is incomplete. Such a "we" is expansive; a commitment to a future not known or knowable, a dependency on others and their descriptions of us. The claim and scope of this "we" has to be discovered and cannot simply be determined or chosen; this is its poetic claim and force.

A wedding is a wedding for the bride and groom when their lives illustrate the promises they make in their wedding. Until then, it is a wedding of mere form. And yet there is no decisive moment until death when one can say that we have illustrated those promises. One can always break these or fail those promises, or find that what one thought was a fulfillment of one's vows was really betrayal or refusal. We can, however, have a sense—gathered in our attitudes of love and care—that suggests how we are fulfilling our vows. A wedding is always being accomplished and never finished. Our wedding vows, therefore, are always posthumous. We must try to hear as a chorus the voices of those who are wed (when we witness a wedding). We are always outside that wedding, or at least always partially outside the accomplishment of the wedding. This is true as well for those who are wedded. This is why partners can have such a different understanding of their lives together and yet remain still together in many ways. We must speak our love and commitment, but we cannot speak with any assurance that we will be heard. This is the posthumous mode.

A wedding aspires, as a ceremony, to effect an interruption of life into a new mode of being in the world: it stages love as an interruption, spoken as a promise and achieved after the fact, but never transparently, with certainty, or even in memory. It is alive in its uncertainty, hence our need to sustain it through our lives and actions.

We are also interrupted by death, a more literal posthumous interruption. As such, we find the dead first as parodies of ourselves, but then in our despair, we can find ourselves parodies of the dead. We can also illustrate life by pretending to be dead. By pretending to be dead we pretend to remove from ourselves that which makes us alive. The more elaborate our pretense, the more we excise life and the more we show what living is.

A poem is a posthumous interruption. The interruptions of death and love give a form for the interruptions of art, the paradigmatic form for me being a poem. The poem that interrupts me, that produces a sense of incompletion, is an event that claims me with a force of necessity that I cannot deny, and often cannot explain.

We are dispersed creatures and collected. Anyone's life is an odd kind of thing. Our lives are often disjunct from who we are. We get interrupted and never recover. The whole of our life, which is where we are each moment, consists of things we have done (actions) and things that have happened to us (events). But it also consists of thoughts and beliefs, experiences and memories, mistakes and confusions; too many aspects to settle into any simple picture. Our lives are nebulous, a mixture of specificity and dispersal amidst so many modes of being alive (thinking, wishing, feeling). That complexity of life is collected in where we are at any particular moment. We are contingently our particularity, which for others can become a necessity of form; our face, the alphabet of our character.

Poems are like this, too: their meaningfulness dispersed, open to witness, unstable and variable, and their particularity collected as the order of words or forms of which they consist. Poems are meaningful in the way faces are. We read and interpret them as a means of making their faces visible, just as we make time visible through our various measurements of change. When we read a poem well, we reveal its face, and in so doing we reveal ourselves; the poem becomes our surrogate face. We speak, but the tone and sensibilities we find through the poem show us in parody. We must make ourselves raw with parody.

In writing and reading poetry, I attempt to keep my life raw enough to allow words to shape it, to show it as gathered in a meaningfulness I do not fully understand. In such rawness, I might be found by a poem that I can take to heart, a poem that will take my heart.

Appendices

Appendix 1

Is There a Unique Poetical Meaning?

If, as seems reasonable, the sense of a sentence is just the thought expressed, and if the logical form of that thought depends on a normative usage of words, then how can nonsense say anything? Why would anyone imagine that the deformation of the normative sense of words, with the resulting obfuscation of thought, could produce any further kind of sense that could matter? And yet it is exactly such deformations that have been and continue to be attempted in varying degrees in modern poetry and literature. The poetry of Paul Celan is exemplary of such aesthetically motivated nonsense, and thus offers a test case for the sense we can discover in nonsense.

Art, as Paul Celan recognizes, "is homage to the majesty of the absurd which bespeaks the presence of human beings" (40). Or again: with poetry, Celan says, we attempt to step "into a realm which is turned toward the human, but uncanny—the realm where the monkey, the automatons and with them… oh art, too, seem to be at home" (42–3). The realm of poetry is a realm of the half-human, a mimic realm of the almost human. His poetry exemplifies this "majesty of the absurd":

> Landshaft mit Urnenwesen.
> Gespräche
> Von Rauchmund zu Rauchmund.

Michael Hamburger translates:

> Landscape with Urn creatures.
> Conversations
> From smoke mouth to smoke mouth.

"Conversations from smoke mouth to smoke mouth": the dead conversing. The fumes of the dead speaking. Celan imagines poems as conversations:

> Das Gesprach, das sich spinnt
> von Spitze zu Spitze,
> angesengt von
> spruhender Brandluft.
>   "Mit Mikrolithen"

Again, Hamburger:

> The Conversation that's spun
> from peak to peak,
> scorched by
> spume air from a fire.

Poems can seem scraped raw, spun into a holy or unholy frenzy, and thus, for Paul Celan, poems and art can form conversations "scorched by spume air from a fire." What sense can this scorching convey? Celan characterizes these poem conversations in a number of ways: "of a voice to a receptive you," a "desperate dialogue," and "a sort of homecoming."[1] If we believe in special forms of sense or what we might call hyper-semantic forms of linguistic sense, we have to not only characterize this special content, but explain how language as the means of conveying this sense does this special work. If it cannot do this special work, is there anything but desperate hope in this desperate dialogue? Is there a unique poetical form of language?

    Celan believed, as Mark Payne puts it, that poems should be a "sudden and unexpected communication from afar... and that [poems] can achieve [an] unexpected utopian communication between author and reader" (3). This communication differs from ordinary communication because it is not face to face ("from afar") and is "utopian." The communication is utopian because it is transhistorical and, in some sense, ideal, not bound to the contingencies of ordinary conversation. It marks a special kind of intimacy of author and reader grounded in a *basic need* for speech and reading. The author's absence and the vagueness of this idea of need make lyric an odd form of communication. So much so that "communication" is used in some different and metaphorical sense to describe how lyrics mean. Thus, "lyric communication" cannot mean communication in the sense that expressing a thought or talking is communicative. This is a problem.

In fact, this is the key problem. Any theory or idea or wish for a special poetical language relies on a belief in a non-normative kind of thinking and thus of speaking. This poetical language is imagined to be unique and supra-meaningful beyond the normative senses of ordinary language. Because feeling is not syntactically bound and is a kind of experience, it is often used as a model for such poetical thinking. In general, poetical modes of communication are meant to say the unsayable, most importantly the complexity of what we experience. If it is cast as a kind of knowledge, then it is of our embodied self and world, what is imagined as experiential rather than conceptual. Consequently, poetical language is often characterized as language that has become more experienced than understood, that challenges, distorts, or disrupts conceptual clarity and coherence. Since this language is still imagined as language, and thus as able to communicate content or thoughts, albeit of a unique or non-rational kind, this kind of poetical language must speak not just a new thought, but a new (or non-rational) *kind* of thought. A new kind of thought is of a sort that cannot be said in ordinary language, or in fact in any kind of language except in (or by means of) the particular poetic form in which it is discovered and revealed.

The poetical experiments to reveal or create this new kind of thought and language take many forms. Not all are worthy of attention. Celan's is.

If one wants to believe, like Celan seems to, that lyric can communicate in some special sense, different than how ordinary words in sentences and phrases mean, then we need to explain how a lyric poem means in this special way, and we also must be able to say something about the nature of this putative lyric content, or else we will just spin in circles.

A lyric poem can express beliefs and feelings; it can be something like a report. As such it would be something meant and said non-fictionally. A poem is repeatable and is formalized, and that removes it from ordinary conversation. This makes a poem more like an oath or deposition. A deposition is a way of formalizing a speaker's responsibility for what is said. A lyric is some other kind of formalization; it is a formalization relative to parameters other than communication or truth.

The formalizations of poetry can partly, but only partly, replace conversational contextual markers. The more poetic form controls what is said, the more difficult it becomes to differentiate what would count as a thought such that it could be communicated by lyric means (again, attempts to do this quickly show themselves to be viciously circular). And if a lyric does not articulate a thought, then lyric expression would not communicate meaningful statements, but attempt to produce effects. Effects are not semantic. When we say that we communicate effects, we mean we cause them. While what I say allows you to understand me, it does not cause you to understand me: that is why language is understood as normative, not causal. Language can cause things, and your understanding of what I say can cause you to do something, but it is your understanding and what follows from it that is the cause for your action. Understanding is not simply accomplished by words. It is nothing so simple, even if the content of what we understand is simple and determinate. Understanding is more like a judgment.

At this point, you could stipulate that lyric is a form of communication, but to do so you would have to show and establish what you mean by *communication*. The lyric, so understood, would have to be bounded by norms, not simply of form but of uptake (of understanding), if it were to count as communication. As such lyric communication would have some role within a community of understanding. It would constitute an idiolect. This would hardly be a new form of communication. Celan seems to imagine that the poem makes its own language community, and in some metaphoric sense that might be true. It would not be a language community, but a community with a certain investment and belief in a particular set of lyrical poems (since what would constitute a lyric could only be established through examples). A community so constituted would be closer to having a religion (shared beliefs) than taking part in a conversation.

The notion of community here remains question-begging. It is difficult to make the argument that we can say things using words in a way that is different in kind from how words ordinarily mean. A lot rests on how one understands the "*how*"—in "how words mean."

If you can say in ordinary ways what is said or meant in the putatively new lyric use of words, then the new lyric way of saying that is not necessary, although it might be convenient. If the new mode of saying is still a form of communication, then you have to be able to know if what you said is what you meant; you have to be able to get wrong what you said. Similarly, to grasp what is said would be to understand (or conform to) the norms of usage. If those norms cannot be taught, then it is not communication—but something else. None of these conditions are met by a lyric language that would operate (whatever that would mean) in a non-ordinary way. To be guided by norms, even if those norms are new, is to use ordinary language.

Poetic language is meant to be non-ordinary. To defend such non-ordinary language, as Payne does in his defense of Celan, requires the defense of the idea that poetic language can produce unique poetic content, which would require that its form be non-normative and hyper-particular, such that to alter the form would be to alter its content. In order to make this work, one must demonstrate that there is a special kind of content that is not just ordinary sentence-meaning in disguise. Payne, for example, characterizes this special, sayable-only-as-lyric mode of communication in two ways:

(1) It produces new semantic possibilities.

(2) It does this because lyric language operates or can operate in new and different ways.

We have to determine what these new semantic possibilities are; and we, at least, have to show how language operates in this poetic way in comparison with how it ordinarily operates.[2] (Although, this use of "operate" is misleading.) A car and an airplane operate differently, but they both can get you to the same *kind* of place, although not always the same place, because of time or the intervention of an ocean. But Chicago and London are both still places. If poetry were like an airplane and ordinary language were like a car, then poetry would be emphatic language—able to leap higher in single bounds.

One thing this analogy exposes is that the operation of language is less comparable to the operation of cars and airplanes than to traveling through space. And both cars and airplanes can do that. If we want a new semantic possibility, something that is not sayable in ordinary language, that would mean that we should be able to get some place that we could not get to by either car or airplane. With poetry, we would be able to drive to heaven and not just to Chicago. Heaven would be a different kind of place than those places to which we can ordinarily travel.

I don't know what this poetic heaven would be. It would not be something we could say using norms of usage. So unless we can say how lyric says what it does, and what it says such that it is not bound by ordinary norms, there are no new semantic possibilities except for the ordinary kinds of thinking up new things and getting others to believe in them. Again, the idea that I am resisting is that poetry can make new kinds of semantic possibilities by virtue of getting language to operate in some special way.

What would it mean to get language to operate in some different, special way? Celan, like Joyce in *Finnegans Wake*, invents new kinds of words. If we can determine or stipulate a sense to such words, then they simply mean like any word does. If we cannot or do not, then they are at best codes or compressed phrases and metaphors. They do not operate in any new way; they are just targets for interpretation. We can see this with one of Payne's examples (and translations):

> Fadensonnen
> über der grauschwarzen Ödnis.
> Ein baumhoher
> Gedanke
> greift sich den Lichtton: es sind
> noch Lieder zu singen jenseits
> der Menschen.

[Threadsuns over the gray-black waste. A tree-high thought gets the light tone: there are still songs to be sung on the far side of mankind.]

"Thread-suns" is a great word-phrase, but it does not mean in some new way, nor does the sentence. "Thread-sun" is evocative and picturesque. The operation of the sentence is the same as it would be if we replaced "thread-sun" with "sun rays" or even "sunny." The meaning of this new word must be derived from its constituent parts and from its role as a noun, a noun that functions as an argument for some predicate, with the verb of that predicate implied and not stated. The word means what it describes relative to the gray-black waste over which these thread-suns would be seen, so that we can imagine how the light of the sun over gray-black waste might appear.

The literal picture gets abstracted into an idea in the next clause: "A tree-high thought gets the light tone." A tree-high thought is a riddle. Thoughts don't have height, so we can only speculate about what could be meant by this phrase. It is not a low thought, but high enough to get illuminated, but not too high so as to disappear in the far above. So it seems to be a human thought of some hope; a sense and feeling that get carried into the next phrase, which is another riddle; "there are still songs to be sung on the far side of mankind." In this final clause, Payne finds his example of a new semantic thought, which is unsayable except poetically, in the phrase "on the far side of mankind." The phrase is meant, as are the phrases from Pindar that he offers, to be a means of experiencing what the poet experiences—by virtue of the poet expressing this experience in a certain obscurity of phrase. How the grasping of a word (or phrase) produces a similar experience of something that is non-linguistic remains unexamined, but is a part of a certain strand of romantic aesthetics. How sharing an experience through the evocation of a phrase alters *how* the phrase means (or operates), as opposed to *what* it means, is more than obscure, it is nonsensical.

Does mankind have a far side? We can come up with an example of this human far side if we treat the phrase as a riddle. We might call it the part of our humanity that is furthest from our humanity. You could imagine some other sense or idea. Whatever you imagine will depend on your notion of humanity. All of this can be said and determined. If the phrase has a sense, then we can describe that sense (it needn't be translatable into a single word). We can collect our sense of what this far side is into a single idea, and call it a concept. If we can distinguish it from other concepts and establish its normative senses through various usages, then it can be used intelligibly. There is nothing odd about any of this. No new mode of speaking is required, just ordinary speaking about something that is vague, a bit gestural, and open to further specification.

To see further how and why there is no unique poetical meaning, let me look at a related example, in which a writer attempts to get language to operate in a different manner through what can seem like syntactic deformations. These syntactic deformations produce a kind of poetic idiolect. While there are poems in which Celan seems to attempt this kind of syntactic deformation, a more overt and clear case is offered by some of the writings of Gertrude Stein.

Stein pursues two primary modes of losing sense. (1) She simplifies the inferential and narrative relation between and among sentences to parataxis, thus obscuring or deranging the relationships between and among sentences; the relation among sentences seems irrational or random. (In addition, she misuses logical connectives, and makes false or confused inferences.) (2) This use of parataxis in order to obscure inferential relations also organizes the syntax of sentences such that the syntactical relations and the underlying logical structure expressed by these relations are either lost or again simplified into parataxis. This internal parataxis, which can result in an ungrammatical succession of words, is only one means of pressuring syntax into nonsense. Her other methods include indeterminate pronoun reference, repetition, substitution of a concept word for an object word, and other substitutions that result in ungrammaticality.

Now we can look at an example. How can we construe the following sentence as somehow meaningful?

> The meaning of this is entirely and best to say the mark, best to say it best to shown sudden places, best to make bitter, best to make the length tall and nothing broader, anything between the half.
>
> (*Tender Buttons*, "A Drawing," 471)

I think one can reasonably have two opposing intuitions about this kind of Steinian sentence. (1) The words and phrases are not combined in conformity with semantic norms, syntactical constraints and logical relations. Thus, they do not mean or constitute a thought. Such sentences alone and in combinations are not truth-preserving. Associations of some kind seem to organize the seemingly intelligible parts of the sentences. Thus, such sentences are expressive in the way an expletive might be or as any set of sounds could be. I'll call this the no-thought intuition. (2) The second and competing intuition is that while there is no linguistic sense to such sentences, they express a specific kind of thought or sense of the world tied to and dependent on the person who says or writes them: a unique thought. I'll call this the nothing-but-thought intuition.

This last possibility is in many ways a desperate hope. Any such sentence expressing such a unique thought does not mean like ordinary, transparent sentences. Such a sentence must articulate some special code known to the person speaking—something like Humpty Dumpty's use of "glory," by which he means "there's a nice knock-down argument for you." Can we, however, learn to speak Steinian, and in so doing, not just imitate the style of her writing, but use her words like we might use the redefined "glory"? If it were just a question of knowing the meaning of strange words or ordinary words with different but still determinate meaning, then the analogy with Humpty Dumpty might be apt (since the meaning of a word would be at issue). But Stein's words are normal English words, simple ones for the most part, and so to learn the thoughts expressed through such sentences would mean learning the grammar of this way of speaking—learning the idiolect. Can we describe this grammar like we could Finnish grammar, that is, describe its transformations relative to English? Could we learn the norms so that we could be corrected when we repeated the wrong kind of noun? Since the answer to all of these questions is no, the content of Stein's sentences might be something we could guess at, but it would be difficult to use the words and their order to stabilize the content (her putative thought) into some intersubjective form.

What has replaced thought in this case is just the person who pretends to speak these words. She only pretends to speak since she, herself, doesn't have any way of thinking through these words themselves, although she might think a lot of things as she said them. She might even think what she says constitutes a set of specific thoughts, but she would be wrong. If Stein read what she had just said, for example, it is unlikely that her thoughts would be the same as the thoughts when she first spoke. How would she know?[3] Also she could not build other thoughts from bits of any of her other sentence, since all she could do would be to correlate some specific thought, expressed in some other language, with a specific set of words. This would be like a code and not like a language. (In other words, the code is only meaningful relative to the mysterious thoughts controlling it, in whatever language or form in which those thoughts are given content. The code cannot be used creatively to construct new thoughts in its controlling language.)

The situation is the same for us. When reading Stein-like nonsense we can translate words into some allegory and justify the form of the sentences as expressive of this allegorical content. Or we can attempt to discover Stein's particular thoughts, associations, or intentions as a way of stabilizing interpretative options. This is either an impossible task or a trivial one. At best we might turn her poems into real codes for which we assume she had the key. We could on the other hand read what she writes as exemplifying a specific aesthetic, which we would articulate and justify. This is a common response: one attempts to articulate and justify her aesthetic by showing how it fits a metaphysical picture or a picture of human psychology.

But if we do not show that aesthetic through the same kind of allegory as suggested in the previous paragraph, we could take the aesthetic as an analogue for a picture of how the world is. This is in fact the most common response to Stein's nonsense. The difficulty of describing special content generally tempts people to appeal to a special kind of experience. This often turns metaphysical. Someone like William Gass, for example, argues that Stein's aesthetic repetitions are justified because life is repetitious, and ultimately her nonsense becomes a way of capturing a metaphysical flux.[4] Stein cannot establish the value of recovering her thoughts. Such a justification would require an argument about what one might derive as a claim or content from her texts, and also a justification and description of this content relative to her aesthetic. Without this, reading Stein's text would remain a form of de-coding, and thus would collapse into allegorical projection, disguised maybe through appeals to some hidden encoded meaning. In all of these cases Stein's writing doesn't mean, but our translations or descriptions of the code mean, and those are articulated not in Steinian nonsense but in ordinary language.

When reading Stein we justify how her sentences mean by determining what they mean; this prompts theorizing about Stein's aesthetic motives and the putative nature of reality. Gass' justification is the most thoughtful version of this kind of theorizing. Celan's poetry, however, does not require the same theorizing (although, he himself borrows Heideggerian inflected ways of speaking, which is a way of giving language itself a kind of mythic metaphysics). When faced with a Celan poem, however, I think our most immediate need is to justify what we take from it (what it says in some sense) by attending to how it is written. Celan's poems encourage recognition or disorientation. Stein's art rests on what she means to say; Celan's art rests on how he says what he says. In some ways, this is the difference between prose and poetry. Whatever poetic distortions Stein accomplishes are part of a prose sensibility. It even conforms to a kind of story logic. We follow the plot of her speaking and her constant circling back. Celan poems can have plots or not, but they emerge as a certain structure of style, of language use.

Celan's poems have a different kind of intimacy and a greater sense of concrete situations and conditions than does Stein's writing. In any case, Payne, in accounting for lyric communication, resists appealing to a general metaphysics or to a special aesthetic experience. Instead, he argues that Celan's poetic language creates new semantic possibilities of poetry, which he also characterizes as breaking new conceptual ground. Lyric poetry, Payne believes, allows a sudden emergence of new conceptual possibilities by means of special poetic formulations. This newness would seem to make it non-normative, but if that is what Payne means, then the newness could have no content that anyone could recognize.

If we imagine, as does Celan, that language can also operate in some non-ordinary way and yet remain meaningful, then we remain, despite Celan's differences with Stein, with my two earlier intuitions: either (1) no thought is communicated or (2) a unique thought (i.e., the nothing-but-thought) is communicated. This second option in the case of Stein leads to metaphysical gestures that turn the unique thought into a rather banal general thought. Payne attempts to construe Celan under this second unique thought option. But his concern is less to show that Celan's putative unique thoughts are expressions of metaphysical ideas, as simply to show how Celan creates new concepts, which are also unsayable except by poetic means. In other words, the unique thought is a unique poem. Does this idea support the idea that one can speak or write a special kind of linguistic content?

* * *

If I am a competent language user, then I can understand sentences I have never heard before. I can communicate a new thought using old words. A new thought, however, is not a new kind of thought requiring a special unique mode of linguistic expression. A new kind of thought that was not repeatable would not be a thought at all; a unique mode of linguistic expression that was not normatively bound could not express a sense (it could not have content), but could only produce effects. We would then have to say in what sense such effects or new meanings could be thoughts. I do not think this can be done.[5]

Poetry could be a specialized form of communication, but that is not for it to be a special way for language to operate. For poetry to be a different kind of language than ordinary language is for it be something other than language.[6]

Faced with this challenge, a common response by those who want to defend a poetic mode of thinking is to assert that poetry says what is unsayable, creating new concepts instead of applying already understood concepts. We might appeal, for example, as Payne does in defending Celan's poetics of the unsayable, to a modest notion of linguistic idealism, specifically Richard Rorty's idea that one can invent new kinds of conceptual discourses.[7] Rorty believes that creative thinkers develop new goals for their language as they invent new ways of speaking. Certainly, one can discover new goals for thinking when one discovers new problems and new distinctions, as Galileo did when he conceptualized inertia as distinct from force. But that is not a new goal for language. It is merely a new distinction that can still be understood using the old language. I don't believe that there can be any such new goals shown by new language that are not themselves part of our general thinking.

We draw the same conclusion in a seemingly inverted way: new ways of speaking need not mean new ways of thinking. Amongst Rorty's examples of Galileo, Yeats, and Hegel, it is really only Hegel who wrote so strangely (or badly) that one would be forgiven for imagining that he had set some new goal for thought that required a new kind of language. I think, however, that Hegel just wrote in contradictory ways, and that his ideas could have been and have been explained without that difficulty.

This does not mean that we cannot find and discover new and important ways of talking and thinking. We can, but they do not alter the logic of how we make sense. If we change our beliefs and ways of conceiving things, we do not need a special language in which to embody or express these beliefs. Mathematics might seem like a counter-example to such a claim, since new mathematics can lead to new conceptual possibilities, which can only be expressed in the new mathematics. Mathematics, however, is not a language in the same sense that English is. We can invent new kinds of mathematics, but only in a highly constrained way and not willy-nilly. We cannot invent a new kind of language, however, in which we can express unique new kinds of thoughts that is still a language. A language must be normatively constrained and learnable; it cannot be unique enough to express a new kind of unique thought or sense and still be a language. As human beings, we are changeable and plastic in a number of ways, but we cannot get to the bottom of language such that we can remake how it works.

Rorty more or less admits that there are no new ways of making sense when he claims that what is made by such thinkers are new vocabularies, that is, new words and new distinctions. Payne quotes with approval Rorty's description of the role of vocabulary in our self-understanding, which includes a personal vocabulary we use to describe what matters most to us, ranging from the common words like "good," "right," and "beautiful," to what he calls the parochial words like "Christ," "England," "professional standards," "kindness," "decency," etc. This is true enough. We do have such words, but they are markers or expressions of belief. They do not form a conceptual scheme. And Rorty knows this. The sense and value of such sets of words are sustained by belief, not by a new linguistic logic.

Lyric cannot be a form of communication of what cannot be said otherwise, unless communication is conceived of as something other than what we do when we use ordinary language. In which case, it would not be communication. And if it is not that, it loses its normative constraints and becomes a form of special pleading for semantic possibilities and new kinds of concepts. These possibilities and concepts are either not really unsayable or the whole notion just becomes a vague gesture toward some mysterious mode of language use. Odd writing can force us to respond and react in many ways, but in so doing we are not understanding anything through some new conceptual mode of expression that can be legitimately called "special lyric communication."

This exposes a problem: either poems whose forms and senses are so distorted such that they cannot be redescribed adequately in ordinary English mean nothing and only have effects or we must understand their meaninglessness in some other way such that they are meaningful, if without semantic content. Poems can always have effects. But what the second option entails is that we read such poems in order to justify their form and nonsense, which means we should read such poems in order to redeem their form and possible senses. The justification of the relationship between the form of a poem and its possible senses constitutes the aesthetics of the poem. Consequently, we need not read the meaning of a poem (especially if its semantic sense becomes ambiguous or obscure), but we should always read the aesthetic of a poem. I made this argument in a different way in Chapter 8.

This does not mean that I dismiss or demean Celan's poetry, far from it. It does mean, however, that we do not need to invent imagined semantic processes to read it. We can take it as a gift, and even treat as part of a conversation, if we can take it up as such. This does not require a special semantics. And when the sense of the poem turns beyond the norms we recognize, we must find a way with the new possible senses it might offer. There will be nothing unsayable about these senses—or the poem—except in the way an action or an event is not fully sayable.

Beyond their charm, their rhetorical elegance, and their mnemonic benefits, many poems *do* matter through their games with sense. Reading such a poem, depending on the poem, might require reading its nonsense. But reading its nonsense does not entail or require either translating it into sense, as if the poem were just words gone amiss, or by imagining its nonsense to be a disguised kind of special sense. In the next appendix chapter, I will explore some ways of reading the tensions and pressures against sense that poems can reveal, without, however, appealing to some special kind of meaning or communication.

Appendix 2

If a Poem Is Not Particular, What Is It?

In ordinary situations of communication, I can fail to say what I mean (and fail to mean what I say). I can also mean (assert or state) the same thing using different sentences. In both of these cases, there is no necessary relationship between what is said and what is meant.

One of the fundamental and primary facts about poems, as commonly understood, is that they are constituted by a particular set of words in a particular order; to alter the words or their order is to make a new poem with some genetic relation to the earlier version. From this idea of the particularity of a poem we might draw two different conclusions. (1) What is said (written) is primary, and what is meant is secondary, since the determinate form of the poem necessarily underdetermines the putative meaning of the poem. Or (2) there exists a special correlation or relationship between the determinate words in their order and a determinate meaning, which because such strict linkage between sentence and meaning is non-ordinary and non-normative, and must be a special kind of meaning. In the previous appendix chapter, I argued against the second conclusion—against the idea that there is some special lyric mode of communication (or meaning). In this appendix chapter, I will investigate the first conclusion, and see what it comes down to: what are the consequences and significance for how we read a poem that follow from the asymmetry between a poem's determinacy of form and the consequent underdetermination of its meaning? This appendix chapter is, therefore, an extension of my argument in Chapter 5 "Is a Poem the Same as Its Words?."

I will simply state my answer to the above question, and then explicate what it means as a way of showing its plausibility and general relevance. My answer: a poem is an abstract of its possible meanings.

Before I explicate what I mean by calling a poem an abstract of its possible meanings, I want to review my conclusions from the fifth chapter, since in that chapter I analyzed the logical consequences of treating a poem as radically defined by its particular words. There I asked whether a poem can be constituted by the words of which it seems to consist. My answer was no—unless the poem ceases to become mere words and nothing special. If we insist on defining the poem by its words, then we are pressured it into three possibilities: (1) we can exclude it from the language; (2) it becomes a name, the target of which we cannot know or refer to (it becomes a parody of a name); or (3) we can understand it as analogous to the words of which it seems to consist. My answer is a version of this third possibility, which I will explore in this chapter. I will show how a poem offers words as meaningful and yet not yet having a meaning, that is, as an abstract of its possible senses.

I begin by offering a prima facie argument in support of my claim that a poem is an abstract of its possible senses. As I have argued earlier, if a poem is constituted as a particular series of words, then those words—call this the form of the poem—are determinate (even if there are editorial questions and various versions of the poem). And if these specific words (what I am calling the form of the poem) underdetermine the putative meaning(s) of the poem as a whole, then the poem, as that set of words, is an abstract of their possible meanings. An abstract offers a redacted version of something more extensive: it shortens, extracts, and thus simplifies in some sense what it is an abstract of. If a poem means simply what it says, then it would not be an abstract of its possible senses. If, however, the particularity of its words underdetermines what the poem can mean, then the words of the poem are an abstract of the possible senses we might discover or assert.

A poem is a shaped node of language, a precipitate, or a seed. We discover what these words are abstracts for by following out possible implications that unfold from our understanding and interpreting a poem in particular ways. Describing a poem as an abstract of its own possible senses is a way of characterizing its words, phrases, and sentences as themselves having possible senses that are only actualized when we redescribe them relative to specific targets. The words in their order and their patterns abstract into the generality of our redescriptions of its possible meanings. The phrases of the poem are meaningful relative to the possible meanings that our readings can produce.

It is possible that we respond to any sentence as if it were an abstract of our possible ways of understanding it. But we need not conclude that this is so. We can describe in numerous ways the meaning intended by someone relative to what is said. The sentences we say generally are guided more by what we are trying to communicate (what we mean) than by their particular form. When the particularity of a sentence is primary, when its form determines what it is, identifies it and constitutes it, and not its meaning or the thought expressed or even the thing referred to by it, then our relation to that sentence mirrors our relation to a poem. Our understanding, no longer guided by truth values, intention, or conversational implicature, has a looser, more connotative relation to the initial sentence, in effect, making that sentence an abstract of our possible ways of understanding.

If we offer an interpretation of a poem, then we display in some way these possible senses and produce an epitome of them. We might do it through how we recite the poem, or by some other display. These too would also require interpretation in order to be understood as interpretations of the poem. By so doing, we offer our reading as the target for the poem, *showing the poem to be the abstract for and of our reading*. Our reading of a poem becomes, in such a case, what I am calling an epitome, an epitome of what we can take as what the poem abstracts. A description of the poem's possible meanings is ideally an epitome of those possible meanings, and as such, an idealized, partially symbolic version of the putative meanings of a string of words. It is symbolic because the meanings we offer of the poem stand for that poem. The poem itself does not symbolize these meanings; it does not stand for them, but allows for them and provides formal limits for our interpretive efforts. Poems are not symbols, our readings are.

What does it mean for our readings to be symbols (of the poems we read)? If a poem is an abstract of its possible senses, then our reading of that poem is an epitome of those senses. By distinguishing between an abstract and an epitome, I am also suggesting a relation between them. A poem in its particularity is an abstract of its possible senses. I read that abstract into a different kind of particularity by producing an interpretative description of those senses determined by my best judgment.

The distinction between an abstract and epitome can be slippery. An abstract of a book or of a scientific experiment, for example, is an epitome of a sort, but a kind with a greater need for comprehensiveness. It is less symbolic than discursive, and thus more like a summary. Such an abstract would be an interpretation as well since it would involve a judgment of what was essential. An abstract can be expansive if its target is an intellectual field. Thus an abstract of chemistry would be a compendium of the essential aspects of chemistry.

An epitome, on the other hand, foregrounds some aspect of a particular thing—some event, person, poem—as representative or encapsulating what that something is; it is a kind of interpretation offered as a symbol.[8] One can provide an epitome of someone's life or character. A gesture can epitomize a person; a sentence can be understood as the epitome of a story. At the height of the Roman empire, during the reigns of Trajan and Hadrian, we might describe the city of Rome as the epitome of the empire, symbolizing the empire by representing it in an idealized—or extreme form—such that the power and life of the city brought together elements of the entire empire in a form that symbolized rather than imitated the empire as a whole.[9]

We evaluate one epitome, one interpretation relative to other possible epitomes and interpretations. Our better or worse evaluations of such epitomes constitute a judgment relative to what we take to be most significant in what we epitomize. Such judgments are complex and open to dispute and further rational evaluation. As accounts of what is significant and bound to reason and judgment, they are neither lies nor fictions.

An interpretation of a poem is an epitome of the poem as an abstract of its possible senses and of those senses relative to our own ways of taking them up, of understanding and responding to them. Our involvement in this taking up of possibilities of sense is at a minimum a set of actions (within our practices of reading), and thus results in a story (which is the mode for describing actions). An epitome of a poem is thus a kind of story made into a symbolic representation of this configuration of particularity and possibility fitted with our interest and involvement with the poem. Because the story would be a kind of symbol of the poem, we can call the epitome a parable.

* * *

I will demonstrate the parabolic nature of our reading of poems, and the abstract nature of a poem, by constructing a parable that is an epitome of a poem understood as an abstract of its possible senses. First, I will make a poem.

The door is open.

That's the poem. Admittedly, it is not very good. It looks surprisingly like the rather ordinary sentence— "The door is open"—although it seems a bit homeless and pointless, unlike saying "The door is open" in a room with an open door. If I add some formal oddities, it might do better as a poem.

Open is the door.

Better, because stranger. But isn't it just a poetic turn of phrase, a little old fashioned, not really very interesting? Anyway, it isn't a poem, is it? It sounds poetic, because the ordinary word order has been distorted. Is that enough to make it a poem? The form of the sentence relative to its implied normative meaning is non-normative, and that might prompt interpretation or at least justification. Maybe I am just being playful with the sounds of the words, trying to be dramatic or mocking. We could imagine that it is a title of a story or a mock or mocking statement. In these last possibilities we would invent a story within which to place the sentence.

There is a rhythm to it—"Open is the door." It begins, or so I hear, with an accent, a stress, then a pause and then a stressed "is," and then the flat, unstressed "the," giving us a kind of skip, to the final stress of "door." The sentence begins and ends with a stress. We could invent an interpretative story to give this formal pattern meaning: the symmetrical pattern of stress simultaneously works against the openness described in the sentence, and the ambiguity or tension between the semantics and the poetic syntax increases our interest. Statements like that make the sentence sound like a poem and not just an affected statement that has lost its context. We could expand the story, and explain the tension as ironic, so that the sentence could be taken to mean that *the door is shut*; or that the door is a metaphor for affections or thinking, so that if said ironically it might mean that someone is closed-minded or indifferent. This makes it less a poem. It becomes a euphemism. If we were to understand the phrase in this way, we would be situating it in some story in which this would make sense. And there is no reason to give this sense priority. Other interpretations might just be to the point, or rather we can't say "Open is the door" has a point unless we again imagine it said by someone in some situation. So even if we assume it means that the door is closed, we don't know what door, nor who is speaking, or why the speaker is saying this simple thing in this complex way. There is not even a door to be closed, unless we ourselves quote the sentence about our own doors.

Once we accept that the sentence is not a statement, and thus that we do not need to establish the situation in which saying it would make ordinary sense, we are allowing it to stand formally complete just as it is. Of course, it is not semantically complete, and that is the point. The formal completeness without any clear sense of definitive sense encourages us to find a sense to the form itself.

In other words, we do not simply explain its oddness away, notice its charm, or reinterpret what it might mean if someone said it. Instead, we begin to imagine ways it could be a means to an end beyond communicating something—that is, we imagine that it is a poem. We do this as long as we accept a distinction between verse and poems, and so imagine that by virtue of being something whole called a poem, the sentence means in some special way. There are no essential definitions of a poem. Since I am stipulating that this poetic sentence is a poem, it is one if I treat it as such.

One might still say, of course, that it is a rather bad and uninteresting poem. I could invent an aesthetic that would show the interest and value of this poem—and others like it—and maybe I could convince you. Or maybe not.

There is no particular way to respond to a poem. We might note what seems different and suggestive—that is its initial interest. Maybe, you start imagining, remembering, associating, or dreaming about some aspect, some feel of the rhythm, the wonderful symmetry of stress, you get a good feeling or have a bad feeling, sing it to yourself, write a poem in response. Who's to say? A poem is a poem partly by virtue of your responses to it. Otherwise, it is noise, or just words gone awry.

If I allow this poetic sentence (so-called) to count as a poem I would refuse myself some normalizing tricks. I would not just be puzzled by its oddness. I would no longer pretend that it was a normal act of communication; nor would I let myself explain away its oddities by formal means, as if it were a title or a joke. None of these refusals would be necessary. The more of them I allow, however, the more the form of the poem becomes something to justify relative to some further way of meaning other than the ordinary options. I begin to redescribe the poetic sentence, in this case, in order to find some pattern that can guide my seeing how it might be meaningful.

I might, for example, start again with the tension between the first and last stress. I could assert that the symmetry produces a sense of closedness, thus pushing against what the sentence seems to say: that the door is open. But how could this difference between poetic sense and normal semantics be significant? I could just say that a closed sentence (a sentence beginning and ending with a stress) creates a new context in which to interpret what the sentence means. I start to redefine, that is redescribe, what the words in the sentence might mean relative to each other. In the poem, the phrase "open is" means that existence is open, exposed—and the door is our entrance into that being. I have made a little allegory: "open is the door" means that we are born into the openness of being. Of course, what "openness" means here is unclear and requires some theory or explication. And from that, the sentence will gain a more expansive connection to things through the way this theory, and the concepts on which it depends, define things in general. The very openness of "openness" turns the sentence into a poetic aphorism, a metaphor. One could call it a poem at this point if one wants. It would be a little vision, a symbolic hedgehog, as Friedrich Schlegel would call it, implying far more than its ordinary sense.

There is nothing in the sentence to determine if it should be taken as I suggest, and there is certainly nothing in it to help us figure out what openness of being might be. Let's say that this openness includes three things. First, openness means (1) to be conscious and cognizant of other forms of being. But it also means (2) to be affected by other beings. And finally, it (3) characterizes a condition of being, a condition of being open to language, not hidden away or invisible to what we might say. These putative meanings are not collected in the sentence. The sentence is an abstract of them, a means of pointing to them through its own form and sense. Of course, I have made up what "openness" means in this case.

But what about the closedness indicated by the beginning and ending stress? The framing stresses, with some creative extrapolation, shape the sentence into a formal entity, separate from its syntax and semantics. It has a soul, a form beyond its body and matter. Its soul, its poetic form, manifests in its rhythm, shows it to be an entity or defines it as a dual space, a space of sound and further feeling. What does that mean? The sentence gains some further import in how we understand and describe this putative sound sense with its attendant concepts. We can understand this sound entity and its conceptual senses as an analogical picture of human beings, who are the entities that exemplify the openness of being we are discovering (or producing) as the sense of the sentence as a poem.

The meanings I am ascribing to the sentence are given through the sentences I use to describe it. I am using them to describe not so much the sentence, but to redescribe my initial descriptions of the sentence (its closedness and openness). I am isolating these meanings among the many possible meanings I could invent, supported by various stories and theories and developed from the resources of the initial sentence. I am naturally treating them as an abstract of these possible senses (senses I discover or invent), and my articulation of these meanings, or even my specific choices amongst them epitomizes those meanings, and through them, the sentence. The difference between the abstract of the sentence and the epitomization of its meanings rests on the way that my description of these meanings has the sentence as its target. It has this as its target through the possible meanings I seem to discover (or ascribe). As an abstract, the sentence is just the reduced form that invokes or allows those possible meanings. (There is an important difference between "invokes" and "allows," but it is not relevant at this point.)

In Milan Kundera's *The Unbearable Lightness of Being*, the lovely and wandering Sabina, while walking through a Paris cemetery, discovers that heavy stones are used to cover the dead in their graves. Horrified, she realizes that she will have to leave the city: "move on, and on again, because were she to die here they would cover her up with a stone, and in the mind of a woman for whom no place is home the thought of an end to all flight is unbearable" (125). "[B]ecause were she to die here they would cover her up with a stone, and in the mind of a woman for whom no place is home the thought of an end to all flight is unbearable": the narrator by this sentence explains her reaction. He offers a theoretical explanation of her motivations and understanding, which, given his sometimes-admitted authority as the creator of his characters, defines Sabina the character. His theory is a description of her beliefs and psychology. Psychology, however, is just a formal vocabulary that allows descriptions to be taken as explanations. It is a way of characterizing, feelings, beliefs, motives, and reasons. Sabina's life—the form given her in the author's narrative descriptions—looks to me to be a commentary on the meaning of "open is the door." "Open is the door," one might say, embodies the idea that life requires this opening, this lightness, the lack of weighted stones, so that the opening of being is lived as continual exile and requires, for Sabina, a pattern of betrayal, a refusal to be situated in space, the enclosing of which is worse than death. Sabina imagines her ghost held down by the stones, finished by that weight. She wants the hope, the imagined sense of herself to continue in its lightness, in the lightness of her ghost.

Sabina's betrayals and exile, her pursuit of lightness, cannot help but take the form of saying no to things, to keep the weight of things away. Sabina's openness is not a way of letting things in but of not letting herself close up; she'd rather expose herself to losing others than lose herself by getting weighted into place. She is the niece to Wallace Stevens' Mrs. Uruguay—always saying no in order to make space for herself:

> ... "I have said no
> To everything, in order to get at myself.
> I have wiped away moonlight like mud..."

In such behavior and attitudes, the world is pollution, weight, and distortion unless kept at a distance.

The counter to Sabina's and Mrs. Uruguay's interpretation of space and weight, their lived reaction to the poetry of "open is the door," can be found in

Mark Antony's denial of the world of Roman responsibility, and his commitment to Cleopatra—an insistence that the space which he shares with her is the true being of things. All else can be lost, but not that:

> Let Rome in Tiber melt, and the wide arch
> Of the ranged empire fall! Here is my space!
>
> (1.1.34-5)

The meaning of "Open is the door," for Antony, requires that he deny the space and house of Rome: its door ("the wide arch") must close by falling, in order to keep his space of love open. His love is a surrealistic painting of nothing but a door in blankness, the world of Rome melted and collapsed, like a Francis Bacon streaming blur of colors in which his space, his open door with Cleopatra, stands free, but opens into nothing. A door open, the open space of which is made in the rhythm of his love of Cleopatra, is his space. Here! "Here is my space!," as he desperately insists.

In my explication of "Open is the door," the openness of being takes two forms: (1) a denial of the limits of space in a life of exile and betrayal (a dislike of stones) or (2) a denial of the inherited order of social space in an insistence on a self-made or a love-made space in which one is found and finds oneself. Being is weight or it is weightless, but in either case it needs space, and space is open or it is not space, and to be open is to be a door open. The poem "Open is the door" is the abstract for these possibilities, which I have collected here. My reading of the poem is an epitomization of these possibilities: a little circle of confirmation and revelation.

My descriptions and redescriptions nest within a hierarchy of abstraction. One can, however, invert the hierarchy. We can either use Antony's speech ("here is my space") to describe "open is the door," or we could use "Open is the door" to describe his speech. In drawing out the conceptual possibilities of my initial descriptions of either, I go back and forth, using aspects of one as friction to clarify and to polish into visibility aspects of the other. The sentence and its initial senses are always the light that implies the sun of its possible meanings, and those meanings are open to many redescriptions. These meanings and their descriptions are not unconstrained, but the constraint is a setup. We understand what Antony says relative to our sense of his anxieties and exaggerations within the play and relative to our thematization of these, of the tension between Roman duty and Egypt passion, and so on. *The sense of a poem is produced when we take the poem as a type of something that we give in our descriptions.*

"Open is the door" is a joke; and while it might be harder to see, so is everything in *Antony and Cleopatra*, all that talk of pleasure boats and the wide arch of the empire, Antony's challenge to Caesar to wrestle him with the strength of his love (3.2.63), the melodrama of Antony's botched death, Cleopatra's shifts and her snakes, and an Octavius Caesar who is a cartoon of a man, the historical model of whom Shakespeare has not even approached. Both *Antony and Cleopatra* and even my "Open Door" poem will matter, even if they retain some humor, when the descriptions of each resonate with us: when we discover that our descriptions of them are descriptions of ourselves. We find the resonating frequency through our choice of concept (space or death, for example), in the pathos of desperation or hope, in whatever allows us to collect the relevant senses of the sentences and situations shown. Whenever we interpret a poem, or read it into a particular sense, we make a parable. All of our reading of poems are parables.

Appendix 3

An Analytical Table of Contents

Chapter 1: Poems of the Everyday

In this first chapter, I investigate some surprising examples of everyday poems, the alphabet, for example, and the phrase "I love you." These are what I call events of form that claim us in particular ways that may or may not involve words. How can we find the poems that will reveal our lives amidst our everyday living? Where do we find poems of revelation? How do they find us? I resurrect these everyday poems: the everyday poems we can sometimes find at weddings, in the dead, in our misunderstandings with words, in the faces of those we love, and in the simplicity of the alphabet.

Chapter 2: Interruptions

Anywhere, anytime, accidents of form and symbol make and reveal poems. These poems of the everyday, however, are not mere decoration. They interrupt us. Incompletions and interruptions create opportunities for poems to happen as revelations or confessions of our ethical commitments. Poems are ethical happenings. I explore such poems of ethical event and the posthumous attitude (and mode of writing) by which we facilitate their visibility and recognize their claim on us.

Chapter 3: *Can We Speak a Poem into Existence?*

Important questions follow from the previous chapter. How can we sustain a posthumous attitude? Can we instigate our own moral interruption? Before I go on with such questions, I take a step back. I have insisted that events of form—certain expressions of love, interruptions that require a posthumous response—are poems; that poems are not necessarily made of words. In this chapter, I argue and demonstrate that poems are more and other than words, and in so doing begin to show that we live amidst revelations to which we have too often become blind. I do this by asking: Can we speak a poem into existence? What is the poem that we might hear or find in our voice, in our tone with words?

Chapter 4: *Epithalamion*

The poems of ethical event, the interruptions of love and death, that erupt in my previous chapters disrupt the everyday as much as they make it up. We attempt to domesticate such events: turn the interruptions of love, for example, into the commitments of marriage. A wedding is an attempt to make an event of form, to make a poem; it must be accomplished. A wedding provides a model for how everyday poems can happen, why they matter, and how difficult they are to take up in a sustaining way.

Chapter 5: *Is a Poem the Same as Its Words?*

In all of the preceding chapters, I have demonstrated that poems should be understood as events of form that may depend on words but need not be constituted by words. An important counter to such an idea would be to insist on a poem's linguistic particularity, to insist that it is made of words and made of particular words. But is it?

If we take a poem as constituted by its particular words in their particular order, we produce a surprising (often ignored) logical pressure on how those words can function and mean. The more explicit we make the logical particularity of a poem, the more logically strange it becomes. In fact, if poems are logically constituted by what they say (their particular words) and not by what they mean, they become parodies of language.

Chapter 6: *Poems and Bombs*

In this chapter, I return to poems of the everyday. A wedding attempts to produce an event, to transform the accidents of a personal relationship into a social necessity. Weddings and their aftermath are political events, infused with the tensions of power. Weddings hope to accomplish a unity. Other political events attempt to create disunity. The detonation of a political bomb is one such event.

The kind of thing a political bomb is shows something about how we are involved with words, and how that involvement constitutes the ground of poetry. Consequently, we can learn something about our literature, our minds, and our everyday aspirations with poems when we look at the extraordinary aspects of political bombs. And by looking at the attempted explosive force of poetry, we might learn something about the aspirations and ironies of terrorist bombs and what they might mean beyond propaganda and fear.

Chapter 7: Crucifixion Can Seem Like Standing in Air

In the previous chapter, I examined everyday moral events that create a kind of poetic hysteria, in particular those events that gather death into some visible form. Such poems that speak death can be given literary form, the best modern example of which is T. S. Eliot's *The Waste Land*.

The poetic events in *The Waste Land* are accomplished through its deformations of sense, its fall into half-sense that gets correlated with being half-dead. Reading *The Waste Land* and asking after its dead, requires that we read how it loses sense, how it fails to mean, even how things—the poem and the things represented within it—do not mean. I ask after its nonsense because I am asking about the dead (its dead and my own). The dead will not answer our inquiries. So we must speak for them. There is more than one way of doing this. I attempt it through impersonation, impersonating my own dying when I read the poem. How I respond to reading my own dying and the summoning of the dead becomes necessarily a moral test that drives me beyond the poem.

Chapter 8: Does Poetry Exist?

My ways of reading *The Waste Land* rests on a general understanding of poems and poetry, which in this chapter I bring to the fore as a conceptual claim. I argue that we cannot read or understand a particular poem without understanding, even if in a de facto fashion, a concept of poetry. We can only read a poem if we also read its poetics. This makes close-reading a rather problematic practice. This continues my earlier argument that we cannot reduce even written poems to the words of which they seem to be made.

In this chapter, I will explain how we can read the concept of a poem by reading a poem, and why we should. In order to establish this claim, I will investigate what kinds of things poems are and the kind of thing poetry is not.

Chapter 9: Where Are Love and Death?

Although *The Waste Land's* dynamic configuration of revelation and parody is specific to it, poems, as a general species, suffer some such configuration of promise and of parody. A poem, as a written target or as a crystallization of form amidst our day, as beauty or love or death or attention or fear, is an unstable site of revelation and parody. As such a site, it provides a crux for our attention and investment, and for our shock and alienation.

This is what everyday poems do. They manifest in form what cannot be manifest otherwise, and they do this when we recognize and discover that they do this, when we are claimed by these forms and by what they show.

A Conclusion in Two Parts

In the preceding chapters, I have concentrated on events of form that interrupt us, primarily the revelations of love and death, as they find us through words and the forms of everyday life. I have called these events poems.

Poems are meaningful in the way that faces are. We read and interpret them as a means of making poems faces visible, just as we make time visible through our various measurements of change. When we read a poem well, we reveal its face; the poem becomes our surrogate face. And in so doing, we reveal ourselves.

Appendices

Appendix 1: Is There a Unique Poetical Meaning?

Can a poem be written such that it has a unique poetical meaning? This question is answered by examining particular theories about the poetries of Paul Celan and Gertrude Stein. The possibilities of meaning and the effects of nonsense are analyzed relative to paradigmatic theories about poetry and language.

Appendix 2: If a Poem Is Not Particular, What Is It?

If a poem is not particular, as I have argued earlier, what is it? The answer to this question leads to a description of a poem as an abstract of its possible senses. Such a notion leads to a way of reading and interpreting written poems by analogy, thus challenging common practices of close reading.

Notes

Preface

1. Poems are not simply academic targets, to be absorbed as illustrations of fashionable theories or beliefs. But this is not to write, as does John Burnside, of "poems and ideas of poetry as they inform, not just 'the life of the mind' but also my own day-to-day existence. For this is where poetry works best, in what Randall Jarrell calls 'the dailiness of life'...." (xi). What Burnside accomplishes is important and useful, but what I explore remains more philosophical, more about the structure of everyday life.

Chapter 1

1. If this chapter had an epigram and motto it would be: "And looked and looked our infant sight away." See Elizabeth Bishop, "Over 2000 Illustrations and a Complete Concordance."
2. A fable need not be fictional or fantasy, even if it can seem fantastic. Sir Thomas Browne describes his life as fabulous in this sense, a life both actual and poetic, although calling it so perplexed Samuel Johnson, since he could find nothing particularly fabulous or poetic about Browne's life: "but what most awakens curiosity, is his assertion, that 'His life has been a miracle of thirty years; which to relate, were not history but a piece of poetry, and would sound like a fable.'" "A piece of poetry" would be a fiction, something unreal, so Johnson diagnoses Browne's sense of his life as distorted and deluded:

   > The wonders probably were transacted in his own mind: self-love, co-operating with an imagination vigorous and fertile as that of Browne, will find or make objects of astonishment in every man's life: and, perhaps, there is no human being, however hid in the crowd from the observation of his fellow-mortals, who, if he has leisure and disposition to recollect his own thoughts and actions, will not conclude his life is some sort a miracle, and imagine himself distinguished from all the rest of the species by many discriminations of nature or of fortune.
   >
   > (488)

   One cannot help but read the mockery here as pointing to what Johnson earlier calls "the farce of life." Johnson struggles to acknowledge a joy unmixed with delusion.

Browne's gesture of wonder and Johnson's deflationary diagnosis, regardless of their merits as accounts of Browne's life, give us two senses of how a life can or cannot be a poem.

3   Thomas Bernhard, *Old Masters*. Trans. Ewald Osers. Chicago: University of Chicago Press, 1985, 1989, 6.

4   Consequently, we should not take poems as given simply by their words. If our belief in art is to be more than our own personal investment, then what we take art to be must be justified. Art lives and matters in its justifications.

5   Nelson Goodman, *Ways of World Making*. NY: Hackett Pub, 1978.

6   I do not think there are necessary conditions, let alone necessary and sufficient conditions, for art to be art. What we take as art is historically contingent (Danto would allow that art is historically contingent but also that it has necessary qualities).

7   But if art is nothing in particular, then all of these explorations of what art is will be just-so-stories, fantasies built from privileged examples. Or art will be understood always as expressive or determined by something else—by society or by psychology or by ideology.

8   Beauty collects our beliefs about goodness. We can believe in the goodness of certain kinds of beauty for no good reason. Beauty is both powerful and strange because the content we give it is so unjustified, and often false; but this does not alter its grip. It just keeps us searching for new senses and forms of its promise and hold. Or maybe we just search for the beauty we think matches us: the beauty we want to match how we hope to be seen and valued. And this can be true about the other qualities we value. There is a quality of mind in a gesture. A radiance in a look; compassion and brilliance in the eyes. These beauties need never fade.

Chapter 2

1   A person diminished in this way, like the Sibyl who asked for eternal life, but forgot to ask for eternal youth, exists almost dead in his or her life. The Sibyl remained aware of her own condition and felt her alienation from others as a source of continual grief. Or it is as if a person has become mere rumor, lost to the accidents of the routes of talk and memory, without any way to resist through their person the cycles of accident and gossip.

2   For excellent accounts of the Chosin campaign, see Martin Russ, *Breakout: The Chosin Reservoir Campaign, Korea 1950*. NY: Penguin, 2000 and Hampton Sides, *On Desperate Ground: The Epic Story of Chosin Reservoir—the Greatest Battle of the Korean War*. NY: Anchor, 2019. For a superb general account of the war, see T.R. Fehrenbach, *This Kind of War: The Classic Korean War History*. NY: Potomac Books, 2001.

3 Private Hubert Edward Reeves, *Chosin*. [Film] Dir. Brian Inglesias, 2010.
4 They were living as if they were dead, but that was not to disregard how they lived. To be worthy of remembrance regardless of whether they would be remembered. To live posthumously is to court anonymity as a means of self-assertion. To live posthumously in this way takes great virtue—at least bravery—and it produces a necessary virtue in the posthumous. Even if the living person was prideful and arrogant, the same person when posthumous is modest, because even if fame finds the posthumous person, he cannot find his fame.
5 The poet speaker demonstrates his integrity through his attentions of seeing but that seeing fails to find its articulation in the poetry.
6 See Trevor Bryce, All quotations concerning the Hittites are from *The Kingdom of the Hittites*. 2nd ed. NY: Oxford University Press, 2006.
7 Ibid., 228.
8 Ibid., 229.

Chapter 3

1 Underlying this observation is a claim about the musicality of poems. There is no necessary musical or metered or other auditory quality to poems. I would say that a certain musicality might be sufficient to make a string of words into a poem, but it is not necessary.
2 Christopher Ricks, *T.S. Eliot and Prejudice*. London: Faber, 1988, p. 133.
3 Ludwig Wittgenstein, *Philosophical Investigations*. 3rd ed. Trans. Elizabeth Anscombe. Cambridge: Blackwell, 1991, p. §78.
4 Ibid., p. 183.
5 Ibid.
6 Ibid.
7 As if it were a person—for the only thing a tone can picture in this case would be the speaker.
8 Cormac McCarthy, *The Road*. NY: Vintage, 2006, p. 74.
9 The father is, in effect, acting posthumously so that his son has a chance to live a life of some kind of greater hope.
10 S.Y. Agnon, *A Guest for the Night*. Trans. Misha Loutish. Madison: University of Wisconsin Press, 1968, pp. 67–8.
11 We read the forms of things, surfaces, appearances (the modes by which whatever exists for us is made manifest), through our intimacy with these, our awareness and reactions—and we call our reactions our experience. Recognition and reaction are our first modes of reading, and thus of giving content to our intimacy.

Chapter 4

1 See Bourbon, *Finding a Replacement for the Soul: Mind and Meaning in Literature and Philosophy*. (Cambridge: Harvard University Press, 2004), chapter 4.
2 My appeal to witnessing is modest and not dependent on any theoretical commitments to a broader notion of witnessing. I want to acknowledge these broader ideas of witness, especially as a response to the Shoah. The primary and secondary literature is extensive. I only mention two authors, because they have informed my own understanding of what it can mean to bear witness separate from any sentimentality or easy moral righteousness. The first of these authors is Primo Levi. The second is Berel Lang. I cannot isolate any of Levi's writings from the others. The core of Lang's understanding of witnessing can be found in *Philosophical Witnessing: The Holocaust as Presence* (The Tauber Institute Series for the Study of European Jewry). Waltham, MA: Brandeis University Press, 2009.

Chapter 5

1 Marianne Moore, *The Complete Poems of Marianne Moore*. NY: Penguin Books, 1981.
2 Malcolm Budd, *Values of Art: Pictures, Poetry and Music*. NY: Penguin, 1996, p. 83.
3 Ibid. For Budd, the particularity of the poem matters because it is that particularity that produces (or facilitates) the poetic experience. According to Budd, the thoughts of the poem could be said in another way, but those thoughts do not constitute the poem—the words do.
4 The meaning of the sentences that make up a story should be distinguished from the meaning of a story. That would be true as well for whatever story might be told or shown or expressed through a lyric poem (let alone a narrative poem). The meaning of a story, however, is different in kind from the meaning of a poem qua poem.
5 John Ashbery, *Selected Poems*. NY: Penguin, 1986.
6 Ben Jonson, *The Complete Poems*. Ed. George Parfitt. NY: Penguin Books, 1996.
7 These attitudes are not aesthetic attitudes of the kind criticized by George Dickie; they are simply a disposition to take something as a poem. See "All Aesthetic Attitude Theories Fail: The Myth of the Aesthetic Attitude," *Aesthetics: A Critical Anthology*. Ed. George Dickie and R.J. Sclafani. NY: St Martin's P, 1977, pp. 342–55.

Chapter 6

1 Nonsense is universally possible. It is not, however, necessary. Harmony is also possible. It is just that harmony like sense has a content that is particular, if not

always determinate. That is what it means for language to be normative and intersubjective. If we did not have norms of correct and incorrect usage, we could not make distinctions, and without distinctions between thoughts and the words that constitute them, we could replace them all willy-nilly, and all would be senseless. Nonsense has no content and is its form is framed relative to the senses that are lost.

2 In sharing with you the form of my friend's skin as meaning *death*, I am not sharing the look or the feeling of my experience; I am not sharing the meaning of his skin. I am sharing the meaningfulness of it.

Chapter 7

1 See Keith H. Basso, *Wisdom Sits in Places: Landscape and Language among the Western Apache*, p. 89.
2 Pound, in the *Pisan Cantos*, exclaims the hopelessness of our situation as human beings continually facing extinction:

> I don't know how humanity stands it
> with a painted paradise at the end of it
> without a painted paradise at the end of it
>
> (*Canto* LXXIV, p. 456)

This wonder at "how humanity stands it" pretends to stand at a distance to this terror and to humanity. If he is not denying his own humanity, then he is asking how he or anyone could be human, not as if it were a choice, but as if it were a burden that we understand as a burden. As such a burden, painted paradise or not will not obviate our responsibility to withstand until "the end of it." This puzzlement is followed by an invocation of Christ's crucifixion, with which the speaking "I" identifies. Christ is an example under which the "I" figures itself as an image of suffering. This is not what Eliot does. "Death by Water" is followed by what seems, at least in part, a description of Christ's crucifixion, where again the relation of any I to such a description is open to interpretation, extrapolation, and guessing. Thus, the passage is simultaneously exemplary and a description floating in the poetic space afforded by the poem—it is not yet a metaphor, although it could be interpreted as one in order to characterize the lyric voice in the last section of the poem or as part of the imagery accruing around sacrificial figures in the poem.

3 Pronouns and names, which, in *The Waste Land*, are also often as indeterminate and indefinite as pronouns, in their semantic sense and in their logical form, identify persons or things. Pronouns and names are markers of persons. The indeterminacy of pronouns and names in the poem does not undermine the sense of these

pronouns and names as identifying or expressing what we would fictionally take as persons, but it does force us to question what is expressed by these pronouns and names in relation to each other. Any "I" within the poem can still be taken to have the ability to say "I said... " or "I believe....". Consequently, the full range of senses of "I" and other pronouns remains, but what is expressed by belief, in saying, in doubting, and so on and what kind of who is believing, saying, doubting, etc. become unclear. The retention of person-talk, of pronouns, names, and intentional vocabulary protects the idea of persons without giving it any stable content that could be understood as picturing consciousness or subjectivity.

For a counter argument, see Michael Levenson, *The Genealogy of Modernism*, pp. 169–75.

4   What that means is that we can all stand in for each other, whether we like it or not. But the I marks a limit, a first person limit that is different from that offered by the third person he, she, and it. Those pronouns objectify that which is referred to by such means within a world of which we are all a part. The first person suggests something different.

5   Such a generalization displaces the force of such statements as "I sat down and wept" from psychological expressiveness to the delimitation of a world—in which these three, and the other quasi-first person statements would pick out someone. What kind of who could that be?

6   Karl Barth, *Epistle to the Romans*. Trans. Edwyn C. Hoskyns. Oxford: Oxford University Press, 1933, iii.21, p. 94

Chapter 8

1   From the flyer for *How to Read. What to Do*, University of Chicago, March 2006.

2   See "Can I Drive My Car from Its Form to Its Movement." *Common Knowledge* 16 (3): 404–16 (2010).

3   The actual trees in a yard are not a state of affairs: such a state is a logical idea determined relative to the propositions we can state or relative to our grasp of the content determined by such a proposition.

4   My appeal to the idea of a natural kind does not entail a robust commitment to any particular doctrine of natural kinds. I am using the notion in order to eliminate possible ways of understanding the kind of thing a poem might be. The most powerful corrective to an unwarranted appeal to natural kind is offered by Ian Hacking in his seminal paper "Natural Kinds: Rosy Dawn, Scholastic Twilight," in O'Hear A (ed) Philosophy of science (Philosophy—Royal Institute of Philosophy Supplement 61). Cambridge University Press: Cambridge, 2007, pp. 203–39. For a review of the topic and a response to Hacking, see Miles MacLeod and Thomas A. C.

Reydon, "Natural Kinds in Philosophy and in the Life Sciences: Scholastic Twilight or New Dawn?," *Biological Theory* 7 (2): 89–99 (2013). See also Hilary Putnam, "The Meaning of 'Meaning'", *Mind, Language and Reality* (Philosophical Papers, Volume 2), Cambridge: Cambridge University Press, 1975. The literature on natural kinds is extensive.

5. I argue for the theory of fiction I put forward here in "The Logical Form of Fiction," in *Finding a Replacement for the Soul: Mind and Meaning in Literature and Philosophy* (Cambridge, Harvard University Press, 2004).

6. Vendler, *The Music of What Happens*, (Cambridge, Harvard UP, 1988), p. 259.

7. The very triviality of taste relative to the logical significance of fictions encourages our ideas of poetry to include vast stretches of intellectual concerns—primarily theories about ontology, mind, language, and politics. So Gertrude Stein uses the idea of actuality as fundamentally flux to justify her aesthetic nonsense. Others appeal to ideas about the imagination and the mind to characterize both how poems are made and what they show. Others appeal to the idea of metaphor or to symbols, or to the idea of poetry as a form of ordinary language. Still others appeal to a political idea of subversion and possibility built out of the new possibilities of poetry. These various ideas can be combined—and put into some kind of hierarchy, although this does not mean that in their combination they are coherent or sensible.

Chapter 9

1. We need no witchcraft to fit death and love to their respective parcels of "accidental and trivial circumstance." The witchcraft of affection, a youthful mix of sentiment and egotism, gives the accidental the tone of the "divine rage and enthusiasm" that produces it. Emerson, in "Love," fits this early mode of youthful love within a Neoplatonic scheme of purification, in which love becomes an intimation of the transcendent. He is too dismissive of earthly love and too sanguine about love as a means to a greater purity of being, but he begins with the actuality of everyday poems, when the contingent gains a kind of necessity.

2. We can analyze a gesture of love to reveal what love is and how it relates to its means of manifestation. Gestures of love offer both an example of how love is manifest and show by analogy show how my beloved can manifest love.

3. But for me, the face of my beloved is not simply an example of love, but a revelation of it. And thus, her face gathers, for me, that complexity of feeling and commitment that is central to love and gives it a form... for me.

4. I do not accomplish or effectuate that person or that love, since both that person and my love for them already exists. When we act for the sake of something, we might be attempting to live up to some ideal, and in so doing we might be expressing some virtue (or vice).

5   See Donagan for an excellent clarification of these distinctions relative to Aquinas.
6   Art provides exemplary objects of a similar unstable shifting and inversion of appearance and reality, not only by showing us our lives shaped and distorted by feelings, but because art lives within this same instability. Poetry is itself like love and sympathy: it carries with it the same potential for dissolution into parody. Thus, it is an expression or form of special meaning, of primary linguistic attention and force or it is nonsense: posturing, rhetoric, delusion. The primary form of the inversion from something to nothing in all art, but especially in the linguistic arts, is the shifting from the sense that art means to a sense that it does not. This is like love turning to death.
7   See in particular Harry G. Frankfurt, "On Caring." In *Necessity, Volition and Love*. Cambridge: Cambridge University Press, 1999.
8   Her particularities, her qualities, provide the means for her recognition and her expressiveness, although one imagines that there exists a wide range of possibilities here, and it would not be easy to say which would be necessary expressions as opposed to accidents of association. It is in this sense that such particularities should be understood as surrogates.

Conclusion

1   Sometimes we ask riddles of riddles. A raven is ostensibly a kind of bird and a writing desk is ostensibly a kind of furniture piece. A poem, however, is a riddle-thing about which we can ask further riddles.
2   If we imagine the points on a number line to be the thousands who wait for its visit, then the answer could be an asymptotic line.
3   See Quine, *Word and Object*. Cambridge: MIT P, 1960 for his arguments for the indeterminacy of translation. Wittgenstein's relevant account of language games and of meaning can be found in *Philosophical Investigations*, 3rd ed. Trans. Elizabeth Anscombe. Cambridge: Blackwell, 1991, remarks 1 through 341.
4   James Boswell. *The Life of Samuel Johnson*. Abridged, with an introduction by Bergen Evans. NY: The Modern Library, 1952.

Appendices

1   Paul Celan, "The Meridian," in *Collected Prose*. Trans. Rosmaire Waldrop. NY: The Sheep Meadow P, pp. 37–56.
2   Ordinarily we say things regardless of how language works. Its working is not our responsibility. For the poet the working of language is his or her responsibility. Payne

believes this poetic attention "allows semantic possibilities to open up that are not available in ordinary language as it usually operates." The poet does attend to how language means, but the question is: how deep can he or she get into the workings of language to change them?

3 In saying this, I am, of course, invoking Wittgenstein's private language argument. See *Philosophical Investigations*, §§244–271. Consequences of this argument are pursued in subsequent remarks.

4 William Gass, Preface to *The Geographical History of America or the Relation between Human Nature and the Human Mind*. Baltimore: Johns Hopkins University Press, 1995, p. 29.

5 Let me use an example to explain why this cannot be done: Should we say that someone playing a trumpet is communicating something that isn't sayable, and assume that what we mean by "communicate" in this case is the same as what I am communicating with these words I am using now? Trumpets make trumpet sounds; they do not offer conceptual or semantic content that we could get right or wrong.

6 One might be tempted to argue that this difference is like that between a statement and a question. But statements and questions both mean in the way that sentences do. And, anyway, you can articulate what a question is asking by making a statement (e.g., "He was asking which x…").

7 Payne appeals to Rorty's arguments in Richard Rorty, *Contingency, Irony, and Solidarity*. Cambridge: Cambridge University Press, 1989, pp. 12–27, 39–43.

8 Epitomes leave things out, of course. But in making an epitome we do not omit things to avoid the consequences of some fact, like when we lie by refusing to reveal something. Omissions, in themselves, are not lies. In deriving an abstract or epitome we must omit, and since the principle of omission is not deception, it is not deceiving. It can be badly done and lead to false conclusions, but this does not make it a lie. If we omit to deceive, we can measure our omissions relative to what we hope to hide or relative to the effect we want to produce, or would produce if we did not omit. Our goals may not all be bad; we may wish to spare someone's feelings. Our deception could be corrected by an account that included what was left out. Euphemisms also can create a verbal distance from the force of fact. As such they might be ways of misleading ourselves, if not in the sense of what is the case, possibly relative to its significance.

9 Another sense of "epitome" brings it closer to an idea of an abstract: the sense that an abstract is a representation or summary version of something. The city of Rome might also be this, but it would be this under a different description, a description more neutral, less symbolic, and more a summary of the empire.

Bibliography

Agnon, S. Y. *A Guest for the Night*. Trans. Misha Loutish. Madison: University of Wisconsin Press, 1968.
Alter, Robert. *The Wisdom Books*. New York: W. W. Norton & Company, 2011.
Ammons, A. R. *A Coast of Trees*. New York: W. W. Norton & Company, 2002.
Ammons, A. R. *Collected Poems, 1951–1971*. New York: W. W. Norton & Company, 1972.
Ammons, A. R. *Sphere: The Form of Motion*. New York: W. W. Norton & Company, 1974.
Ashbery, John. *Selected Poems*. New York: Penguin, 1986.
Aubrey, John. *Aubrey's Brief Lives*. Ed. Oliver Lawson Dick. London: Secker and Warburg, 1949.
Austin, J. L. *How to Do Things with Words*. Cambridge: Harvard University Press, 1962, 75.
Barth, Karl. *The Epistle to the Romans*. Trans. Edwyn C. Hoskyns. Oxford: Oxford University Press, 1933.
Basso, Keith H. *Wisdom Sits in Places: Landscape and Language among the Western Apache*. Albuquerque: University of New Mexico Press, 1996.
Bernhard, Thomas. *Old Masters*. Trans. Ewald Osers. Chicago: University of Chicago Press, 1985, 1989.
Bishop, Elizabeth. *The Complete Poems: 1927–1979*. New York: Farrar Straus Giroux, 1979.
Boswell, James. *The Life of Samuel Johnson*. Abridged, with an introduction by Bergen Evans. New York: The Modern Library, 1952.
Bourbon, Brett. "The Accident and Substance of Modern Poetry." *Ligget* (December 2006).
Bourbon, Brett. "Can I Drive My Car from Its Form to Its Movement." *Common Knowledge* 16.3 (Fall 2010).
Bourbon, Brett. "Consequences of Particularity." *Philosophy and Literature* 41.2 (January 2018).
Bourbon, Brett. *Finding a Replacement for the Soul: Mind and Meaning in Literature and Philosophy*. Cambridge: Harvard University Press, 2004.
Bourbon, Brett. "Response to Mark Payne." *Modern Philology* 105.1 (October 2007).
Bourbon, Brett. "What Can My Nonsense Tell Me about You?" in *Literature and Philosophy*. Ed. David Rudrum. London: Palgrave Macmillan Press, 2006.
Bourbon, Brett. "What Is a Poem?" *Modern Philology* 105.1 (October 2007).
Browne, Sir Thomas. *The Major Works*. Ed. C. A. Patrides. London: Penguin, 1977.
Bryce, Trevor. *The Kingdom of the Hittites*. 2nd ed. New York: Oxford University Press, 2006.
Budd, Malcolm. *Values of Art: Pictures, Poetry and Music*. New York: Penguin, 1996.
Burnside, John. *The Music of Time: Poetry in the Twentieth Century*. Princeton: Princeton University Press, 2021.

Bush, Ronald. *T. S. Eliot: A Study in Character and Style*. New York: Oxford University Press, 1984.

Carroll, Lewis. *The Annotated Alice*. Notes by Martin Gardner. New York: Meridian, 1960.

Celan, Paul. *Poems of Paul Celan: A Bilingual German/English Edition*, rev. edn. Trans. Michael Hamburger. New York: Persea, 2002.

Celan, Paul. "The Meridian." In *Collected Prose*. Trans. Rosmaire Waldrop. New York: The Sheep Meadow Press, pp 37–56.

Chosin. [Film] Dir. Brian Inglesias, 2010.

Clark, T. J. *The Sight of Death: An Experiment in Art Writing*. New Haven: Yale University Press, 2006.

Conrad, Joseph. *The Secret Agent*. London: Penguin, 1963, 1984.

Danto, Arthur. *After the End of Art: Contemporary Art and the Pale of History*. Princeton: Princeton University Press, 2014.

Dickie, George. "All Aesthetic Attitude Theories Fail: The Myth of the Aesthetic Attitude." In *Aesthetics: A Critical Anthology*. Ed. George Dickie and R. J. Sclafani. New York: St Martin's P, 1977.

Donagan, Alan. *Human Ends and Human Actions: An Exploration of St. Thomas' Treatment*. Milwaukee: Marquette University Press, 1985.

Donne, John. *The Poems of John Donne*, 2 Volumes. Ed. Herbert Grierson. Oxford: Oxford University Press, 1912.

Eliot, T. S. *The Poems of T. S. Eliot*. Eds. Christopher Ricks and Jim McCue. New York: Farrar, Straus and Giroux, 2018.

Eliot, T. S. *The Use of Poetry and Use of Criticism*. Cambridge: Harvard University Press, 1986.

Elliot, George. *Middlemarch*. London: Penguin, 1994.

Emerson, Ralph. *Essays and Poems*. New York: Library of America, 1983, 1994, 1996.

Fehrenbach, T. R. *This Kind of War: The Classic Korean War History, Fiftieth Anniversary Edition*. NY: Potomac Books, 2001.

Fingarette, Herbert. *Revisions, Changing Perspectives in Moral Philosophy*. Ed. MacIntyre and Hauerwas. South Bend: Notre Dame University Press, 1983.

Frankfurt, Harry G. "On Caring." In *Necessity, Volition and Love*. Cambridge: Cambridge University Press, 1999.

Gass, William. Preface to *The Geographical History of America or the Relation between Human Nature and the Human Mind*. Baltimore: Johns Hopkins University Press, 1995.

Goodman, Nelson. *The Ways of World Making*. Cambridge, NY: Hackett Pub., 1978.

Hacking, Ian. "Natural Kinds: Rosy Dawn, Scholastic Twilight." In *Philosophy of Science (Philosophy—Royal Institute of Philosophy Supplement 61)*. Ed. A. O'Hear. Cambridge: Cambridge University Press, 2007, pp. 203–39.

Hill, Geoffrey. *Broken Hierarchies: Poems 1952–2012*. Ed. Kenneth Haynes. New York: Oxford UP, 2012.

Johnson, Samuel. *The Life of Sir Thomas Browne*. In *The Major Works*. Ed. C. A. Patrides. London: Penguin, 1977.
Jonson, Ben. *The Complete Poems*. Ed. George Parfitt. New York: Penguin Books, 1996.
Joyce, James. *Finnegans Wake*. New York: Penguin, 1999.
Kant, Immanuel. *Critique of the Power of Judgment*. Trans. Paul Guyer and Eric Mathews. Cambridge: Cambridge University Press, 2000.
Kenner, Hugh. *The Invisible Poet*. London: Taylor & Francis Books Ltd, 1965.
Kierkegaard, Soren. *Fear and Trembling/Repetition: Kierkegaard's Writings, Vol. 6*. Princeton: Princeton University Press, 1983.
Kundera, Milan. *The Unbearable Lightness of Being*. Trans. Michael Henry Heim. New York: Harper Perennial, 1984.
Lang, Berel. *Philosophical Witnessing: The Holocaust as Presence* (The Tauber Institute Series for the Study of European Jewry). Waltham, MA: Brandeis University Press, 2009.
Levenson, Michael H. *The Genealogy of Modernism*. Cambridge: Cambridge University Press, 1986.
Levi, Primo. *The Complete Works of Primo Levi*. Ed. Ann Goldstein. New York: Liveright, 2015.
Lewis, C. S. *An Experiment in Criticism*. Cambridge: Cambridge University Press, 2012.
MacLeod, Miles and Thomas A. C. Reydon. "Natural Kinds in Philosophy and in the Life Sciences: Scholastic Twilight or New Dawn?" *Biological Theory* 7.2 (2013): 89–99.
MacLow, Jackson. *Words nd Ends from Ez*. Los Angeles: Sun & Moon Press, 1989.
McCarthy, Cormac. *The Road*. New York: Vintage, 2006.
Moore, Marianne. *The Complete Poems of Marianne Moore*. New York: Penguin Books, 1981.
Murdoch, Iris. *Existentialists and Mystics: Writings on Philosophy and Literature*. New York: Penguin, 1999.
Payne, Mark. "Ideas in Lyric Communication: Pindar and Paul Celan." *Modern Philology* 105.1 (October 2007).
Putnam, H. "The Meaning of 'Meaning.'" In *Mind, Language and Reality* (Philosophical Papers, Volume 2). Cambridge: Cambridge University Press, 1975.
Pound, Ezra. The *Cantos of Ezra Pound*. New York: New Directions Book, 1950.
Quine, W. V. *Word and Object*. Cambridge: MIT Press, 1960.
Ricks, Christopher. *T. S. Eliot and Prejudice*. London: Faber, 1988.
Rorty, Richard. *Contingency, Irony and Solidarity*. Cambridge: Cambridge University Press, 1989.
Russ, Martin. *Breakout: The Chosin Reservoir Campaign, Korea 1950*, New York: Penguin, 2000.
Shakespeare, William. *Antony and Cleopatra*. 3rd Series. Ed. John Wilders. New York: Arden, 1995.
Shakespeare, William. *Hamlet*. 2nd Series. Ed. Harold Jenkins. New York: Arden, 1982.
Sides, Hampton. *On Desperate Ground: The Epic Story of Chosin Reservoir—the Greatest Battle of the Korean War*. New York: Anchor, 2019.

Spenser, Edmund. *The Yale Edition of the Shorter Poems of Edmund Spenser*. Ed. William A. Oran, et al. New Haven: Yale University Press, 1989.

Stein, Gertrude. *Selected Writings of Gertrude Stein*. Ed. F. W. Dupee and Carl Van Vechten. New York: Vintage, 1990.

Stevens, Wallace. *Collected Poetry and Prose*. New York: The Library of America, 1997.

Tomlinson, Charles. *Collected Poems*. Cambridge: Oxford UP, 1984, 1985.

Valéry, Paul. *The Collected Works of Paul Valery. Volume 10. History and Politics*. New York: Pantheon Books, 1962.

Vendler, Helen. *The Music of What Happens: Poems, Poets, Critics*. Cambridge: Harvard University Press, 1989.

Virgil, *Aeneid*. Trans. Robert Fagles. New York: Penguin Classics, 2008.

Walcott, Derek. *Collected Poems, 1948–1984*. New York: Farrar Straus Giroux, 1986.

Wittgenstein, Ludwig. *Philosophical Investigations*, 3rd ed. Trans. Elizabeth Anscombe. Cambridge: Blackwell, 1991.

Wolheim, Richard. *Art and Its Objects: With Six Supplementary Essays*. Cambridge: Cambridge University Press, 1980.

Index

action 34–6, 48, 51, 105, 116–19, 158 *See also* ethics and love
Agnon, S.Y. (*A Guest for the Night*) 6–7, 10, 38, 168 n. 10
alphabet, the ix–x, 1–6, 13–14, 26, 127, 134–5, 139, 162
Alter, Robert 21
Ammons, A. R. ("Easter Morning") 9, 15–21, 136
Analogy 18–20, 31, 66–8, 88, 145, 148–9, 154, 159, 165, 172 n. 2
  apprehension of 35, 125–6, 130
  as poem 3–6, 37–41, 107–10, 130–5
  interpretation of 76–8, 82, 85–6, 91, 95
Apache, naming of the landscape 85, 170
Ashbery, John 7, 57, 169 n.5
Aspect 32–3, 104
  of face 126
  of love 112–13, 120–4, 134
  of poem 109, 111
  of words x
  of world 10
Austin, J. L. x, 58

Barth, Karl ix, 95, 171 n.6
beauty 4–6, 10, 18, 21, 39, 74, 75, 111, 126, 132, 165, 167 n. 8
Bernhard, Thomas 2
Bishop, Elizabeth 166 n. 1
Boswell, James 173
Browne, Sir Thomas 166 n. 2
Budd, Malcolm 56, 169 n. 3
Burnside, John 166 n. 1

Carroll, Lewis 86, 129
  Alice's Adventures in Wonderland 70–3
Celan, Paul 141–52, 165, 173 n. 1
ceremony 18, 35–8, 44–5, 50–1, 137–8
Chosin Reservoir, Battle of 32–3
Clark, T. J. 111–12
close Reading 153–62, 165

Danto, Arthur 167 n.6
death ix, 8, 50, 69, 94, 160, 162–5, 170 n. 2, 172 n. 1, 173 n. 6
  and the dead 8, 13, 18, 21, 85, 86, 88, 90, 91, 95–6, 108, 113–14
  as interruption 21–6, 36
  parody 95, 96, 113, 126, 138, 164
  as poem 76, 80–2, 85–9, 108–15, 126, 133–9
Dickie, George 169 n. 7
Donne, John 114
  "Aire and Angells" 115, 119

Eliot, T.S. (*The Waste Land*) x, 30, 85–96, 111, 164–5
Emerson, Ralph 19, 23, 111–12, 172 n. 1
ethics viii–x, 1, 7, 11–12, 26, 40, 52, 162–3
  ethical judgement 35
  and love 120–1
event(s) viii, 13, 15, 29, 53, 64, 66–7, 75, 80–2, 86, 100, 111, 150, 153
  events and actions 35, 37, 43, 47, 69
  events and analogy 6–11, 50, 75, 134
  events of form 7, 29, 31, 35–7, 46–8, 55, 69, 80, 86, 126–7, 133–5, 162–5
  see also poems
  events of recognition 126
everyday poems viii–x, 5–7, 31–5, 135, 162–5, 172 n. 1

face(s) viii, 2, 6, 13, 25–7, 29–36, 39–41, 65, 80, 112–16, 118–21, 133–5, 172 n. 3
  of love 126, 127, 134, 162
  of poems 9, 123–27, 139, 165, 168 n. 11
  of words viii, 30, 31, 34, 35, 126, 165
faith 36–7, 43, 52, 137
  fiction 14, 34, 49, 61, 92, 98, 104–7, 143, 156, 166–7, 171 n. 3, 172 n. 5
fictionalization 45–6
Fingarette, Herbert 22
Frankfurt, Harry G. 121

Gass, William 149
god (s) x, 13, 21, 22, 26, 38, 39, 51-2, 77, 91-5, 116
gods 24, 81, 124
Goodman, Nelson 3

Hacking, Ian 173 n. 4
Hill, Geoffrey 13
Hittites 23-5
hysteria 49, 80-2, 85, 164

'I love you' viii, 1-7, 9, 11-12, 52-3, 81-2, 121-2, 127, 135, 162
impersonation 86, 88, 90, 94, 164
incomplete (and incompletion) 13-19, 22, 26, 34-5, 41, 43, 137-8, 162
interpretation ix, 2, 4, 11, 26, 64-7, 81-2, 85, 93, 101, 105, 146, 170 n. 2
  as description 110, 124
  of poetics 64, 98, 107, 110
  relative to epitome 155-62
interruption viii, 13, 15, 19, 22-6, 29, 135-8, 162, 163

job 33-4
Johnson, Samuel 100, 135, 166 n. 2, 167 n. 2
Jonson, Ben 58-60
Joyce, James 145

Kant, Immanuel 5, 74-5, 82
Kierkegaard, Soren 14
Kundera, Milan 160

Levi, Primo 169 n. 2
Lewis, C. S. 39
logical form 30, 105-6, 118, 141, 170 n. 3, 172 n. 5
love viii, 1-19, 41, 35, 37-40, 76-7, 95, 135-8, 160-2, 165 See also 'I love you'
  love of children 112-14, 117-21
  manifesting 29, 112, 133 see also analogy
  parodies of 86, 163, 173 n. 6
  romantic love 111, 115-17, 119-27, 136, 172 n. 1-4
  and weddings 44-5, 47-54, 137-8
love poems 11, 39

MacLow, Jackson 97-8
marriage ix, 43-54, 76-8, 137, 163
mathematics 65, 75, 151

McCarthy, Cormac (*The Road*) 36-7
meaning 2-6, 9, 12, 32-4, 68, 75, 88, 90, 110, 114, 165
  of love 40-1, 48, 50-2
  of a story or poem 56-67, 98, 105-6, 132, 147, 153-62, 173 n. 6
  of sentences and words 119-27, 132, 141-53
  of things 80-2, 170 n. 2
meaningfulness ix, 11, 124, 125, 135, 139
  See also faces and poems
  of actions 36-7, 39-41
  of words 9, 30-5, 38-41, 102-6, 118-21, 134-9
Middlemarch (Elliot, George) 56
Moore, Marianne 55
morality 19, 38, 49-52, 59, 60, 121, 164
  moral courage 23
  moral interruption 29, 78, 82, 85-6, 135, 163-4
  moralistic 12, 21, 100
Murdoch, Iris 39

names 52, 63, 67-8, 81, 85-7, 90-5, 124-5, 130, 170 n. 3
natural kind 103-4, 171 n. 4 See also Hacking, Ian
necessity 10, 26, 43, 45, 62, 79, 104, 120-3, 163
  contingent necessities 5-6, 81-2, 111-14, 127, 133-9, 172 n. 1
nonsense x, 1, 10, 17, 49, 50, 61, 65, 92, 141, 170 n. 1

parody 34, 50-1, 65-8, 95-6, 111, 113, 126-7, 139, 154, 165, 173 n. 6
particularity 4, 17, 20, 26, 29-30, 89-94, 124-7, 130-5, 139, 163, 169 n. 3
  of a poem 3-6, 67, 97, 103, 106, 110
  of a sentence 55-6, 60-7, 153-6
Payne, Mark 142, 145-52, 173 n.2, 174 n.7
poems ix, x, 1-9, 11-16, 23, 25-6, 46, 109-12, 142-62, 163-5 See also everyday poems
  as events viii, 29-31, 55, 69-70, 85-6, 111, 124-7, 133-9 (see also events of form)
  form 38, 58, 133, 143, 159
  general descriptions of 55-62, 34-40, 107-8, 119, 133, 135, 139, 167 n.4, 172 n. 7

our intimacy with 67, 109, 132–5, 142, 150
poetry ix, x, 1–9, 12, 16, 23, 39–41, 46–50, 66–70, 139, 164, 166 n.1, 173 n. 6
  idea of poetry 56–7, 60, 94–6, 98–9, 106–10, 131, 166 n.2, 172 n. 7
  as language 29–30, 34, 141–5, 150–1
  non-existence of 59–60, 97–110
poetics 40, 151, 164
political bombs 69–70, 73
posthumous writing 13–15, 20, 22–6, 162
Pound, Ezra 94, 98, 170 n. 2
pronoun 87, 89–96, 106, 147, 170 n. 3, 171 n. 3

Quine, W. V. x, 64, 132, 173 n. 3

revelation viii–ix, 4, 6–7, 10, 29, 31, 49, 111–12, 118, 126, 132–5, 160–5, 172 n. 3
Ricks, Christopher 29–30
ritual 19, 36, 43–4, 50–1, 89, 92, 95
Rorty, Richard 151–2, 174 n. 7

Secret Agent, The (Joseph Conrad) 73–9, 82–3
sentences 3, 5, 9, 11, 92, 98, 114, 135, 141–3, 162, 174 n. 6 *See also* particularity

as poems 9, 30, 32–4, 102–4, 112, 130, 132–4, 157
intimacy with 67, 132
meaning of 56–68, 110, 145–61, 169 n. 4
Shakespeare, William *Antony and Cleopatra* 161–2
Shakespeare, William *Hamlet* 46–9
Spenser, Edmund 43
Stein, Gertrude 147–50, 165, 172 n.7
Stevens, Wallace 8–9, 127, 160
surrogate 11, 34, 94, 109, 114, 121–5, 127, 136–9, 165

time 7, 14, 88, 112, 123, 129–30, 137, 165
Tomlinson, Charles 10–11
tone 5, 29–35, 37, 40–1, 48, 124–4, 134–5, 139, 146, 160, 163, 168 n. 7

Valéry, Paul 13
Vendler, Helen 16, 107

Walcott, Derek 135
Watteau 135–6
wedding ix, 2, 37, 43–53, 69, 62–5, 137–8, 162–4
witnessing 50–1, 169 n. 2
Wittgenstein, Ludwig x, 32–4, 64, 87, 132, 168 n.3, 173 n. 3, 174 n. 3
Wolheim, Richard 109

www.ingramcontent.com/pod-product-compliance
Lightning Source LLC
Chambersburg PA
CBHW061834300426
44115CB00013B/2380